INTELLIGENT IMAGE DATABASE SYSTEMS

SERIES ON SOFTWARE ENGINEERING AND KNOWLEDGE ENGINEERING

Series Editor-in-Chief
S K CHANG (*University of Pittsburgh, USA*)

Vol. 1 Knowledge-Based Software Development for Real-Time Distributed Systems
Jeffrey J.-P. Tsai and Thomas J. Weigert (Univ. Illinois at Chicago)

Vol. 2 Advances in Software Engineering and Knowledge Engineering
edited by Vincenzo Ambriola (Univ. Pisa) *and Genoveffa Tortora* (Univ. Salerno)

Vol. 3 The Impact of CASE Technology on Software Processes
edited by Daniel E. Cooke (Univ. Texas)

Vol. 4 Software Engineering and Knowledge Engineering: Trends for the Next Decade
edited by W. D. Hurley (Univ. Pittsburgh)

Vol. 6 Object-Oriented Software: Design and Maintenance
edited by Luiz F. Capretz and Miriam A. M. Capretz (Univ. Aizu, Japan)

Forthcoming titles:

Acquisition of Software Engineering Knowledge
edited by Robert G. Reynolds (Wayne State Univ.)

Monitoring, Debugging, and Analysis of Distributed Real-Time Systems
Jeffrey J.-P. Tsai, Steve J. H. Yong, R. Smith and Y. D. Bi (Univ. Illinois at Chicago)

INTELLIGENT IMAGE DATABASE SYSTEMS

editors

S K Chang
University of Pittsburgh, and
Knowledge Systems Institute, USA

E Jungert
Swedish Defense Research Establishment,
Sweden

G Tortora
Universita di Salerno, Italy

World Scientific
Singapore • New Jersey • London • Hong Kong

Published by

World Scientific Publishing Co. Pte. Ltd.

P O Box 128, Farrer Road, Singapore 912805

USA office: Suite 1B, 1060 Main Street, River Edge, NJ 07661

UK office: 57 Shelton Street, Covent Garden, London WC2H 9HE

British Library Cataloguing-in-Publication Data
A catalogue record for this book is available from the British Library.

ISBN 981-02-2390-0

This book is printed on acid-free paper.

Printed in Singapore by Uto-Print

PREFACE

This book is the result of a workshop primarily concerned with Symbolic Projection which is a qualitative spatial reasoning technique originally developed as a technique for iconic indexing. Later on, Symbolic Projection turned out to be useful for spatial reasoning as well. The workshop took place in August 1993 in Bergen, Norway, in connection with the 1993 IEEE Symposium on Visual Languages. We are grateful to the following people who contributed the various chapters that constitute this book: T. Arndt, A. Del Bimbo, D. J. Buehrer, C. C. Chang, J. Hildebrandt, F. J. Hsu, T. F. Hwang, R. Kuppanna, S. Y. Lee, Y. Li, S. M. Ling, S. C. Orphanoudakis, G. Petraglia, E. G. M. Petrakis, C. Schlieder, M. Sebillo, Q. Shi, K. Tang, C. R. Tseng, M. Tucci, E. Vicario, D. Yan, and W. P. Yang. Most chapters are based upon papers presented at the workshop, and a few are reprinted from journals with permission from the publishers so that the book can be more comprehensive.

Intelligent image information systems will in the future be concerned with the handling of large quantities of images and of other types of spatial information coming from various sources like, for instance, sensors. Thus new techniques for handling, analysis and fusion of such information will be necessary. This is due to the fact that the traditional techniques used today will not be able to solve the, in the future, upcoming problems — neither in real time nor reasonably quickly. Many of the problems of concern are temporal as well, and as a consequence, they have to be dealt with by using techniques that are spatio/temporal. Other problems of importance require techniques for similarity retrieval, shape recognition and determination of spatial relations, etc. Of particular interest when dealing with these classes of problems are techniques based on spatial and/or spatio/temporal reasoning. Therefore, the purpose of this book is to illustrate such reasoning techniques, primarily based on Symbolic Projection.

In particular, spatial reasoning techniques will have a large impact on future image information systems and databases. However, there are other application areas that will benefit from these techniques as well; among them are, for instance, geographical information systems, and to a large degree systems where sensor data fusion will play an important role. Examples of the latter are robotics and systems for environmental assessment.

Special thanks are due to Tracy Yu and May Look of World Scientific who edited the book.

Shi-Kuo Chang, Erland Jungert and Genoveffa Tortora

CONTENTS

SPATIAL REASONING, IMAGE INDEXING AND RETRIEVAL USING SYMBOLIC PROJECTIONS

S. K. CHANG, E. JUNGERT and G. TORTORA

This book covers the principles and recent research results in intelligent image database systems design. As the title indicates, the book places special emphasis on spatial reasoning and the techniques for image indexing and retrieval, mainly based upon the Theory of Symbolic Projection. In addition, applications of the theory and techniques to intelligent image database systems design are also discussed.

With the recent advances in multimedia computing and distributed multimedia systems, image database system has become increasingly important because it is one of the centerpieces for distributed multimedia systems. In general, an image database system is a combination of three basic components: the first component deals with image processing for the extraction of information from physical images, the second component is responsible for the storage and management of the original images and the extracted information, and the third component is concerned with the user interface for querying the database. Thus, in order to increase the capabilities of image database systems, it is important to consider the problem of how images are stored and how images are retrieved.

To make an image database system more flexible and more intelligent, the spatial knowledge embedded in images should be preserved by the data structure used to store them. The symbolic description of visual information such as shape or spatial relations is a very difficult task using the traditional approaches. Attempts to describe this information textually can lead to representations that are either too general or too complex. As an example, let us consider the neighborhood relationship. It is a spatial relation whose meaning can be derived only by analyzing the image and comparing the surrounding spaces according to a particular spatial interpretation of the image. Such relation is difficult to describe by text alone.

1

In traditional database systems, the use of indexing to facilitate database accessing has been well established. Analogously, image indexing techniques have been studied during the last decade to facilitate image information retrieval from an image database. The use of icons as picture index is the basic principle of the iconic indexing methodologies developed to this aim. With this approach, the index of an image is a picture itself, which is best suited to hold visual information and to allow different levels of abstraction and management.

The Theory of Symbolic Projection is introduced in the first part of the book. Chapter 2 is an abridged version of the original paper that first proposed the concept of 2D strings. This basic theory has been extended toward the solution of three main problems: a) the description of spatial relations among objects of different sizes and shapes for 2D image databases, b) the description of three dimensional pictures and, c) the description of image sequences.

In order to describe more accurately the spatial relations among objects of different sizes and shapes, it is necessary to consider the objects with reference to their beginning point and ending point along the x- and y-direction. Chang and Jungert [1] extended the idea of symbolic projections by introducing the cutting mechanism concept and defining a knowledge structure for image databases. In order to establish the relations among the objects in terms of spatial operators, they partition the original image by drawing cutting lines at the beginning and ending points of the overlapping objects, thereby, decomposing the image into many smaller subpictures. In this representation, called generalized 2D string [1], every subpart is referred to by the same name of the whole object.

The generalized 2D string provides an indexing mechanism for objects of different sizes and shapes. However, this approach and most of the existing retrieval methodologies are based on pictorial indexing mechanisms that describe images with a fixed orientation. Likewise, during the retrieval process, the result of every comparison depends on the orientation of the query. In applications like medical image database systems, one would reasonably expect to be able to have solution to queries without worrying too much about the possible erroneous storing of plates, for example, in the reverse direction. Moreover, in many cases, more freedom in the filing of images with respect to the orientation is required since the visual information contained in them is independent of any orientation, as for example in the management of images under a microscope. In this case, the orientation of this kind of pictures is not meaningful at all, therefore, this pictorial information should be stored independently of any specific orientation. In other words, the iconic index should be normalized with respect to reversion and rotation. In chapter 3, Petraglia, Sebillo, Tucci and Tortora address the issue of normalizing the iconic index and introduce the concept of virtual image as a solution.

An approach to the representation of 3D pictures, called 3D string, is presented in chapter 4 by Chang and Li. The ambiguity of this representation is discussed with respect to the properties of the pictures. The reconstruction problem has been faced and algorithms for 3D string matching are also given. Finally, interesting open problems are pointed out.

In chapter 5, Lee and Hsu introduce a more efficient cutting mechanism for a new spatial knowledge representation, called the 2D C-string. Based upon the generalized 2D string, the 2D C-string preserves all the spatial information of an image by drawing the least possible number of cutting lines. This leads to a compact representation of the image and allows an image database system to efficiently represent and handle pictures of arbitrary complexity. This knowledge structure also leads to the possibility of similarity retrieval, and finally spatial reasoning. This chapter also initiates the second part of this book, focused on spatial reasoning.

Efficient methods for spatial reasoning are becoming more and more necessary in a large variety of applications in which not only spatial, but lately also temporal data, must be combined and manipulated in various ways. The demand for such methods are fueled by ever more increasing data volumes represented in greater resolution. Methods that can handle and analyze data of many tera-bytes are becoming more and more necessary. The data quantities that must be handled will most likely grow for a long time to come. The reason for this, which at the same time is a challenge, is that spatial data sources of various types are being developed and coming into use for a large number of applications. Examples of such sources are sensors that can generate images with different characteristics. Common to all these sensors are that they are being installed on various types of platforms which then produce extremely large quantities of data. It must also be pointed out, that it is no longer sufficient just to analyze sensor data coming from just a single sensor. Methods that can support fusion and filtering of data from many different sources will be required. Furthermore, methods for reduction of data such that loss of information is minimized are required as well. Needless to say, all these methods that must be developed should be efficient, otherwise they are of no interest. At this time, however, there is a shortage of methods that can help us solve all these problems and, for this reason, further research is required. Symbolic projection is one step in this direction.

All reasoning methods must be based on some kind of model or theory and spatial reasoning is no exception to this. The foundation is be the same although the reasoning technique is influenced by the underlying spatial concept [2]. To carry this further, in spatial analysis, the underlying space is generally relying on Euclidean geometry. However, the drawback with this type of geometry is not that it cannot serve as a theory for reasoning. The drawback, taking the discussion above into account, is that it does not consider the data reduction problem, or that it cannot handle the massive quantities of data that in the future need be analyzed. The major drawback is that these problems cannot be solved within a reasonable amount of time using Euclidean geometry. For this reason, other methods must be considered. Clearly, such methods cannot go beyond Euclidean geometry; on the contrary, such methods must be well founded in Euclidean geometry, which for many reasons can be considered universal.

The main question is thus, where to go in order to solve these problems? The classical solution is to build up a search strategy that can be used to build up some kind of indexing technique that eventually can make it possible to prone off unnecessary branches in the search space at the earliest possible stage. In image processing and related areas, such methods are called iconic indexing and, for instance, Symbolic Projection was originally developed for this purpose. Iconic indexing methods may, however, be of different types, but common to them all is that they are founded in techniques allowing both reduction of data and dead-ends to be pruned off early. Later when closer to the final solution, methods based on the use of high resolution data can be applied to more acceptable data quantities, thus in the end, leading to correct and optimal results. Spatial projection was originally introduced for this purpose and displays metric information in qualitative form. In other words, this method, which is symbolic, is reasoning in qualitative terms. Here again, we can talk about a method that is reducing data while the relevant information is kept. Furthermore, this method is founded in the Euclidean geometry as well.

A good theory should always guarantee that it leads to correct inferences established by soundness and completeness of the method in a qualitative way [3]. In spatial reasoning there should be no exception. Hence, inferred relationships must always respond to these two requirements. There are also other less important but nevertheless not neglectable requirements needed for identification of certain object attributes and relations. Obviously, there is a need for various conceptualizations, corresponding to some kind of formal language, that eventually will allow for a set of inference techniques that can carry out the reasoning process and finally, can infer whatever result that is needed. Through a large set of applications, this has again and again been demonstrated by Symbolic Projection, that is, it has been shown that the method is founded on a formal language using conceptualizations from the symbolic projections. It is not only possible to use the method for identification of a large number of relations and properties, it can also be used in a manner that demonstrates both completeness and soundness.

It has already been mentioned that Symbolic Projection is a fundamental method that performs reasoning in a qualitative way. A corner stone in qualitative reasoning is that reasoning can be performed by reducing data without loss of information. However, the technique should also contain other useful characteristics. For instance, Freksa [4] argues that higher cognitive mechanisms employ qualitative rather than quantitative mechanisms even if the knowledge originally is available in quantitative forms through perception. Furthermore, qualitative knowledge can be viewed as that aspect of knowledge which critically influences decisions. That is to say, methods based on qualitative knowledge will thus support development of various kinds of decision support tools. Symbolic reasoning is one method that can be used for this purpose.

The work by Allen [5] is concerned with qualitative temporal reasoning and has had an impact on much of the later work that has been done in the area of qualitative spatial reasoning. The reason for this is, that the basic set of temporal relations that was introduced by Allen can directly be mapped into the spatial area. Hence, many similarities between spatial and temporal reasoning can be pointed out in a large number of approaches. However, temporal reasoning is simpler to deal with in that it just includes a single dimension and therefore, is more or less related to a linear problem while it turns out that spatial reasoning problems are much more complex.

It may not be clear from this discussion that creating methods for solving problems on a very high abstraction level is not sufficient. This is due to the fact that sooner or later, any method despite which level of abstraction it works on, must use basic data in full resolution, that is, we are not allowed to forget the bits and pieces. Hence, we should not just be concerned with the qualitative aspects of the problem, we must also spend a great deal of our efforts on basic data such that both levels will work hand in hand allowing for efficiency from start to end or from top to bottom. In symbolic reasoning, it has been demonstrated that one such basic data structure is run-length-code.

In this discussion, the qualitative aspects of symbolic reasoning has been in focus, but other really important aspect have been pointed out as well, such as the requirements for soundness and completeness of this method. There is also a further aspect of great importance that must be taken into consideration in spatial reasoning and, that is, due to the enormous data quantities that in the future must be analyzed, basically all reasoning methods must allow reduction of data without loss of information. Clearly, Symbolic Projection is in this regards no exception.

Two types of ordering information about a finite set of points are studied in chapter 6. Some properties of ordering information help in analyzing the Symbolic Projection approach to spatial reasoning. Then the problem of rotation invariance is addressed. The design of rotation-invariant extensions of Symbolic Projection are discussed. Finally, panorama is introduced as a representation of ordering information which can be used as a rotation invariant index to symbolic descriptions of point configurations.

In chapter 7, two approaches concerned with object relations seen from a moving object are analyzed. In the first approach, the agent itself is of no concern when reasoning about the view as seen by the agent. Simple aspects of symbolic projections are used, while most other aspects are based upon novel concepts. The second approach is based entirely upon Symbolic Projection. Common to both approaches are the basic technique of qualitative reasoning.

The third part of the book deals with image indexing and retrieval. The joint representation of time and space is relevant in many research areas, including spatial-temporal reasoning, video sequence representation and content-based indexing and querying. In chapter 8, Bimbo and Vicario introduced an original language for symbolic representation of the contents of dynamic scenes. This language incorporates and extends concepts of Temporal Logic to deal in a uniform way with both time and space, and supports metric qualifiers for distance and speed.

The 2D string is one of a few representation structures originally designed for use in an image database environment. In chapter 9, a generalized approach for 2D string based indexing, which avoids an exhaustive search through the entire database of previous 2D string based techniques, is proposed. The classical framework of representation of 2D strings is also specialized to the cases of scaled and unscaled images. Index structures for supporting retrieval by content, utilizing the 2D string representation framework, are also discussed. The performance of the proposed method is evaluated using a database of simulated images and compared with the performance of existing techniques of 2D string indexing and retrieval. The results demonstrate a very significant improvement in retrieval performance.

Chapter 10 considers the problem of how to efficiently retrieve pictures from a large image database. A query should retrieve all input pictures which satisfy a given pattern expression, where this pattern expression may involve Boolean operators applied to a given set of permissible subpatterns. The number of permissible subpatterns determines whether a simple linear search, hashing, or a decision-tree would give the best performance. For on the order of 1,000,000 patterns or more, the decision-tree algorithm presented in this chapter has the advantage of being able to rule out the most non-matching patterns without performing any disk accesses. The whole indexing structure can usually be stored in the main memory, making it possible to access the needed data with a single disk access. How the decision-tree algorithm works on 2D strings is described in detail.

Chapter 11 presents two image retrieval algorithms for 2D strings. The first one improves the retrieval efficiency, while the second one reduces the space requirement. The performance analysis shows that the two methods perform much better than previous works, especially when the image database is large.

The last two chapters dealing with applications constitute the fourth part of the book. In chapter 12, a prototype multimedia database system incorporating iconic indexing is described. Iconic indexing is a technique which assists in a fast and easy retrieval of related images from an image database by providing a mechanism for content-based queries. This indexing technique is extended to deal with multimedia data in a uniform matter. In the prototype system, the system can use object or speech recognition to automatically generate an index, if such techniques are available. Otherwise, the system works interactively with the user to generate the index. Audio index, image index, and video index can thus be constructed in a unified framework, thus supporting content-based retrieval of multimedia objects through media specific indexing. Although the work needs to be extended to deal with complex queries involving more than one data type, it illustrates the potential applications of iconic indexing.

Finally, in chapter 13, a prototype system for querying ship data through a graphical user interface is described. Queries use symbolic descriptions of component objects of the ships and the objects' relative positions. The basic approach is to encode 3D structure via pairwise spatial relations in a standard relational database. This allows one to take advantage of efficient searches based on standard SQL queries.

This book was the result of a workshop on spatial reasoning, held in conjunction with the 1993 IEEE Symposium on Visual Languages. The discussion papers were extensively revised, and several reprints are included so that the book will comprehensively cover the important contributions to the Theory of Symbolic Projection, and techniques for spatial reasoning, image indexing and retrieval. We thank all the authors for their patience and hard work, which made this volume possible. A related book [6] covers the spatial reasoning and theoretical issues in greater depth.

References

1. S. K. Chang and E. Jungert, "Pictorial data management based upon the theory of symbolic projections", *Journal of Visual Languages and Computing* **2**, 3 (September 1991) 195–215.
2. A. Frank, "Qualitative spatial reasoning about distances and directions in geographical information systems", *Journal of Visual Languages and Computing* **3** (1992) 343–371.
3. T. R. Smith and K. K. Park, "Algebraic approach to spatial reasoning", *Int. Journal of Geographical Information Systems* **6**, 3 (1992) 177–192.
4. C. Freksa and R. Rhrig, "Dimensions of qualitative reasoning", *Qualitative Reasoning and Decision Technologies*, eds. N. P. Carret and M. G. Singh (CIMNE, Barcelona, 1993) pp. 483–492.
5. J. F. Allen, "Maintaining knowledge about temporal intervals", *Comm. ACM* **26**, 11 (Nov 1983) 832–843.
6. S. K. Chang and E. Jungert, *Symbolic Projection for Image Information Retrieval and Spatial Reasoning* (Academic Press, 1996).

ICONIC INDEXING BY 2D STRINGS

SHI-KUO CHANG

Department of Computer Science
University of Pittsburgh
Pittsburgh, PA 15260

QING-YUN SHI and CHENG-WEN YAN

Departrment of Mathematics and Information Science Center
Peking University
Beijing, China

In this chapter, we describe a new way of representing a symbolic picture by a two-dimensional string. A picture query can also be specified as a 2D string. The problem of pictorial information retrieval then becomes a problem of 2D subsequence matching. We present algorithms for encoding a symbolic picture into its 2D string representation, reconstructing a picture from its 2D string representation, and matching a 2D string with another 2D string. We also prove the necessary and sufficient conditions to characterize ambiguous pictures for reduced 2D strings as well as normal 2D strings. This approach thus allows an efficient and natural way to construct iconic indexes for pictures.

Index terms — Iconic indexing, pictorial information retrieval, string matching algorithms, two-dimensional string representation.

1. Introduction

In pictorial information retrieval, we often want to retrieve pictures satisfying a certain picture query, for example, "find all pictures having a tree to the left of a house". Previous approaches for pictorial information retrieval include relational database queries [4], query-by-examples [2], quad-trees [12], etc. In this chapter, we present a new way of representing a picture by a 2D *string*. A picture query can also be specified as a 2D string. The problem of pictorial

This work was supported in part by the National Science Foundation under Grants ECS-8305566 and MCS-8306282, and by an AT&T Foundation Grant. This chapter is primarily based upon a paper with the same title, which appeared in *IEEE Transactions on Pattern Analysis and Machine Intelligence*, Vol. PAMI-9, No. 3, May 1987, 413–423. The permission to reprint this paper was authorized by IEEE.

information retrieval then becomes a problem of 2D subsequence matching. This approach thus allows an efficient and natural way to construct *iconic indexes* for pictures [13].

In Sec. 2, we describe the 2D string representation as the symbolic projection of a picture, and define absolute 2D string, normal 2D string, and reduced 2D string. Section 3 presents algorithms for picture reconstruction from 2D string, and defines the augmented 2D string. Picture matching by 2D subsequence matching is discussed in Sec. 4. Section 5 outlines the methodology of iconic indexing. The problem of ambiguous pictures and their characterization is analyzed in Sec. 6. In Sec. 7, we summarize the algorithms and ambiguity results for the various 2D string representations proposed in this chapter, and discuss the proposed methodology in a broader perspective.

2. 2D String Representation of Symbolic Pictures

Let V be a set of symbols, or the vocabulary. Each symbol could represent a pictorial object (a named object such as "house", "tree", etc.) or a pixel.

Let A be the set $\{$"="$,$ "<"$,$ ":"$\}$, where "=", "<", and ":" are three special symbols not in V. These symbols will be used to specify spatial relationships between pictorial objects.

A *1D string* over V is any string $x_1 x_2 \cdots x_n, n \geq 0$ where the x_i's are in V.

A *2D string* over V, written as (u, v) is defined to be

$$(x_1 y_1 x_2 y_2 \cdots y_{n-1} x_n, \quad x_{p(1)} z_1 x_{p(2)} z_2 \cdots z_{n-1} x_{p(n)})$$

where

$$x_1 \cdots x_n \quad \text{is a 1D string over } V.$$

$$p : \{1, \ldots, n\} \to \{1, \ldots, n\} \quad \text{is a permutation over} \{1, \ldots, n\}.$$

$$y_1 \cdots y_{n-1} \quad \text{is a 1D string over} A.$$

$$z_1 \cdots z_{n-1} \quad \text{is a 1D string over} A.$$

We can use 2D strings to represent pictures in a natural way. As an example, consider the picture shown in Fig. 1.

The vocabulary is $V = \{a, b, c, d\}$. The 2D string representing the above picture f is:

$$(a = d < a = b < c, \quad a = a < b = c < d)$$

$$= (x_1 y_1 x_2 y_2 x_3 y_3 x_4 y_4 x_5, \quad x_1 z_1 x_3 z_2 x_4 z_3 x_5 z_4 x_2)$$

where

$x_1 x_2 x_3 x_4 x_5$	is	$adabc$.
$x_1 x_3 x_4 x_5 x_2$	is	$aabcd$.
p	is	13452 .
$y_1 y_2 y_3 y_4$	is	$=<=<$.
$z_1 z_2 z_3 z_4$	is	$=<=<$.

In the above, the symbol "$<$" denotes the left-right spatial relation in string u, and the below-above spatial relation in string v. The symbol "$=$" denotes the spatial relation "at the same spatial location as". The symbol "$:$" denotes the relation "in the same set as". Therefore, the 2D string representation can be seen to be the *symbolic projection* of picture f along the x- and y-directions.

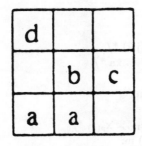

Fig. 1. A picture f.

A *symbolic picture* f is a mapping $M \times M \to W$, where $M = \{1, 2, \ldots, m\}$, and W is the power set of V (the set of all subsets of V). The empty set $\{\ \}$ then denotes a null object. In Fig. 1, the "blank slots" can be filled by empty set symbols, or null objects. The above picture is:

$$f(1,1) = \{a\} \qquad f(1,2) = \{\ \} \qquad f(1,3) = \{d\}$$
$$f(2,1) = \{a\} \qquad f(2,2) = \{b\} \qquad f(2,3) = \{\ \}$$
$$f(3,1) = \{\ \} \qquad f(3,2) = \{c\} \qquad f(3,3) = \{\ \}$$

We now show that given f, we can construct the corresponding 2D string representation (u, v), and vice versa, such that all left-right and below-above spatial relations among the pictorial objects in V are preserved. In other words, let R_1 be the set of left-right and below-above spatial relations induced by f. Let R_2 be the set of left-right and below-above spatial relations induced by (u, v). Then R_1 is identical to R_2, for the corresponding f and (u, v).

It is easy to see that from f, we can construct the 2D string (u, v). The above example already illustrates the algorithm. In the formal algorithm, we will first construct 2D string (u', v') where u' and v' contain symbols in W. Then, u' and v' can be rewritten as follows: if we see a set $\{a, b, c\}$, we write "$a : b : c$." If we see a null set $\{ \}$, we simply remove it (i.e. we write a null string). We can rewrite "$= <$", "$<=$", and "$<<$" to "$<$", and "$==$" to "$=$", so that redundant spatial operators are removed. The operators "$=$" and "$:$" can also be omitted. The algorithm now follows:

```
Procedure 2Dstring(f,m,u,v,n)·
begin
    /*we assume f is m by m square picture*/
    n = m × m;
    for j from 1 until m
        for k from 1 until m
        /* we are looking at f(j,k) */
        /* construct string x1 ... xn */
            begin
            i = k + (j − 1) m;
            xi = f(j,k);
        /* construct string x_{p(1)} ... x_{p(n)} */
            p(i) =j + (k − 1) m;
            end
    /* construct y string and z string */
        for i = 1 until n−1
            if i is a multiple of m
                then yi = zi = ' < '
                else yi = zi = ' = ';
    /* rewrite strings u and v*/
    while strings u and v contain rewritable substrings
        apply the rewriting rules (see following explanation):
                r1. {a1,a2, ..., ak} is rewritten as a1: a2: ... :ak
                    {} is rewritten as (null string)
                r2. ' = = ' is rewritten as ' = '
                    ' = < ' is rewritten as ' < '
                    ' < = ' is rewritten as ' < '
                    ' << ' is rewritten as ' < '
```

r3. ' = ' is rewritten as (null string)

r4. ' : ' is rewritten as (null string) /* reduced string only* /;

end

As an example, for the picture f shown in Fig. 1, if we apply the procedure "2D string" without the rewriting rules, we obtain:

$$(\{a\} = \{ \} = \{d\} < \{a\} = \{b\} = \{ \} < \{ \}$$
$$= \{c\} = \{ \}, \{a\} = \{a\} = \{ \} < \{ \} = \{b\}$$
$$= \{c\} < \{d\} = \{ \} = \{ \}). \qquad (1)$$

Now we apply rewriting rule r1 to obtain:

$$(a = = d < a = b = < = c =, a = a = < = b$$
$$= c < d = =)$$

(absolute 2D string). $\qquad (2)$

Since the 2D string of (2) contains all the spatial operators, it is a precise encoding of the picture f. The 2D string of (2) is called an *absolute 2D string*. This coding is obviously inefficient. In fact, one string suffices to represent f precisely. Therefore, we can apply rewriting rule r2 to obtain:

$$(a = d < a = b < c, a = a < b = c < d). \qquad (3)$$

In the above 2D string representation, we only keep the *relative* positioning information, and the *absolute* positioning information is lost. If we also omit the "=" symbols by applying rewriting rule r3, we obtain:

$$(ad < ab < c, aa < bc < d) \qquad \text{(normal 2D string)}. \qquad (4)$$

The same procedure can be applied to pictures whose "slots" may contain multiple objects (i.e. object sets). For example, if in Fig. 1, $f(1, 3)$ is $\{d, e\}$ instead of $\{d\}$, then the 2D string representation is:

$$(ad : e < ab < c, aa < bc < d : e)$$
$$\text{(normal 2D string with sets)}. \qquad (5)$$

The 2D strings of (4) and (5) are called *normal* 2D *strings*. If the ":" symbols are also omitted by applying rewriting rule r4, we obtain the following *reduced* 2D string:

$$(ade < ab < c, aa < bc < de)$$

$$\text{(reduced 2D string)}. \tag{6}$$

We note that in a reduced 2D string representation, there is no apparent difference between symbols in the same set and symbols not in the same set. In the above example, the local substring (i.e. substring between two "<"s, or one "<" and an end-marker) "adc" might also be encoded as "acd", "dac", "dca", "cad", or "cda". In other words, for reduced 2D strings, a local substring is considered to be equivalent to its permutation string.

3. Picture Reconstruction from 2D String

From the 2D string (u, v), we can reconstruct f. As an example, suppose the 2D string is $(x_1x_2 < x_3x_4 < x_5, x_2x_3x_4 < x_1x_5)$. We first construct the picture shown in Fig. 2(a), based upon 1D string u, by placing objects having the same spatial location (i.e. objects related by the "=" operator) in the same "slot". Next, we utilize 1D string v to construct the final picture. The algorithm now follows.

```
Procedure 2Dpicture (f, m1, m2, u, v, n)
begin
    /*find out the size of the picture*/
    m1 = 1 + number of ' < ' in string u;
    m2 = 1 + number of ' < ' in string v;
    /* find out the x-rank and y-rank of each object*/
    for i from 1 until n
        begin
        x-rank of xᵢ = 1 + number of ' < ' preceding xᵢ in u;
        y-rank of x_p(i) = + number of ' < ' preceding x_p(i) in v;
        end
    /*we construct an m1 by m2 picture f*/
    for j from 1 until m1
        for k from 1 until m2
            f(j, k) = the set of all objects
                    with x-rank j and y-rank k;
end
```

In the procedure "2Dpicture," we assume the permutation function p is given. If all the objects in a 2D string are distinct, the permutation function

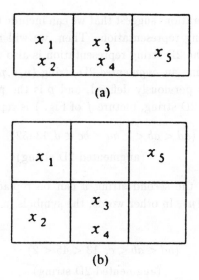

(a)

(b)

Fig. 2. A picture f.

p is unqiue. If, however, there are identical symbols in the 2D string, then in general there are many permutation functions. For example, the picture f of Fig. 1 has 2D string representation $(u, v) = (ad < ab < c, aa < bc < d)$. Let the u string be "$x_1 < x_3 x_4 < x_5$." Then the v string is either

$$\text{"}x_1 x_3 < x_4 x_5 < x_2\text{"}$$

$$\text{or} \quad \text{"}x_3 x_1 < x_4 x_5 < x_2\text{"} .$$

We can use either permutation function in the above procedure "2Dpicture," which will always reconstruct a picture. However, the reconstructed picture could be different from the original picture. In the above example, the reconstructed picture is actually unique and unambiguous. However, this may not always be the case. The problem of ambiguity will be treated in Sec. 4.

Another consideration is the uniqueness of the 2D string representation. As stated above, given any 2D string (u, v) and its permutation function p, the procedure "2Dpicture" will always reconstruct a picture. However, only for the reduced 2D string representation, the 2D string generated from the reconstucted symbolic picture is always identical to the original 2D string, because the local substrings and their permutation strings are considered equivalent.

The above considerations suggest that we can include the permutation function p in the 2D string representation. Then, we will have no ambiguity in reconstruction, and the 2D string representation is also unique.

Therefore, we define an *augmented* 2D string (u, v, p), where (u, v) is the reduced 2D string as perviously defined, and p is the permutation function. With the augmented 2D string, picture f of Fig. 1 is represented by:

$$(ad < ab < c, aa < bc < d, 13452)$$

$$\text{(augmented 2D string)}. \tag{7}$$

In actual coding, the second string v can be replaced by $w = p(1)z(1)$ $p(2)z(2) \cdots z(n-1)p(n)$. In other words, the symbols in v are replaced by the permutation indexes:

$$(ad < ab < c, \ 13 < 45 < 2)$$

$$\text{(augmented 2D string)}. \tag{8}$$

We will use the notation (u, v, p) to denote an augmented 2D string, although in actual coding we will use (u, w). For augmented 2D strings, the procedure "2Dpicture" can be applied directly, by including p as an additional input parameter. Procedure "2Dstring" should be replaced by the following procedure:

```
Procedure 2DstringA(f, m; u, w)
begin
    /*we assume f is m by m square picture */
n = 0;
for i from 1 until m do
    begin
        for j from 1 until m do
            begin
                if f(i, j) is not empty
                    for s in f(i, j)
                    begin
                        n = n + 1
                        q(i,j) = q(i,j) ∪ {n}
                    end
            end
    end
l = 0; u ='null' /* 'null' denotes null string */
for i from 1 until m do
```

```
begin
    for j from 1 until m do
        begin
            if f(i, j) is not empty
            l = l + size-of(f(i, j))
            u = u.f(i, j) /* '.' denotes concatenation operator */
            end
        if i < m and l < n
            u = u. <
    end
    k = 0; w = 'null'
    for j from 1 until m do
    begin
        for i from 1until m do
            begin
                if f(i, j) is not empty
                k = k + size-of(f(i, j))
                w = w.q(i, j)
                end
            if j < m and k < n
                w = w. <
        end
end
```

The above procedure "2DstringA" generates an augmented 2D string representation, where the function size-of(S) returns the number of elements in a set S.

4. Picture Matching by 2D String Matching

Two-dimensional string representation provides a simple approach to perform subpicture matching on 2D strings. The *rank* of each symbol in a string u, which is defined to be one plus the number of " < " preceding this symbol in u, plays an important role in 2D string matching. We denote the rank of symbol b by $r(b)$. The strings "$ad < b < c$" and "$a < c$" have ranks as shown in Table 1.

A substring where all symbols have the same rank is called a *local substring*.

A string u is *contained* in a string v, if u is a subsequece of a permutation string of v.

Table 1. Ranks of strings.

		String v			String u	
a	d	$< b$	$< c$	a	$< c$
1	1	2	3	1	2

A string u is a *type-i 1D subsequence* of string v, if, 1) u is contained in v, and 2) if $a_1 w_1 b_1$ is a substring of u, a_1 matches a_2 in v and b_1 matches b_2 in v, then

$$\text{(type-0) } r(b_2) - r(a_2) \geq r(b_1) - r(a_1)$$
$$\text{or } r(b_1) - r(a_1) = 0$$
$$\text{(type-1) } r(b_2) - r(a_2) \geq r(b_1) - r(a_1) > 0$$
$$\text{or } r(b_2) - r(a_2) = r(b_1) - r(a_1) = 0$$
$$\text{(type-2) } r(b_2) - r(a_2) = r(b_1) - r(a_1).$$

Now we can define the notion of type-i ($i = 0, 1, 2$) 2D subsequence as follows. Let (u, v) and (u', v') be the 2D string representation of f and f', respectively. (u', v') is a *type-i 2D subsequence* of (u, v) if, 1) u' is type-i 1D subsequence of u, and 2) v' is type-i 1D subsequence of v. We say f' is a type-i subpicture of f .

In Fig. 3, $f1$, $f2$, and $f3$ are all type-0 subpictures of f; $f1$ and $f2$ are type-1 subpictures of f; only $f1$ is a type-2 subpicture of f. The 2D string representations are:

$$f \ (ad < b < c, a < bc < d)$$
$$f1 \ (a < b, a < b)$$
$$f2 \ (a < c, a < c)$$
$$f3 \ (ab < c, a < bc).$$

Therefore, to determine whether a picture f' is a type-i subpicture of f, we need only to determine whether (u', v') is a type-i 2D subsequence of (u, v). The picture matching problem thus becomes a 2D string matching problem.

For augmented 2D strings, we can define the notion of 2D subsequence as follows: (u', v', p') is a type-i 2D subsequence of (u, v, p), if 1) (u', v') is a type-i 2D subsequence of (u, v), and 2) if x'_i of u' matches x_j of u, then

$$x'_{p'(i)} \text{ of } v' \text{ matches } x_{p(i)} \text{ of } v.$$

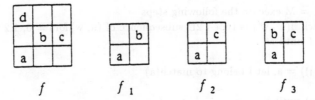

Fig. 3. Picture matching example.

In type-1 subsequence matching, each local substring in u should be matched against a local substring in v. In Table 1, substring "a" in u is a subsequence of "ad" in v, and substring "c" in u is a subsequence of "c" in v. Notice the skipping of a rank is allowed in type-1 subsequence matching. Therefore, the type-1 subsequence matching problem can be considered as a two-level subsequence matching problem, with level-1 subsequence matching for the local substrings, and level-2 subsequence matching for the "super-string" where each local substring is considered as a super-symbol, and super-symbol u_1 matches super-symbol v_1 if u_1 is a subsequence of v_1. See procedure "2Dquery1" in Appendix A.

Type-2 subsequence matching is actually simpler, because the rank cannot be skipped. That is to say, if local substring u_1 of u matches local substring v_1 of v, then local substring u_i of u must match local substring v_i of v for any i greater than 1. In the example shown in Table 1, $v =$ "$a < c$" is not a type-2 subsequence of "$ad < b < c$."

The following is a procedure for $i = 0$, 1 or 2 augmented 2D string matching. By applying procedure "2DmatchA", we can check if (u', w') can be a type-i 2D subsequence of (u, w) for $i = 0$, 1 or 2. A similar procedure "2Dmatch" can be written to handle absolute, normal, or 2D reduced string matching. For type-0 and type-1 matching, the procedure 2DmatchA is inexact, and there may exist a few instances in the answer set which do not actually match the query. An exact algorithm has been proposed to list all matched subsequences [8], with any number of object properties [11].

Procedure 2DmatchA(u', w'; u, w; i)
begin
1.convert(u', w') to (x', r', s', p') = (x'(1)$\cdots$x'(N), r'(1)$\cdots$r'(N), s'(1)$\cdots$s'(N),
   p'(1)$\cdots$p'(N)) using procedure CA(u', w'; x', r', s', p')
   convert(u, w) to (x, r, s, p) = (x(1) $\cdots$ x(M), r(1) $\cdots$ r(M), s(1) $\cdots$ s(M),
   p(1) $\cdots$ p(l))
      using procedure CA(u, w; x, r, s, p)

while $N <= M$ execute the following steps
    /* check if(u', w') is type-i 2D subsequence of (u, w) for $i = 0, 1, 2$ */
2.for j from 1 until M
  begin
     if $x(p(j)) = a$, let j belong to match(a)
  end
  for n from 1 until N
  begin
     $MI(n) = match(x'(p'(n)))$
  end
3.for n from 1 until $N - 1$
  begin
     $MC = \{ \}$ /* $\{ \}$ denotes empty set */
     while k belongs to $MI(n)$ and j belongs to $MI(n + 1)$
     begin
        call subroutine $d(n + 1, j; n, k)$
        if return "yes"
        let k belong to $a(j, n + 1, 1)$
     while $n > 1$
     begin
        $AP = a(k, n, 1)$
        for m from 2 until n
        begin
           $a(j, n + 1, m) = \{ \}$
           while *la* belongs to AP
           begin
              call subroutine $d(n + 1, j; n - m + 1, la)$
              if return "yes"
                let *la* belong to $a(j, n + 1, m)$
           end
           $AP = \{lp \mid$ whenever *la* belongs to $a(j, n + 1, m)$ such that
                      lp belongs to both $a(la, n - m + 1, 1)$ and $a(k, n, m)\}$
        end
     end
     if all $a(j, n + 1, m), m = 1, \ldots, n$ are not empty
        let j belong to MC
  end
     if MC is empty
        emit "no" and stop
     else $MI(n + 1) = MC$
  end
  emit "yes"
  end

```
subroutne d(m, j; n, k)
begin
    if j = k
        return "no"
    if [r(p(j)) - r(p(k))][r(p'(m)) - r(p'(n))] ≥ 0 and
            (when i = 0) [s(j) - s(k)][s'(m) - s'(n)] ≥ 0
                        | s(j) - s(k) | ≥ | s'(m) - s'(n) |
                        | r'(p(j)) - r(p(k)) | ≥ | r'(p' m)) - r' (p'(n)) |
            (when i = 1) s(j) - s(k) ≥ s'(m) - s'(n) > 0 or s(j) - s(k) =
                        s'(m) - s'(n)=0
                        | r(p(j)) - r(p(k)) | ≥ r'(p'(m)) - r'(p'(n)) | > 0 or
                        r(p(j)) - r(p(k)) = r'(p'(m)) - r'(p'(n)) = 0
            (when i = 2) s(j) - s(k) = s'(m) - s'(n)
                        r(p(j)) - r(p(k)) = r'(p'(m)) - r'(p'(n))
        return "yes"
    else
        return "no"
end

procedure CA(u, w; x, r, s, p)
begin
    /* convert (u, w) = (u(1)...u(L), w(1)...w(K)) to (x, r, s, p) = (x(1)...x(N),
        r(1)...r(N), s(1)...s(N), p(1)...p(N)) */
    m = 0
    for l from 1 until L
    begin
        if u(l) ≠ ' < '
            x(l - m) = u(l)
            r(l - m) = m + 1
        else m = m + 1
    end
    n = 0
    for k from 1 until K
    begin
        if w(k) ≠ ' < '
            s(k - n) = n + 1
            p(k - n) = w(k)
        else n = n + 1
    end
end
```

This procedure can be divided into there major steps. Step 1 converts (u, w) and (u', w') to (x, r, s, p) and (x', r', s', p'), respectively, in which string

x over A consists of symbols appearing in the u string, r is the corresponding rank string, s is another rank string corresponding to string y which consists of symbols appearing in the v string, and p is the permutation function. The same is true for (u', w') and (x', r', s', p').

Step 2 constructs the initial matching tables $\mathrm{MI}(n) = \{j|$ whenever $y(j) = x(p(j)) = x'(p'(n)) = y'(n)\}$ for $n = 1, 2, \ldots, N$.

Step 3 checks if there can be a type-i subsequence in (u, w), which matches (u', w').

Procedure "2DmatchA$(\cdot)$" has running time of $O(M) + O(N^2 * lp^3)$, where lp denotes the maximal length of matching tables $\mathrm{MI}(n), n = 1, \ldots, N$. In fact, Steps 1 and 2 can be completed in time $O(M) + O(N)$. For each j in $\mathrm{MI}(n+1)$, the construction of $a(j, n+1, m), m = 1, \ldots, n$, in Step 3 needs time $O(n * lp^2)$. Since the number of elements contained in $\mathrm{MI}(n+1)$ is no greater than lp, and the length of n loop is $N - 1$, so the time spent by Step 3 is $O(N^2 * lp^3)$. And the total time spent by this procedure is $O(M) + O(N^2 * lp^3)$.

Through a little modification, procedure "2DmatchA" can be used to list all type-2 2D subsequences in (u, w) that matches (u', w') and all type-0 and type-1 subsequences with possibly a few extra instances. See Appendix A.

5. Iconic Indexing

The 2D string representation is ideally suited to formulating picture queries. In fact, we can easily imagine that the query can be specified graphically, by drawing an iconic figure on the screen of a personal computer. The graphical representation can then be translated into the 2D string representation using the procedure "2Dstring" described in Sec. 2. This approach combines the advantage of the query-by-example approach, where a query is formulated by constructing an example, and the concept of icon-oriented visual programming systems [6].

Pictorial information retrieval is then transformed into the problem of 2D subsequence matching. The query, represented by a 2D string, is matched against the *iconic index*, which is the 2D string representation of a picture. Those pictures whose iconic indexes match the qurey 2D string are retrieved.

The iconic index not only can be used in pictorial information retrieval, but also provides an efficient means for *picture browsing*. Since we can reconstruct a picture from its 2D string representation, we can apply procedure "2Dpicture" to construct an icon sketch from the *iconic index*. In this picture browsing mode, we need only access the icoinc indexes, instead of retrieving the actual images from the pictorial database. For some applications, the picture browsing technique might be very useful.

To construct the icoinc index, we can proceed as follows. First, we apply edge detection and boundary detection techniques to construct icon sketches. The icon sketches are then classified into objects, and translated into 2D string representation. The location of each object is its centroid for areal objects, or the central point of its medial axis for objects. The icon sketches can be displayed in a browsing mode for user visualization. However, the retrieval is actually by 2D subsequence matching.

We have implemented 2D string matching algorithms described in previous section using the C programming language on both workstations and personal computers. Some experimental results will now be described. Figure 4 shows

Fig. 4. A digitized picture of lakes.

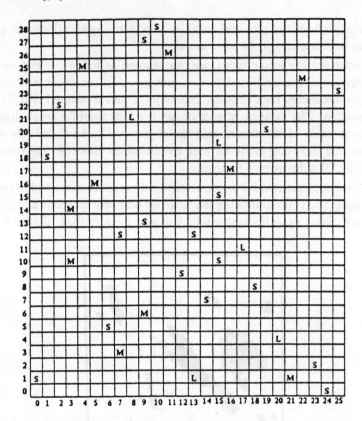

Fig. 5. A symbolic picture of lake objects.

a picture, which is a map overlay of lakes. This picture was digitized, and the lake objects were classified into small lake, medium-sized lakes, and large lakes. The resultant symbolic picture is shown in Fig. 5. The user can specify a query by a qurey pattern, as shown in Fig. 6. Figures 6(a)–(c) are quries to retrieve type-0, type-1, and type-2 subpictures respectively. By applying the 2D string matching algorithms, the matched subpictures are found. When there are several matched subpictures, the results (the coordinates of retrieved objects) are all displayed.

The above approach is applicable to pictures containing objects whose convex hulls are mutually disjoint, so that the objects have only left-right and below-above spatial relations. More complex objects need to be segmented first, so that they can be described in terms of the constituent objects.

```
QUERY PATTERN ( TYPE-0 )
.L
L.

RESULT:
•(13,1) (20,4)
•(13,1) (17,11)
•(13,1) (15,19)
                          (a)
```

```
QUERY PATTERN ( TYPE-1 )
L. .
.L.
. .L

RESULT:
•(20,4) (17,11) (15,19)
•(20,4) (17,11) (8,21)
•(20,4) (15,19) (8,21)
•(17,11) (15,19) (8,21)
                          (b)
```

```
QUERY PATTERN ( TYPE-2 )
S.
                .M
RESULT:
•(7,3) (8,5)
•(11,26) (10,26)
                          (c)
```

```
QUERY PATTERN ( TYPE-0 )
. .L
.Z.
L. .

RESULT:
•(13,1) (20,4)
•(13,1) (14,7) (15,10) (17,11)
•(13,1) (14,7) (15,19)
                          (d)
```

```
QUERY PATTERN ( TYPE-1 )
.L. .
. .Z.
. . .L
L. . .

RESULT:
•(13,1) (20,4) (18,8) (17,11)
•(13,1) (20,4) (18,8) (17,11) (16,17) (15,19)
•(13,1) (17,11) (16,17) (15,19)
                          (e)
```

```
QUERY PATTERN ( TYPE-2 )
. . . .L. . .
. . . . . . .
. . . . . . .
. . . .Z. .
. . . . . . .
. . . . . . .
. . . . . . . .
. . . . ,. .L
. . . . . . .
. . . . . . .
L. . . . . . .

RESULT:
•(13,1) (20,4) (18,8) (17,11)
                          (f)
```

Fig. 6. Picture queries and results.

Fig. 7. Encompassing objects (a) and their segmentation (b).

As an example, for objects that encompass other objects, such as the objects "a" and "b" shown in Fig. 7(a), we can describe their relations by regarding them to be in the same "slot". Notice the size of the "slots" can be defined arbitrarily.

The 2D string for Fig. 7(a) is (adc, abc). If the object "b" is segmented into objects "x" and "y," as shown in Fig. 7(b), the 2D string representation becomes $(x < ay < c, xa < yc)$. Aerial objects should be segmented into primitive constituent objects. Linear objects such as roads, riverways should be segmented into line segments. Point objects, of course, need not be further Avolo segmented.

The approach for *hierarchical 2D string encoding* is outlined below:

```
Procedure 2Dindex(picture, u, v)
begin
    /*objects recognition*/
    recognize objects in the picture:
    find minimum enclosing rectangular (MER) of each object;
    /*decomposition*/
    while the MERs overlap
        begin
            segment overlapping objects into constituent objects;
            find MER of each segmented object;
        end
    /*now all objects are disjoint*/
    find centroid of each object;
    find 2D string representation using Procedure 2Dstring
end
```

6. Characterization of Ambiguous Pictures

We define a picture f to *be ambiguous* if there exists a different reconstructed picture g from its 2D string representation (u, v).

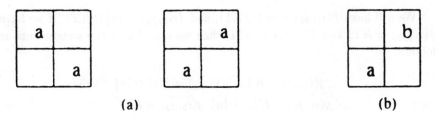

Fig. 8. Ambiguous picture (a) and unambiguous picture (b).

The ambiguity problem for binary pictures was first treated in [3]. The same technique can be applied to the general case, by regarding the binary picture as a special case, where the vocabulary set V contains a single symbol, say "a". For example, as shown in Fig. 8(a), the 2D string $(a < a, a < a)$ has ambiguous reconstruction. However, if the symbols are distinct, as shown in Fig. 8(b), there is no ambiguity.

Since an absolute 2D string represents a picture precisely, it cannot be ambiguous. An augmented 2D string is also unambiguous. Therefore, we should investigate normal and reduced 2D string representation.

For reduced 2D strings, we can prove the following theorem.

Theorem 1. *Let F be the class of all symbolic pictures without subpatterns of the form:*

$$
\begin{array}{cc}
a & a \\
a & a
\end{array}
$$

A symbolic picture f in F is ambiguous under the reduced 2D string, if and only if the reduced 2D string contains the subsequence $(a < a, a < a)$ where "a" is some symbol in V.

Proof. Suppose $(a < a, a < a)$ is a subsequence of (u, v), the 2D string representation of f. If we apply the procedure "2Dpicture" to reconstruct the picture, we will find x- and y-indexes i_1, i_2, j_1, j_2, for the subsequence $(a < a, a < a)$.

$$\text{The subsequences: } (a < a, a < a)$$
$$x - \text{and } y - \text{indexes: } i_1 i_2 j_1 j_2$$

We will have $f(i_1, j_1) = \{a\} \cup K11$, and $f(i_2, j_2) = \{a\} \cup K22$. If we have $f(i_1, j_2) = K12$ and $f(i_2, j_1) = K21$, then we can change the assignments as follows:

$$g(i_1, j_1) = K11, g(i_2, j_1) = K21 \cup \{a\}$$
$$g(i_1, j_2) = K12, \cup \{a\}, g(i_2, j_2) = K22.$$

This would construct a differenct picture g with the same 2D string representation, unless the four Kij's all contain "a" — which is impossible, because $K11$ and $K22$ do not contain "a".

Now suppose the picture f is ambiguous. Let its 2D string be (u, v). If the symbols x_i in u are all distinct, then f cannot be ambiguous. Therefore, there must be at least two identical symbols in string u (or string v). Let this symbol be "a". We construct a new picture g, where

$$g(i, j) = f(i, j) \cap \{a\}.$$

In other words, we only preserve the symbol "a" in $f(i, j)$. For some "a", g must be ambiguous. By the results proven in [3], g must contain a "switching component," as illustrated in Fig. 8(a). Therefore, the 2D string of f contains a subseqence $(a < a, a < a)$.   □

The above condition is for reduced 2D strings. For normal 2D strings, we have the following result.

Suppose f and g are symbolic pictures, Q and $Q_i(l = 1, 2, \ldots, k)$ are sets over V. Suppose f and g satisfy the following conditions:

(i) $Q = Q_1 \cup Q_2 \cup \cdots Q_k$ and $Q_i \cap Q_j = \{\}$ for $i \neq j$

(ii) $g(i, j) = f(i, j) - Q$

(iii) $g(i, j_l) = f(i, j_l) \cup Q_l$ for $l = 1, 2, \ldots, k$.

We define moving operation $O[r(i) : j(Q) \to j_1(Q_1), \ldots, j_k(Q_k)](f) = g$.

If we interchange the roles of i and j, we can see that the moving operation $O[c(j) : i(Q) \to i_1(Q_1), \ldots, i_k(Q_k)](f) = g$.

Let $O_1, O_2, O_3, \ldots, O_n$ be moving operations. We define $O_1, O_2, O_3, \ldots, O_n(f) = O_1, (O_2, (O_3(\cdots O_n(f)) \cdots)$

We define $fr(i)$ as the string obtained by concatenating all the symbols in $f(i, 1), f(i, 2), \ldots, f(i, m)$ in sequence, $fc(j)$ as that by concatenating all the symbols in $f(1, j), f(2, j), \ldots, f(m, j)$, where m is the size of $f \cdot fr(i)$ and $fc(j)$

are called a "row string" and a "column string", respectively, and both are called "segment string". Now we give the definition of the *ambiguous loop* for the normal 2D string as follows. Suppose

$$(i_1, j_1), (i_2, j_1), (i_2, j_2), \ldots, (i_k, j_k), (i_1, j_k)$$

is a sequence of indexes to the elements in f. If we connect the indexes one to another with straight lines, we get a loop. If there exists a set Q over V such that:

$$fc(j_1) = g_1 c(j_1), \text{ where } g_1 = O[c(j_1) : i_1(Q) \rightarrow i_2(Q)](f)$$
$$fr(i_2) = h_2 r(i_2), \text{ where } h_2 = O[r(i_2) : j_1(Q) \rightarrow j_2(Q)](f) \cdots$$
$$fc(j_k) = g_k c(j_k), \text{ where } g_k = O[c(j_k) : i_k(Q) \rightarrow i_1(Q)](f)$$
$$fr(i_1) = h_1 r(i_1), \text{ where } h_1 = O[c(i_1) : j_k(Q) \rightarrow j_1(Q)](f)$$

then there is an ambiguous loop, denoted by

$$\{(i_1, j_1)(i_2, j_1)(i_2, j_2) \cdots (i_k, j_k)(i_1, j_k); Q\}.$$

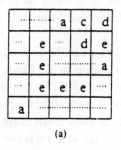

(a)

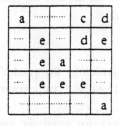

(b)

Fig. 9.

For example, Figs. 9(a) and (b) have the same normal 2D string. This ambiguity comes from the dotted loop.

Theorem 2. *A symbolic picture f is ambiguous under the normal 2D string if and only if there exists an ambiguous loop in f.*

Proof. Suppose the ambiguous loop is

$$\{(i_1, j_1)(i_2, j_2) \cdots (i_k, j_k)(i_l, j_k); Q\}.$$

We will prove that f and g have the same 2D string, where

$$g = O[c(j_1) : i_1(Q) \to i_2(Q)]O[c(j_2) : i_2(Q) \to i_3(Q)]$$
$$\cdots O[c(j_k) : i_k(Q) \to i_1(Q)].$$

Since the 2D string is a row by row and column by column representation, if two pictures have the same "row strings" and the same "column strings," they have the same 2D string. Therefore, we only need to check if f and g have the same "segment strings."

The pictures f and g may only differ at rows $i_1, i_2, \ldots, i_k$ and columns $j_1, j_2, \ldots, j_k$, and it is straightforward to prove f and g cannot be different at those rows and columns.

If f and g are different, but with the same 2D string, we can prove that there must exist an ambiguous loop in f. First, we search f and g columm by column at the same time. Let $f(i1, j1)$ be the first element found to be different from g. Without loss of generality, suppose $f(i_1, j_1)$ is nonempty and $g(i_1, j_1)$ is empty. We conclude that there must exist an $f(i_2, j_1)$ such that $f(i_2, j_1) = \{\ \}, g(i_2, j_1) = f(i_1, j_1)$ and $fc(j_1) = gc(j_1)$. We can repeat this procedure until we have found an ambiguous loop. Since the picture is finite, this procedure will terminate. □

7. Discussion

This chapter presents a methodology for symbolic picture representation by 2D strings. Table 2 summarizes the important properties of various 2D string representations.

The proposed methodology for symbolic picture representation by 2D strings supports pictorial information retrieval in a natural way. It has the advantage of pictorial-qurey-by-example [2], but avoids the lengthy processing

Table 2. Summary of 2D string representation.

string type	normal 2Dstring	absolute 2Dstring	reduced 2Dstring	augmented 2Dstring
example string	(a:bc < a, a:ba < c)	(a:b = c < a = a:b = a < c =)	(abc < a, aab < c)	(abc < a, 124 < 3)
picture to string	procedure 2Dstring	procedure 2Dstring	procedure 2Dstring	procedure 2DstringA
string to picture	procedure 2Dpicture	procedure 2Dpicture	procedure 2Dpicture	procedure 2Dpicture
string match	procedure 2Dmatch	procedure 2Dmatch	procedure 2Dmatch	procedure 2DmatchA
ambiguity condition	Theorem 2 ambiguous loop	unambiguous	Theorem 1 ($a < a, a < a$) subsequence	unambiguous

time to retrieve information from a relational database. The iconic index provides a natural index to a pictorial database, thereby reducing search time. On the other hand, since a symbolic picture can be reconstructed from 2D string representation, the iconic index can also be used in a *browsing mode* for visualization of the symbolic pictures. Therefore, it also has some of the advantages of the quad-trees, in that a visualization of a crude picture is possible. However, the quad-tree approach cannot handle symbolic pictures easily. Therefore, the 2D string representation of a symbolic picture has advantages over both the relational database approach and the quad-tree approach.

We have implemented all the algorithms reported in this paper using the C programming language on a personal computer equipped with an image processing board, a camera, and a video monitor. APC-based experimental image information system has been implemented, combining the 2D string approach for iconic indexing, and the relational database approach for storing pictorial attributes. The user can digitize an image and store it on hard disk or floppy diskette. The user can index the image by an image name, a set of keywords, and the 2D string. These indexes are stored in a relational database. In addition to direct retrieval by image id, the user can also retrieve images by image name, keywords, or a pictorial query (2D string). The experimental image information system is intended for teleconferencing, computer-assisted teaching, and office document storage/retrieval applications.

There are many interesting topics requiring further investigation. We have recently extended the basic methodology to include to spatial reasonning and rule-based visualization of symbolic pictures [7]. We are currently working on: efficient algorithms for 2D subsequence matching, iconic indexing and applications, characterization of ambiguous pictures, query processing by 2D subsequence matching, 3D scene description and recognition [1], similarity measures for symbolic pictures based upon longest common 2D subsequences [9], [10], and symbolic pyramid structures which combine quad-trees with the 2D string representation.

Appendix A. Query Processing by 2D String Matching

Let f be a symbolic picture represented by 2D string (u, w). We are often faced with the problem "find all subpictures in f that match a query symbolic picture". This problem can be converted to a problem of 2D string matching, by adding the following statements right to the end of loop 4 in procedure "2DmatchA" in Sec. 4, we can obtain all type-i ($i = 0, 1, 2$) 2D matched subsequences plus possibly a few extra instances for $i = 0$ or 1:

```
. . . . . . . . .
for j in MI(N)
begin
    R(N) = j
    list(j, N − 1)
end
subroutine list(j,n)
begin
    if n = 0
        begin
            output R /* output results */
            return
        end
    for k in a(j, n + 1, 1) ∩ a(j, N, N − n)
        begin
            R(n) = k
            list(k, n − 1)
        end
end
```

The time complexity is appoximately $N_m * N$, where N_m is the number of matched subsequences.

The following procedure "2Dquery1" is a procedure to list all the type-1 matched subpatterns using the two-level matching method discussed in Sec. 4.

```
Procedure 2Dquery1(u', w'; u', w')
begin
global x(), r(), s(), p(), x'(), r'(), s'(), p'(), min(), z(), match()
1.convert (u', w'), to (x', r', s', p') = (x'(1) ··· x'(N), r'(l) ··· r'(N),
          s'(l), ..., s'(N),
          p'(1) ··· p'(N)) using procedure CA(u', w'; x', r', s', p')
2.convert (u, w) to (x, r, s, p) = (x(1) ··· x(M), r(1) ··· r(M), s(1) ··· s(M),
          p(1) ··· p(M))
          using procedure CA(u, w; x, r, s, p)
   while N ≤ M execute the following steps
   /* list all the type-i (i=0, 1) subpatterns of (u,w) which match (u', w') */
3.curb(front,back)
3.for j from 1 until M              /* construct match tables */
          begin
                  if x(p(j))=a, let j belong to match (a)
          end
4.for a in V                        /* V is symbol set */
          begin
                  let min (a) be pointer to the first element in match (a)
          end
5.n = 1
6.a = x'(p'(0))
7.for j in match(a) from the one pointed by min(a) until the last one
          begin
                  z(j) = j                /* keep matched position */
                  min(a) points to the element in match(a) next to j
                  begin
                          head = 1
                          call procedure query1(n, j, head)
                  end
          end                            /* end of loop 7 */
end

query1(n, k, head)
begin
1.b = x'(p'(n + 1))
2.if match(b)= {}
          stop                          /* no match */
3.if s'(n + 1) − s'(n) > 0
          head = n + 1
4.for j in match(b) from the one pointed by min(b) until the last one
```

```
        begin
            if s'(n + 1) − s'(n) = 0 and s(j) − s(k) > 0
                return(head)
            call procedure check(n + 1, j; n, k)
            if return "yes"
                begin
                    z(n + 1) = j    /* keep matched position */
                    if n = N − 1       /* if it is the end */
                        begin
                            output matching result using z()
                            continue
                        end
                    else
                        begin
                            tp = min(b)      /* tp is a temporary pointer */
                            min(b) points to the elements in match (b) next to j
                            call procedure query1 (n + 1, j, head)
                            min(b) = tp
                            if value(query1) ≠ n + 1
                                return(value(query1))
                        end
                end
            end
        end                     /* end of loop 3 */
    return (n)
end

curb(front, back)
/* generate front and back curb for every symbol in (u', w') */
begin
    for i from 1 until N
        q(p'(i)) = i              /* reverse permutation function */
    for i from 1 until N
        begin
            n = p'(i)
            for k from n − 1 until 1
                find the first k such that s'(q(k)) ≤ s'(n)
            if such k does not exist
                front(i) = null
            else front(i) = q(k)
            for k from n + 1 until N
                find the first k such that s'(q(k)) < s'(n)
            if such k do not exist
                back(i) = null
```

```
            else back(i) = q(k)
        end
end

check(m, j; n, k)
/* check if j is a candidate after k */
f = from(m)
b = back(m)
switch()
    case f ≠ null and b ≠ null :
        if s(j) − s(k) ≥ s'(m) − s'(n) > 0 or s(j) − s(k) = s'(m) − s'(n) = 0
            r(p(z(m))) − r(p(z(f))) ≥ r'(p'(m)) − r'(p'(f)) > 0
                or r(p(z(m))) − r(p(z(f))) = r'(p'(m)) − r'(p'(f)) = 0
            r(p(z(b))) − r(p(z(m))) ≥ r'(p'(b)) − r'(p'(m)) > 0
                or r(p(z(b))) − r(p(m))) = r'(p'(b)) − r'(p'(m)) = 0
            return "yes"
        else
            return "no"
    case f = null and back(m) ≠ null :
        if s(j) − s(k) ≥ s'(m) − s'(n) > 0 or s(j) − s(k) = s'(m) − s'(n) = 0
            r(p(z(b))) − r(p(z(m))) ≥ r'(p'(b)) − r'(p'(m)) > 0
                or r(p(z(b))) − r(p(z(m))) = r'(p'(b)) − r'(p'(m))) = 0
            return "yes"
        else
            return "no"
    case f ≠ null and b = null :
        if s(j) − s(k) ≥ s'(m) − s'(n) > 0 or s(j) − s(k) = s'(m) − s'(n) = 0
            r(p(z(m))) − r(p(z(f))) ≥ r'(p'(m)) − r'(p'(f)) > 0
                or r(p(z(m))) − r(p(z(f))) = r'(p'(m)) − r'(p'(f)) = 0
            return "yes"
        else
            return "no"
end
```

In the procedure "query1", suppose we have found matches for first n elements of $p'(\ )$, k is the match of $a = x'(p'(n))$, and let $b = x'(p'(n+1))$. At this time, $min(b)$ points to the element in $match(b)$ from which we start to find match for $b = x'(p'(n+1))$. Given an element j in $match(b)$, we use procedure to check if j matches $b = x'(p'(n+1))$. If the answer is "yes", we set $min(b)$ to the element next to j and go on. In procedure "check", procedure "curb" is invoked. Here, we briefly demonstrate the definition of front and back curbs using an example. Suppose Fig. 10 is the symbolic pictures of (u', w').

We have

symbol	front curb	back curb
a	null	null
b	a	null
c	a	b
d	a	c
e	b	null

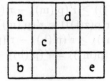

Fig. 10.

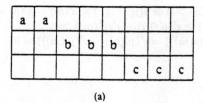   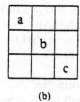

(a)   (b)

Fig. 11.

The worst case of procedure "2Dquery1" is illustrated in Fig. 11, where every combination of a, b, and c in Fig. 11(a) is a type-1 match for Fig. 11(b). Therefore, the worst case running time of procedure is

$$| \text{match}(x'(1))| * | \text{match } (x'(2))|$$

$$* \cdots * | \text{match } (x'(N))|.$$

In practice, through using min( ), the running time of "query1" is close to that of listing all matched subpatterns. Procedure "2Dquery1" is a two-level matching algorithm. We first find match for the present local substring. Whenever the local substring match fails, we do not have to process further, and can proceed to next local substring. Therefore, it needs less time than "one-level" matching.

The following procedure "2Dquery2" generates all type-2 match subpatterns:

```
Procedure 2Dquery2(u′, w′; u, w)
begin
global x(),r(),s(),p(), x′(), r′(), s′(), p′(), min(), z(), match()
1. convert (u′, w′) to (x′, r′, s′, p′) = (x′(1) ··· x′(N), r′(1)···r′(N),s′(1)···s′(N′),
       p′(1)···p′(N′)) using procedure CA(u′, w′; x′, r′, s′, p′)
2. convert (u, w) to (x,r,s,p) = (x(1)···x(M), r(1)···r(M),s(1)···s(M),p(1)···p(1))
       using procedure CA(u,w; x,r,s,p)
   while N ≤ M execute the following steps
/* list all the type-2 subpatterns of (u, w) which match(u′, w′) */
3. for j from 1 until M              /* construct match tables */
       begin
            if x(p(j))=a, let j belong to match(a)
       end
4. for a in V                        /* V is symbol set */
       begin
            let min(a) be pointer to the first element in match(a)
       end
5. n = 1
6. a = x′(p′(1))
7. for j in match(a) from the one pointed by min(a) until the last one
       begin
            z(j) = j                 /* keep matched position */
            min(a) points to the element in match(a) next to j
            call procedure query2(n,j)
       end                           /* end of loop 7 */
end

query2(n, k)
begin
1. b = x′(p′(n + 1))
2. if match(b) = { }
       stop                          /* no match */
3. for j in match(b) from the one pointed by min(b) until the last one
       begin
            if j < k
                continue
            if s(j) − s(k) = s′(n + 1) − s′(n) and r(p(j)) − r(p(k)) =
            r′(p′(n + 1)) − r′(p′(n))
                begin
                    z(n + 1) = j     /* keep matched position */
```

```
            if n = N - 1              /* if it is the end */
               begin
                  output matching result using z( )
                  return
               end
            else
               begin
                  tp = min(b)          /* tp is a temporary pointer */
                  min(b) points to the element in match(b) next to j
                  call procedure query2(n + 1, j)
                  min(b) = tp
                  return
               end
            end
      end                        /* end of loop 3 */
   return
end
```

In the above procedure, for every j in match $(x'(p'(1)))$, we search each element of $p()$ at most one time by using min(). Thus, the total running time is no more than $O (| \text{match} (x'(p'(1)))| * M)$. Let $mf = \min \{| \text{match}(a)| -$ number of a in $x'()|a$ in $V\}$ and denote such a by S. We can find the smallest n in $O(M)$ time such that $S = x'(p'(n))$, denote such n by na. If we start to match at na in two directions, it is easy to see that the time complexity is $O(mf^*M)$. In practice, we expect the value of mf to be very small, i.e. the matching problem has a very "narrow strait". To answer questions such as "Is this pattern a subpattern of picture f?" we canterminate the procedure "2Dquery" wherever we find a match.

In query processing, a query may allow for *variables*, such as $(a < x < c, b < x)$ meaning "what object 'x' is to the right of 'a' and to the left of 'c' and above 'b'?" Notice the above query $(a < x < c, b < x)$ is not a valid 2D query string. We can call it a partial 2D string. The following procedure is a generalized matching algorithm allowing for variables in 2D query strings, so that queries of the above type can be processed.

Procedure 2DqueryZ(u', v'; u, w; i)
begin
1. convert u', and v' to $(x', r') = (x'(1)\cdots x'(N), r'(1)\cdots r'(N))$ and $(y', s')=$
   $(y'(1)\cdots y'(N'), s(1)\cdots s'(N'))$ using procedure C(u';x',r') and

$C(v'; y', s')$ respectively

convert (u,w) to $(x,r,s,p) = (x(1)\cdots x(M), r(1)\cdots r(M), s(1)\cdots s(M), p(1)\cdots p(M))$
using procedure $CA(u, w; x, r, s, p)$

/* set up initial matching tables */

2. for j from 1 until M
 begin
  if $x(p(j)) = a$, let j belong to matcy(a) and $p(j)$ belong to matcx(a)
 end
 $MI(0) = \{0\}$
 $MI(N + 1) = \{M + 1\}$
 for n from 1 until N
 begin
  if $x'(n) \neq$ 'z'
   $MI(n) = matcx(x'(n))$
  else indz = n
  $mi = \min\{j \mid j$ belongs to $MI(indz - 1)\ \}$
  $ma = \max\{j \mid j$ belongs to $MI(indz + 1)\ \}$
  $MI(indz) = \{j \mid$ whenever $mi < j < ma\ \}$
 end
 $MI'(0) = \{0\}$
 $MI'(N' + 1) = \{M + 1\}$
 for n from 1 until N'
 begin
  if $y'(n) \neq$ 'z'
   $MI'(n) = matcy(y'(n))$
  else ind'z = n
   $mi = \min\{j \mid j$ belongs to $MI'(ind'z - 1)\ \}$
   $ma = \max\{j \mid j$ belongs to $MI'(ind'z + 1)\ \}$
   $MI'(ind'z) = \{\ j \mid$ whenever $mi < j < ma\ \}$
 end
 /* construct $MX(n), n = 1,\ldots,N$ */

3. $MP = MI(1)$
 for n from 2 until N
 begin
  $MC = \{\}$ /* $\{\}$ denotes empty set */
  while j belongs to $MI(n)$ and k belongs to MP such that $j > k$ and
   (when $i = 1$) $r(j) - r(k) \geq r'(n) - r'(n - 1) > 0$ or $r(j) - r(k)$
   $= r'(n) - r'(n - 1) = 0$
   (when $i = 2$) $r(j) - r(k) = r'(n) - r'(n - 1)$
   let j belong to MC and k belong to $f(j,n)$
  if MC is empty
   emit "zset is empty" and stop
  else $MP = MC$
 end

MX(N) = MC

for n from N − 1 to 1

begin

    MX(n) = { k | whenever k belongs to f(j, n + 1) for some j

    in MX(n + 1) }

end

/* construct MY(n), n = 1, ..., N' */

4. MP = MI'(1)

    for n from 2 until N'

    begin

        MC = {}

        while j belongs to MI'(n) and k belongs to MP such that j > k and

               (when i = 1) s(j) − s(k) ≥ s'(n) − s'(n − 1) > 0 or s(j) − s(k)

               = s'(n) − s'(n − 1) = 0

               (when i = 2) s(j) − s(k) = s'(n) − s'(n − 1)

            let j belong to MC and k belong to f'(j, n)

        if MC is empty

            emit "zset is empty" and stop

        else MP = MC

    end

    MY(N') = MC

    for n from N' − 1 to 1

    begin

        MY(n) = { k | whenever k belongs to f'(j, n + 1) for some j in

        MY(n + 1)}

    end

    /* find out the variable set to answer the query */

5. zset = { p(j) | whenever p(j) belongs to MX(indz) and j belongs to MY(ind'z) }

    emit zset

end

procedure C(u; x, r)

begin

    /* convert u = u (l) ··· u(L) to (x,r) = (x(1) ··· x(N), r(1) ··· r(N) */

    m = 0

    for l from 1 until L

    begin

        if u (l) ≠ '< '

            x(l − m) = u(l)

$$r(l - m) = m + 1$$
else m = m + 1
end
end

Similar to the analysis of the pervious algorithms, procedure "2DqueryZ" has a running time of $O(N^*lp)$, where lp is the maximal length of tables MI(n).

References

1. P. J. Basl and R. C. Jain, "Three-dimensional object recognition", *ACM Comput. Surveys* **17**, 1 (Mar. 1985) pp. 75–145.
2. N. S. Chang and K. S. Fu, "Query-by-pictorial-example", *Proc. COMPSAC 79, IEEE Comput. Soc.* (1979) pp. 325–330.
3. S. K. Chang, "The reconstruction of binary patterns from their projections", *Commun. ACM* **14**, 1 (Jan. 1971) pp. 21–25.
4. S. K. Chang and T. Kunii, "Pictorial database systems", *Computer (Special Issue on Pictorial Information Systems)*, Ed. S. K. Chang (Nov. 1981) pp. 13–21.
5. S. K. Chang and S. H. Liu, "Indexing and abstraction techniques for pictorial databases", *IEEE Trans. Pattern Anal. Machine Intell.* (July 1984) pp. 475–484.
6. S. K. Chang and O. Clarisse, "Interpretation and construction of icons for man-machine interface in an information system", in *IEEE Proc. Languages for Automation* (Nov. 1–3, 1984) pp. 38–45.
7. S. K. Chang and E. Jungert, "A pictorial data structure for spatial reasoning using orthogonal symbolic projections", *Proc. FJCC'86*, Dallas, TX (Nov. 2–6, 1986).
8. J. Drakopoulos and P. Constantopoulos, "An exact algorithm for 2D string matching", Technincal Report 21 (1989), Institute of Computer Science, Foundation for Research and Technology, Heraklion, Greece.
9. D. S. Hirschberg, "Algorithms for the longest common subsequence problem", *J. ACM*, **24** (1977) pp. 664–675.
10. J. W. Hunt and T. G. Szymanski, "A fast algorithm for computing longest common subsequences", *Commun. ACM*, **20** (1977) pp. 350–353.
11. E. G. M. Petrakis, "Image representation, indexing and retrieval based on spatial relationships and properties of objects", Ph.D. thesis, Technical report FORTH-ICS/TR-075 (1993), Institute of Computer Science, Foundation for Research and Technology, Heraklion, Greece.
12. H. Samet, "The quadtree and related data structures", *ACM Comput. Survey*, **16** (2) (June 1984) pp. 187–260.
13. S. L. Tanimoto, "An iconic/symbolic data structuring scheme", *Pattern Recognition and Artificial Intelligence*, Ed. C. H. Chen (Academic, New York 1976).

A NORMALIZED INDEX FOR IMAGE DATABASES

G. PETRAGLIA, M. SEBILLO, M. TUCCI and G. TORTORA

Dipartimento di Informatica ed Applicazioni
University of Salerno
I-84081 Baronissi, Salerno, Italy
E-mail: jentor@udsab.dia.unisa.it

The use of picture icons as picture indexes is the basic issue of the iconic indexing methodologies developed for advanced visual database applications. Most of the pictorial indexing methodologies developed so far describe images with meaningful orientation. However, in many cases, more freedom in the filing of images with respect to the orientation is required since the visual information contained in them is independent of any orientation or simply should not be affected by possible erroneous storing, for example in the reverse direction. The conventional methodologies based on orthogonal projections do not allow recognition of the identity between two indexes corresponding to an image and its reverse, even though their visual content is essentially the same.

We define a mapping between images and indexes that satisfies the property of *normalization*. In particular, we deal with the problems of reversing and rotation of images, which represent the two fundamental manipulations in the 2D space. An indexing methodology based on the Indexed 2D C-string is presented to overcome the limitation of the first problem. The transformation law called TX-6 allows us to obtain the index of a reverse image starting from the index of the original one.

Then, to obtain the rotation invariance, we introduce a system of polar axes that substitutes the Cartesian one, and totally inherits all the properties of orthogonal indexes. Finally, we define a structured index which represents the second level of normalization of an IDBS, because it describes an image considering its visual information rather than its external characteristics.

1. Introduction

One of the most important problems to be considered in the design of image database systems is how images are stored in the image database to model and access pictorial data [2, 4, 16]. In general, many advanced applications require that the image objects and their implicit information are converted into a pictorial knowledge structure able to support spatial reasoning and flexible information retrieval. To make an image database more flexible and faster, the spatial knowledge embedded in images should be preserved by the data structure used to store them [6].

43

In traditional database systems, the use of indexing to allow database accessing has been well established. Analogously, picture indexing techniques have been studied during the last decade to facilitate pictorial information retrieval from a pictorial database. The use of picture icons as picture indexes is the basic issue of the iconic indexing methodologies developed to this aim [17]. With this approach, the index of an image is a picture itself, which is suited to hold visual information and to allow different levels of abstraction and management [5, 7]. The Query-by-Pictorial-Example [1], is a methodology to express queries by a symbolic image containing the required objects and spatial constraints among them.

Chang *et al.* introduced the generalized 2D string (2D G-string) [3, 9]. A cutting mechanism segments the image by drawing cutting lines along the x- and y- directions at the beginning and ending points of the objects, so decomposing the image into many smaller subpictures.

A more efficient cutting mechanism has been introduced by Lee *et al.*, who proposed a new spatial knowledge representation, the 2D C-string [10]. It preserves all the spatial information of an image by drawing the least possible number of cutting lines. Both in the 2D G-string and in the 2D C-string representations every subpart is referred to by the same name of the whole object. To distinguish the multiple occurrences of the same symbol, a new iconic index, the *indexed 2D C-string*, has been introduced in [14]. This allows us to extract the spatial relations among whole objects, starting from the index, by the Atomic Relation Extraction Method AREM, which produces the set of the atomic relations (*virtual image*) corresponding to a given indexed 2D C-string by analysing the relations among the subparts of the objects in the image.

Most of the retrieval methodologies developed so far are based on pictorial indexing mechanisms that describe images with meaningful orientation. That is to say, those iconic indexes are constructed by scanning the image along pre-defined x- and y- directions. Pre-defining the x- and y- directions does not affect the filing process because an iconic index describes correctly the visual information in terms of objects and spatial relations. Likewise, during the retrieval process, the result of every comparison depends on the orientation of the query. On the other hand, let us consider an application like a medical image database system. The indexes associated with x-ray photographs should guarantee that answers to queries are independent of the possible erroneous storing of plates, for example in the reverse direction. The conventional methodologies based on orthogonal projections do not allow the recognition of the identity between two indexes corresponding to an image and its reverse, even though their visual contents are essentially the same.

Moreover, in many cases, more freedom in the filing of images with respect to the orientation is required since the visual information contained in them is independent of any orientation. In such cases, an iconic index like those discussed earlier is not sufficient to guarantee that the solution to a query is exhaustive. As an example, let us consider the management of images under a microscope. In most cases the orientation of this kind of pictures is not meaningful at all. Therefore, this pictorial information should be stored independently of any specific orientation. Consequently, the retrieval process must be rotation invariant.

In this chapter, we aim to define an association (mapping) between images and indexes that satisfies the property of *normalization*. In particular, we present an iconic index which is normalized with respect to reversing and rotation of images.

In particular, we overcome the limitation of the first problem by defining a transformation law over virtual images, called TX-6, which allows one to obtain the index of a reverse image starting from the index of the original one.

The second manipulation we consider concerns the rotation of images. The representation by orthogonal projections does not solve the problem of rotation invariance, because rotation modifies the relationship among pairs of objects. Then, in order to obtain the rotation invariance, we define a new index which represents the second level of normalization of an IDBMS, and allows matching by similarity.

In Secs. 2 and 3 we recall the existing iconic indexing methodologies. The normalized iconic indexing approach with respect to reversing and rotation is then presented in Sec. 4.

2. Iconic Indexing for Pictorial Retrieval in Image Databases

Retrieving pictures that satisfy high level spatial queries is an important issue of image database systems. An example of high level pictorial information retrieval could be "find all pictures showing a tree to the left of a house". In general, we consider queries for retrieving all the images containing a given subpattern, i.e. all the images where some objects appear in a specified spatial arrangement.

Chang *et al.* have introduced an iconic indexing method based on the 2D string representation [5]. As a first step to obtain an iconic index for a real image, the logical contents of the images are recognized and a symbolic picture is associated with the real image. A symbolic picture is a two dimensional matrix of symbols. Each object of the real image is represented by a symbol located in the centroid of the object. Then, the iconic index for the image is a compact representation of the symbolic picture obtained by projecting its symbols along the x- and y-directions.

2.1. *Definition*

Given a set V of t symbols, a (reduced) 2D string (u, v) over V is defined as a pair of strings:

$$(x_1 y_1 x_2 y_2 \ldots y_{t-1} x_t, x_{p(1)} z_1 x_{p(2)} z_2 \ldots z_{t-1} x_{p(t)})$$

where $x_i \in V$ and y_i, z_i are either "$<$" or is the empty string and $p : \{1, \ldots, t\} \rightarrow \{1, \ldots, t\}$ is a permutation function.

A 2D string can be derived from a symbolic picture by projecting the symbols of the picture by rows and by columns. The symbol '$<$' denotes the left-right spatial relation in u, and the below-above spatial relation in v. The symbol '$=$' denotes the spatial relation "at approximately the same spatial location as". For compactness, the symbols "$=$" are dropped, therefore two adjacent symbols are considered to be separated by the symbol "$=$".

The 2D string representation is also well suited to formulate queries. In fact, following the Query-by-Example approach, a query can be specified as an image drawn on the screen of a computer. The graphical representation of the image can be translated into a 2D string which is used as an index to access the database.

However, the 2D string iconic index is not sufficient to give a complete description of the spatial knowledge for complex images, since every object is considered as a point, i.e. the reference point for an object corresponds to its centroid. Thus, an image with many objects of complex sizes and shapes such as the one shown in Fig. 1 is not completely described by the 2D string.

In particular, in Fig. 1 if we project the borders of the objects A and D along the x- and y-directions, the resulting x-projection of the object A is partly contained in the x-projection of the object D, because the left border of A is overlapped by the right border of D. Therefore, this spatial relationship,

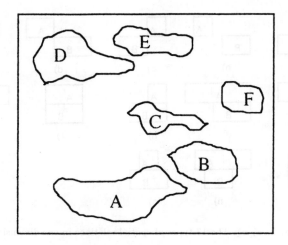

Fig. 1. A complex picture.

which is called *partly overlapping*, cannot be completely described by the 2D string either.

In order to describe more accurately the spatial relations among objects of different sizes and shapes, it is necessary to consider the objects with reference to their beginning point and ending point along the x- and y-direction.

To reach this aim, a more reliable knowledge structure for reasoning about spatial aspects has been introduced by Jungert *et al.* in [9]. They describe an algebra for symbolic image manipulation and transformation which is based both on the generalized empty space object e and a set of three elementary relational operators $G = \{<, =, |\}$, where the new spatial operator '$|$' stands for the *edge to edge with* relation, where A $|$ B means that the right (resp. top) border of the object A has the same projection of the left (resp. bottom) border of the object B.

The image is partitioned both parallel to the x- and y-coordinate axes and the partitions are performed at all the extreme points of all the present objects. In particular, since an extreme point is either a concave or a convex object-point, the generalized empty space e is used to distinguish an interval between two partition-lines which is derived by a convex object-point. Differently, the presence of a concave object-point can produce ambiguity during the reconstruction process. Then, the set of spatial operators G can describe the 13 types of spatial relationships shown in Fig. 2.

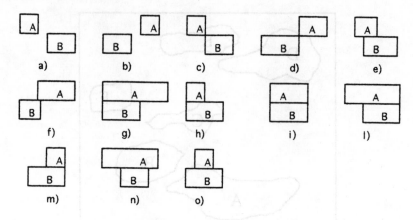

Fig. 2. a)–o): The 13 types of spatial relations in one dimension.

Along this line, Chang *et al.* [3, 8] extended the idea of symbolic projections introducing the cutting mechanism concept and defining a knowledge structure for pictorial databases. In order to establish the relations among the objects in terms of spatial operators they partition the real image by drawing cutting lines at the beginning and ending points of the overlapping objects, thereby decomposing the image into many smaller subpictures where each subpart is referred to by the same name of the whole object.

Formally, they introduced the knowledge structure called generalized 2D string (2D G-string), which is defined as follows.

2.2. *Definition*

The *knowledge structure* of the 2D G-string is a 5-tuple $(S, C, E_{\mathrm{op}}, e, \text{`( )'})$ where

(1) S is the set of symbols in symbolic pictures of interest,
(2) C is the cutting mechanism, which consists of cutting lines at the borders of the objects along the x- and y- projections,
(3) $E_{\mathrm{op}} = \{\text{`='}, \text{`<'}, \text{`|'}\}$ is the set of extended spatial operators,
(4) e is a special symbol which represents an area of any size and any shape, called *empty-space* object, and
(5) '( )' is a pair of separators which are used to describe a set of symbols as one local body.

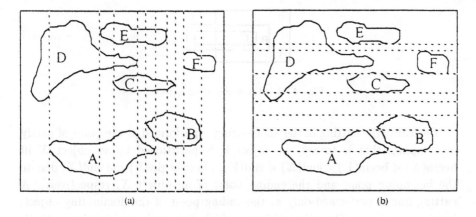

Fig. 3. The 2D G-string cutting mechanism.

The application of the 2D G-string cutting mechanism is shown in Fig. 3. However, the empty-space object e can be omitted to simplify the string representation. The string corresponding to the projection along the x-direction is D | A = D | A = D = E | A = C = D = E | A = C = E | A = B = C = E | B = C = E | B = C | B | B = F | F and the string corresponding to the projection along the y-direction is A | A = B | B < D | D = C | D = F | D | D = E.

The 2D G-string iconic index is a more effective representation of an image, but it requires a high storage overhead because the number of subparts of an object derived by the cutting mechanism is dependent on the number of the beginning and ending lines of other objects which are partly overlapping with it.

A more efficient cutting mechanism has been introduced by Lee *et al.* in the knowledge structure of 2D C-string [10].

3. 2D C-string and the Transformation Laws

Consider three objects, say A, B and C, arranged as shown in Fig. 4. The object A is called the dominating object because it is partly overlapping with the objects B and C, i.e. the beginning borders of the objects B and C are contained in the x-projection of the object A. On the contrary, B is not dominating compared with C, because it contains C completely, i.e. the x-projection of the object B contains both the beginning and the ending borders of C.

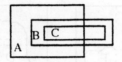

Fig. 4. *A* is the dominating object.

Basically, the cutting of the 2D C-string is performed at the point of partly overlapping, that is to say, an object Y is partitioned by an object X iff begin(X) < begin(Y) < end(X) < end(Y), where begin(X) and end(X) denote the beginning point and the ending point of an object X, respectively. A cutting line is performed only at the ending point of the dominating object, keeping it intact. The other objects, which are partly overlapping with it, are cut.

As an example, for the picture in Fig. 5 the cutting mechanism determines three lines along the x-direction (Fig. 5(a)), since D, A and B are dominating A, E and F, respectively; while only one line along the y-direction (Fig. 5(b)) is performed, since A is dominating B.

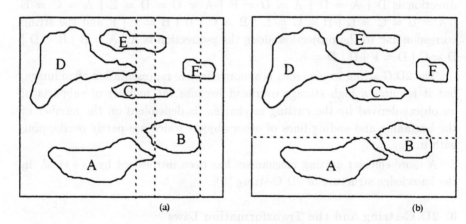

(a)   (b)

Fig. 5. The 2D C-string cutting mechanism.

The 2D C-string methodology considers the following set of spatial operators {'<', '|', '=', '[', ']', '%', '/' }. In Table 1 the meaning of the operators, together with their definition in terms of the beginning and ending points of the objects involved, is recalled.

Table 1. The definitions of 2D C-string spatial operators.

Notation	Meaning	Condition
A < B	A disjoins B	end(A) < begin(B)
A = B	A is the sameas B	begin(A) = begin(B)
		end(A) = end(B)
A I B	A is edge to edge with B	end(A) = begin(B)
A % B	A and B have not the	begin(A) < begin(B)
	same bounds and A	end(A) > end(B)
	contains B	
A [B	A and B have the	begin(A) = begin(B)
	same begin bound and	end(A) > end(B)
	A contains B	
A] B	A and B have the same	begin(A) < begin(B)
	end bound and A	end(B) = end(B)
	contains B	
A / B	A is partly overlapping	begin(A) < begin(B)
	with B	< end(A) < end(B)

The following transformation laws allow one to express some operators in terms of others. It is worth noting that the operator '/' (*partly overlapping*) can be expressed as a composition of the remaining operators:

(TX-1) $A = B \iff B = A$

(TX-2) $A [B \iff A = B | A$ or $B = A | A$

(TX-3) $A] B \iff A | A = B$ or $A | B = A$

(TX-4) $A\% B \iff A | A = B | A$ or $A | B = A | A$
$$\iff A] B | A$$
$$\iff A | A [B$$

(TX-5) $A / B \iff A | A = B | B$ or $A | B = A | B$
$$\iff A] B | B$$
$$\iff A | B [A$$

Finally, let us recall the definition of 2D *C*-string.

3.1. *Definition*

The *knowledge structure* of the 2D C-string is a 5-tuple $(S,\ C,\ R_{\text{glob}},\ R_{\text{loc}},\ `(\ )'\ )$ where

(1) S is the set of symbols in symbolic pictures of interest,
(2) C is the cutting mechanism, which consists of cutting lines at partly overlapping points,
(3) $R_{\text{glob}} = \{`<',\ `|'\ \}$ is the set of global relational operators,
(4) $R_{\text{loc}} = \{`=',\ `[',\ `]',\ `\%'\ \}$ is the set of local relational operators, and
(5) $`(\ )'$ is a pair of separators which are used to describe a set of symbols as one local body.

A 2D C-string (u, v) over S is a pair of strings

$$(x_{i_1} y_{i_1} x_{i_2} y_{i_2} \ldots y_{i_{(t-1)}} x_{i_t},\ x_{j_1} z_{j_1} x_{j_2} z_{j_2} \ldots z_{j_{(s-1)}} x_{j_s})$$

where $x_{i_k},\ x_{j_h} \in S$ are objects or subparts of objects of S and $y_{i_m},\ z_{j_n} \in R_{\text{glob}} \cup R_{\text{loc}}$ are relational operators, for $1 \leq k \leq t,\ 1 \leq m \leq t-1,\ 1 \leq h \leq s$ and $1 \leq n \leq s-1$.

As an example, the 2D C-string representation (u, v) for the picture of Fig. 5 is :
u: D] A] E] C | A = C = E] B | B = (C [E < F) | F,
v: A] B | B < D] (C | F < E).

The 2D C-string allows one to efficiently represent and handle pictures of arbitrary complexity. However, it is not easy to define types of matching between 2D C-strings, like those considered for the 2D strings [12].

Moreover, each occurrence of a symbol concerns its different subparts, even if it is referred to by the name of the whole object. Consequently, it is not possible to distinguish the multiple occurrences of the same symbol within the string because the concept of object is substituted by the concept of subpart.

The limitations of the 2D C-string with respect to the matching problem are overcome in [14], where the indexed 2D C-string and the Atomic Relation Extraction Method (AREM) are introduced. The indexed 2D C-string is able to maintain information about the different subparts of the same object. AREM is used to extract the set of the spatial relations holding between each pair of objects. Such relations are called *atomic relations* and the set of objects and atomic relations corresponding to an image is called *virtual image*.

The main difference between the 2D C-string and the indexed 2D C-string is in the cutting mechanism, which, besides partitioning the objects, numbers the derived subparts in a progressive way both along the x- and the y- directions, independently. The spatial operators of the indexed 2D C-string are defined like those of the 2D C-string (see Table 1).

Then, the indexed 2D C-string (u, v) over S is defined as a pair of strings:

$$(x_{i_1} y_{i_1} x_{i_2} y_{i_2} \ldots y_{i_{(t-1)}} x_{i_t}, \; x_{j_1} z_{j_1} x_{j_2} z_{j_2} \ldots z_{j_{(s-1)}} x_{j_s})$$

where x_{i_k} and $x_{j_h} \in S$ are objects or subparts of objects of S, y_{i_m} and $z_{j_n} \in R_{\text{glob}} \cup R_{\text{loc}}$ are relational operators, $1 \le k \le t$, $1 \le m \le t-1$, $1 \le h \le s$ and $1 \le n \le s-1$.

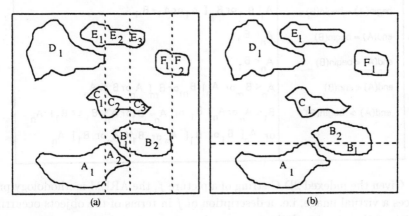

Fig. 6. The indexed 2D C-string cutting mechanism along the x-projection (a), and the y-projection (b).

As an example, the indexed 2D C-string (u, v) for the image depicted in Fig. 6 is:

u: D_1] A_1] E_1] C_1| $A_2 = C_2 = E_2$] B_1| $B_2 = (C_3 \; [E_3 <F_1)|$ F_2,

v: A_1] B_1| $B_2 < C_1 <D_1\% \; (F_1 < E_1)$.

In general, given the objects A and B where A is the dominating object, let $\{A_1, \ldots, A_n\}$ and $\{B_1, \ldots, B_m\}$ be the sets of their subparts derived from the cutting mechanism of the indexed 2D C-string. The spatial relations holding between (A_1, B_1), (A_n, B_m), and (A_n, B_1) are said *characteristic relations*, while the subparts A_1, B_1, A_n and B_m are said *characteristic subparts*. In the previous example, the characteristic subparts along the x-projection are D_1, A_1, E_1, C_1, B_1, F_1, A_2, E_3, C_3, B_2 D_1, and F_2.

Table 2 describes the correspondence between the characteristic relations of two objects A and B and the relations holding between their borders.

Table 2. The correspondence between the conditions on the borders and the conditions on the characteristic relations.

Condition on the borders	Condition on the characteristic subparts
begin(A) < begin(B)	$A_1 < B_1$ or $A_1] B_1$ or $A_1 \% B_1$ or $A_1	B_1$
end(A) > end(B)	$B_m < A_n$ or $A_n[B_m$ or $B_m	A_n$ or $A_n \% B_m$
end(A) = end(B)	$A_n] B_m$ or $B_m] A_n$ or $A_n = B_m$
begin(A) = begin(B)	$A_1[B_1$ or $B_1 [A_1$ or $A_1 = B_1$
end(A) = begin(B)	$A_n	B_1$
end(A) < begin(B)	$A_n < B_1$
end(A) < end(B)	$A_n < B_m$ or $A_n	B_m$ or $B_m[A_n$ or $B_m \% A_n$
end(A) > begin(B)	$B_1 < A_n$ or $A_n] B_1$ or $A_n = B_1$ or $A \% B_1$ or $B_1	A_n$ or $A_n[B_1$ or $B_1[A_n$ or $B_1 \% A_n$ or $B_1] A_n$

Given the indexed 2D C-string of a picture f, the AREM methodology produces a virtual image, i.e. a description of f in terms of the objects occurring in it and the atomic relations among them.

Let us recall the definition of virtual image [14].

3.2. Definition

A virtual image P is a pair (Ob, Rs) where
$Ob = \{ob_1, \ldots, ob_n\}$ is a set of entities;
$Rs = (Rs_x, Rs_y)$ is a pair of sets of the form $\{r(p_i, p_w) | r \in R_{glob} \cup R_{loc}$, where p_i, p_w are objects in $Ob\}$. Each $r(p_i, p_w)$ in Rs_x (resp. Rs_y) represents a spatial relation between a pair of objects in Ob along the x-projection (resp. y-projection).

In the representation given by the virtual image, the atomic relations represent the spatial arrangement of the objects; this elementary information is independent of the spatial arrangement of the other pairs of objects. On the contrary, the iconic indexes based on the cutting mechanism partition overlapping objects deriving smaller subparts and the spatial relations among the subparts can be different from the one holding between whole objects.

Then, in order to derive the virtual image starting from the indexed 2D C-string, we propose the Atomic Relation Extraction Method (AREM), which is based on the spatial operators defined in Table 2 and consists of two major steps:

(1) obtain all the spatial relations among subparts from the indexed 2D C-string thanks to the picture algebra laws introduced in [11], and
(2) derive all the atomic relations starting from the spatial relations over the characteristic subparts obtained from the first step.

Let us consider the picture of Fig. 6. In the first step, the indexed 2D C-string (u, v) is decomposed by iteratively applying the laws of the picture algebra. In the following some iterations of AREM are shown in detail for the first component u.

Initially, u: $D_1]$ $A_1]$ $E_1]$ $C_1|$ $A_2 = C_2 = E_2]$ $B_1|$ $B_2 = (C_3[$ $E_3 < F_1)|$ F_2. The Distributive Law DL-2 is applicable, since $r_{(k-1)k} =$ '$=$' is a local operator, $r_{m(m+1)} =$ '$|$' is a global operator and the substrings:

(1) $D_1]$ $A_1]$ $E_1]$ $C_1|$ $A_2 = C_2 = E_2]$ B_1 $|$ B_2,
(2) $B_2 = (C_3[$ $E_3 < F_1)$,

are in the forms (TL-5) and (DL-1) respectively. Moreover, there exists $r_{(s1-1)s1} =$ '$|$' which is a global operator. Then the following three strings are obtained:

u.1: $C_3[$ $E_3 < F_1$,
u.2: $D_1]$ $A_1]$ $E_1]$ $C_1|$ $A_2 = C_2 = E_2]$ $B_1|$ $B_2[$ $C_3[$ $E_3|$ F_2,
u.3: $D_1]$ $A_1]$ $E_1]$ $C_1|$ $A_2 = C_2 = E_2]$ $B_1|$ $B_2]$ $F_1|$ F_2.

Then, the Transformation Law TL-0 can be applied to the u.1 string, since it represents a 2D C-string which relates three spatial objects: $s_1 = C_3$, $s_2 = E_3$, $s_3 = F_1$
so we derive three binary relations:

u.1.1 : $C_3[$ E_3,
u.1.2 : $E_3 < F_1$,
u.1.3 : $C_3 < F_1$.

Conversely, the Transformation Law TL-5 can be applied both to $u.2$ and $u.3$ since $r_{(sk-1)sk} = $ '|' is a global operator, and the other $r_{(i-1)i}$ are local operators. Therefore, we have the following two sets of three substrings:

$u.2.1 : D_1] A_1] E_1] C_1| A_2 = C_2 = E_2] B_1$

$u.2.2 : A_2 = C_2 = E_2] B_1| B_2[C_3[E_3| F_2$

$u.2.3 : D_1] A_1] E_1] C_1 < B_2[C_3[E_3| F_2$

and

$u.3.1 : D_1] A_1] E_1] C_1| A_2 = C_2 = E_2] B_1$

$u.3.2 : A_2 = C_2 = E_2] B_1| B_2[C_3[E_3| F_2$

$u.3.3 : D_1] A_1] E_1] C_1 < B_2] F_1| F_2$

Then, by applying the picture algebra laws iteratively, we derive all the binary relations among each pair of objects and/or subparts.

For the sake of clarity, the following table gathers the binary relations among subparts of C, D, E and F produced by the complete application of the first step. In the table, they are divided with respect to their arguments: in each column the binary relations found between each pair of objects are reported.

C vs E	C vs F	D vs E	D vs C	E vs F	D vs F
$C_3 [E_3$	$C_3 < F_1$	$D_1] E_1$	$D_1] C_1$	$E_1 < F_1$	$D_1 < F_1$
$E_1] C_1$	$C_3 < F_2$	$D_1	E_2$	$D_1 < C_2$	$E_1 < F_2$	$D_1 < F_2$
$C_2 = E_2$	$C_2 < F_2$	$D_1 < E_3$	$D_1 < C_3$	$E_2 < F_1$	
$E_1	C_2$	$C_1 < F_2$			$E_2 < F_2$	
$C_1	E_2$	$C_2 < F_1$			$E_3 < F_1$	
$C_2	E_3$	$C_1 < F_1$			$E_3 < F_2$	
$E_2	C_3$					
$E_1 < C_3$					
$C_1 < E_3$					

In the second step, the atomic relations are obtained by verifying the conditions on the characteristic subparts.

For the previous example, the characteristic relations between C and E are $E_1] C_1$, $C_3[E_3$ and $C_1 < E_3$. Then, according to Table 2, we have

$E_1] C_1 \Rightarrow$ begin(E) < begin(C),
$C_3[E_3 \Rightarrow$ end(E) < end(C),
$C_1 < E_3 \Rightarrow$ end(E) > begin(C).

Finally, according to Table 1, we can conclude that E/C, since the condition

begin(E) < begin(C) and end(E) < end(C) and end(E) > begin(C)

is satisfied.

The atomic relations holding between the other pairs of objects are derived analogously:

C vs F	($C_1 <F_1$, $C_3 <F_2$, $C_3 <F_1$) $\Rightarrow$ C<F
D vs E	($D_1]E_1$, $D_1 <E_3$, $D_1]E_1$) $\Rightarrow$ D/E
D vs C	($D_1]C_1$, $D_1 <C_3$, $D_1]C_1$) $\Rightarrow$ D/C
E vs F	($E_1 <F_1$, $E_3 <F_2$, $E_3 <F_1$) $\Rightarrow$ E<F
D vs F	($D_1 <F_1$, $D_1 <F_2$, $D_1 <F_1$) $\Rightarrow$ D < F

Then, the atomic relations corresponding to the objects C, D, E and F obtained from the u string are: C<F, E/C, D/E, D/C, E<F and D<F. Analogously, the process is applied to the v string so obtaining the atomic relations corresponding to the objects C, D, E and F along the y-projection.

At this point, AREM derives the corresponding virtual image (Ob, Rs) as illustrated below:

$Ob = \{A, B, C, D, E, F\},$

$Rs_x = \{(D/A), (D/E), (D/C), (D < B), (D < F), (A/C), (A/E), (A/B),$
$\qquad (A < F), (B/F), (C/B), (C < F), (E/C), (E/B), (E < F)\},$

$Rs_y = \{(A/B), (A < C), (A < D), (A < E), (A < F), (B < C), (B < D),$
$\qquad (B < E), (B < F), (C < D), (C < E), (C/F), (F|D),$
$\qquad (D/E), (F < E)\}.$

4. Normalized Iconic Indexing

Many advanced applications require that image objects and their implicit information be converted into a pictorial knowledge structure able to support spatial reasoning and flexible information retrieval.

In particular, it may be necessary to perform various transformations, so that the desired image knowledge can be easily accessed, visualized, and/or manipulated. The transformations include: rotation, translation, reversing, change of point of view, projection from 3- to 2-D views, etc. Therefore, the capability of preserving the similarity between an image and a manipulation of it is an important requirement for an iconic index to be reliable. In case of images in which objects are considered as points, the problem of rotation invariance has been faced by using a graph-like representation called *point panorama graph* (see [15] for details). In the case of complex objects, the conventional methodologies based on orthogonal projections do not allow the recognition of the identity between two indexes corresponding to an image and one of its manipulations.

Our aim is to define an association (mapping) between images and indexes that satisfies the property of *normalization*, i.e. a mapping which avoids the problem of information loss and recognizes the similarity existing among images when they have been manipulated by the above specified transformations, i.e. rotation along a fixed axis and rotation around a fixed point.

In particular, we deal with the problems of reversing and rotation of images, which represent two fundamental manipulations in the 2D space.

As a matter of fact, let us consider the storing of photographic images or slides, where the visual content can be extracted even though the image is analyzed according to the reverse orientation. In particular, let us consider again an x-ray photograph which has been erroneously stored according to the reverse direction. It cannot be retrieved unless the query is also proposed according to the reverse direction, because the conventional methodologies based on the orthogonal projections do not allow the recognition of the identity between two indexes corresponding to an image and its reverse.

The second manipulation we are considering concerns the rotation of images. In many cases, more freedom in the filing of images with respect to the orientation is required since the visual information contained in them is independent of any orientation. In such cases, an iconic index like those discussed earlier is not sufficient to guarantee that the solution to a query is exhaustive.

As an example, let us consider the management of images under a microscope. The orientation of this kind of pictures is not meaningful at all, since the only possible reference point is the center of the visual visible circular image. Therefore, this pictorial information should be stored independently of any specific orientation. Consequently, the retrieval process must be rotation invariant.

4.1. Normalizing with respect to reversing

Now we present an indexing methodology whose aim is to consider the requirements presented earlier. In particular, we overcome the limitations of the first problem by defining a transformation law, called TX-6, which allows one to obtain the index of a reverse image starting from the index of the original one. Then, in order to verify if a picture f is obtained by reversing another one g, it is sufficient to compare the virtual image of f, say V_f, to the one obtained by transforming the virtual image of g, say V_g, via TX-6. In other words, it is sufficient to verify whether V_f matches with TX-6(V_g).

Let us consider the pictures in Fig. 7. They have the same visual contents, but the corresponding u components of the indexed 2D C-string are obtained scanning the image according to different x-directions. The u component obtained by scanning the image along the x-direction from left to right (see Fig. 7(a)) is:

$u : D_1]A_1]E_1]C_1|A_2=C_2=E_2]B_1|B_2=(C_3[E_3 <F_1)| F_2,$

while the u' component, corresponding to the scanning from right to left (see Fig. 7(b)) is

$u': F_1]B_1|B_2]C_1]E_1]A_1|A_2=C_2=E_2]D_1|D_2[A_3[E_3.$

Then, the string u' cannot be derived from the string u even if they describe the same visual information. Let us observe that the spatial operators are

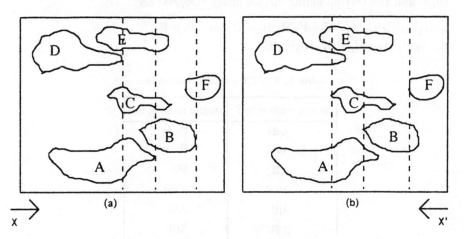

(a)   (b)

$x \longrightarrow$ $\longleftarrow x'$

Fig. 7. Two different scannings of the same picture.

defined in terms of conditions over their borders (beginning point and ending point). Then, when reversing the scanning direction, the beginning point of an object is exchanged with the ending point of the same object. Moreover, when evaluating the indexed 2D C-string of the reverse image, the cutting mechanism determines different cutting lines.

On the contrary, AREM derives the atomic relations independently of the performed cutting lines. Then, the virtual image of the reverse picture can be directly obtained from the atomic relations of the original one. Starting from this observation, the transformation law TX-6 can be easily derived.

To fix our ideas, given a picture f, let Rs_x be the set of the atomic relations on the objects in f along the x-axis. Let f' be the picture obtained by reversing f along the y-axis and Rs_x the set of its atomic relations along the x-axis. The transformation law TX-6 relates the atomic relations in Rs_x to the ones in Rs_x. The same law applies to the set of atomic relations along the y-axis when reversing along the x-axis as well.

In Table 3, the definition of TX-6 is given by the correspondence between each atomic relation in f and its corresponding one in f'. In order to show the correctness of the correspondences in TX-6, let us consider the first one in the table. Let A and B be two objects in f, then, A < B in f holds iff $\text{end}_f(A) < \text{begin}_f(B)$ from the definition; by reversing f we obtain: $\text{end}_{f'}(B) < \text{begin}_{f'}(A)$ and then B < A in f'.

As an example, consider the picture of Fig. 7(a). Its indexed 2D C-string (u, v) and the corresponding virtual image (Ob, Rs) are:

u :D$_1$]A$_1$]E$_1$]C$_1$|A$_2$=C$_2$=E$_2$]B$_1$|B$_2$=(C$_3$[E$_3$ <F$_1$)| F$_2$,
v : A$_1$]B$_1$|B$_2$ <C$_1$]F$_1$|F$_2$|D$_1$]E$_1$|E$_2$.

Table 3. The TX-6 transformation law.

atomic relation in f	atomic relation in f'
A<B	B<A
A=B	B=A
A|B	B|A
A%B	A%B
A[B	A]B
A]B	A[B
A/B	B/A

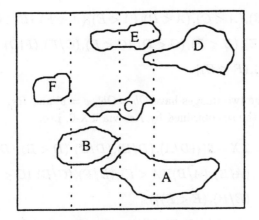

Fig. 8. A reversion of the image of Fig. 7.

$Ob = \{A, B, C, D, E, F\}$,

$Rs = (Rs_x, Rs_y)$where

$Rs_x = \{(D/A), (D/E), (D/C), (D < B), (D < F), (A/C), (A/E), (A/B),$

$\quad (A < F), (B/F), (C/B), (C < F), (E/C), (E/B), (E < F)\}$,

$Rs_y = \{(A/B), (A < C), (A < D), (A < E), (A < F), (B < C), (B < D),$

$\quad (B < E), (B < F), (C < D), (C < E), (C/F), (F|D),$

$\quad (D/E), (F < E)\}$.

Figure 8 shows the image obtained by reversing the picture of Fig. 7 along the y-axis, its indexed 2D C-string (u', v') is the following:

u': $F_1]B_1|B_2]C_1]E_1]A_1|A_2=C_2=E_2]D_1|D_2$ $[A3[E3,$
v': $A_1]B_1|B_2 <C_1]F_1|F_2|D_1]E_1|E_2$.

By applying the AREM methodology to this indexed 2D C-string, the following virtual image (Ob', Rs') is obtained

$Ob' = \{A, B, C, D, E, F\}$,

$Rs'_x = \{(A/D), (E/D), (C/D), (B < D), (F < D), (C/A), (E/A), (B/A),$

$\quad (F < A), (F/B), (B/C), (F < C), (C/E), (B/E), (F < E)\}$,

$$Rs'_y = \{(A/B), (A < C), (A < D), (A < E), (A < F), (B < C), (B < D),$$
$$(B < E), (B < F), (C < D), (C < E), (C/F), (F|D),$$
$$(D/E), (F < E)\}.$$

Of course, the two images have $Ob = Ob'$, $v = v'$ and $Rs_y = Rs'_y$.
Let us evaluate the set obtained by Rs_x via TX-6, i. e.

$$TX - 6(Rs_x) = TX - 6(\{(D/A), (D/E), (D/C), (D < B), (D < F), (A/C),$$
$$(A/E), (A/B), (A < F), (B/F), (C/B), (C < F), (E/C),$$
$$(E/B), (E < F)\})$$
$$= \{(A/D), (E/D), (C/D), (B < D), (F < D), (C/A), (E/A),$$
$$(B/A), (F < A), (F/B), (B/C), (F < C), (C/E),$$
$$(B/E), (F < E)\}$$
$$= Rs'x.$$

Then, it is proved that a virtual image is a normalized index with respect
to the reversing operation along the axes, or equivalently, with the respect to
the reversing scanning direction.

4.2. *Normalizing with respect to rotation*

We have just presented a first level of normalization for the conventional
methodologies based on the orthogonal projections, which solves the problem of independence with respect to the reversion. On the other hand, the
representation by orthogonal projections does not solve the problem of rotation invariance, because any rotation can modify the relationship among a pair
of objects. In order to obtain the rotation invariance with respect to the center
of the image, as in the case of images under microscope, we introduce an index
based on a system of polar axes which substitutes the Cartesian one, and inherits important properties of orthogonal indexes, such as the transformation
laws TX-1 to TX-5.

Here we present a solution to the rotation invariance requirement, thus
representing a further level of normalization of an IDBMS.

A solution to the problem of rotation invariance is obtained by associating
any image in the image database with a complex iconic index. Such iconic index

is actually a pair (2R string, 2D string) where the first index, the 2R string [13], looses the information about the orientation so maintaining rotation invariant information and the second index, the 2D string [5], preserves information about the original storing orientation.

The iconic index 2R *string* is defined with respect to a settled object. It uses a system of polar axes whose origin, *the rotation center*, coincides with the centroid of the settled object.

Without loss of generality, the rotation center can be the centroid of the object which is closest to the center of the image, while the *rotation line*, given by the half-line with respect to which the scanning is performed, is shown in the picture 10(b), provided that it does not cross any object, otherwise the initial position of the rotation line is considered to be the first one in the clockwise direction for which this condition holds. If, even rotating the half-line, the condition is not successful, the rotation center is moved to the next object encountered when moving from the center of the image to outside. Once the rotation center has been selected, the object to which it belongs is ignored in the successive cutting phases.

Then the 2R string is obtained by a cutting mechanism in which the cutting lines along the x- and y-direction are replaced by circles having the *rotation center* as center and radial segments around the rotation center, i.e. cutting lines along the ring-direction *(c-direction)* and sector-direction *(s-direction)*, respectively.

For each object the beginning point and ending point along the sector-direction are defined by considering the radial segments which are tangent to the object itself (see Fig. 9(a)), the beginning point and the ending point along the ring direction are defined by the concentric circles which are tangent to the object (Fig. 9(b)).

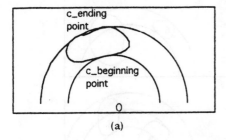
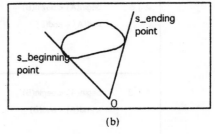

Fig. 9. The beginning points and the ending points along the c- and s-direction.

Table 4(a). Definitions of 2R string spatial operators along the c-direction.

Notation	Condition	Meaning
A < B	end(A) < begin(B)	
A = B	begin(A) = begin(B) end(A) = end(B)	
A | B	end(A) = begin(B)	
A % B	begin(A) < begin(B) end(A) > end(B)	
A [B	begin(A) = begin(B) end(A) > end(B)	
A] B	begin(A) < begin(B) end(A) = end(B)	
A / B	begin(A) < begin(B) < end(A) < end(B)	

Table 4(b). Definitions of 2R string spatial operators along the *s*-direction.

Notation	Condition	Meaning
A < B	end(A) < begin(B)	
A = B	begin(A) = begin(B) end(A) = end(B)	
A I B	end(A) = begin(B)	
A % B	begin(A) < begin(B) end(A) > end(B)	
A [B	begin(A) = begin(B) end(A) > end(B)	
A] B	begin(A) < begin(B) end(A) = end(B)	
A / B	begin(A) < begin(B) < end(A) < end(B)	

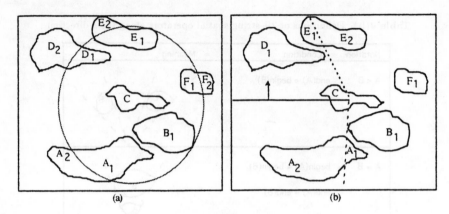

Fig. 10. The 2R string cutting mechanism.

Then, by analogy with the indexed 2D C-string, we can describe every spatial relation in terms of conditions over the beginning point and the ending point along the s-direction and the c-direction, which are again fundamental features of the objects. In Tables 4(a) and 4(b) the new set of spatial relations are defined. For example, the *disjoint* relation "$<$" along the c-direction is satisfied, i.e. A$<$B, if the ending point of A precedes the beginning point of B when moving from the rotation center to outside.

For the example of Fig. 10 only a cutting line is performed along the c-direction because the object B is partly overlapping with A, while two cutting lines are drawn along the s-direction because the object D is partly overlapping with E and the object B is partly overlapping with A. The 2R string with respect to the object C is given by the following pair (c, s):

$$c : B_1] \; A_1 \;] \; D_1 \; = \; F_1 \;] \; E_1 \; | \; D_2 \; [\; A_2 \; [\; F_2 \; [\; E_2,$$
$$s : D_1 \;] \; E_1| \; E_2 \; < \; F_1 \; < \; B_1 \;] \; A_1 \; | \; A_2 \; < \; D_1.$$

To prove the rotation invariance of the 2R string it is sufficient to observe that the beginning point and the ending point of an object do not change when the image is rotated. Consequently, the spatial relations are unchanged as well. That is to say, if an image is represented by the 2R string r_1, the same image, when rotated, determines a 2R string r_2 from which r_1 can be easily derived. As an example, let us consider the picture in Fig. 11 whose 2-R string is

$$c: B_1] \; A_1 \;] \; D_1 \; = \; F_1 \;] \; E_1| \; D_2 \; [\; A_2 \; [\; F_2 \; [\; E_2,$$
$$s: F_1 \; < \; B_1 \;] \; A_1| \; A_2 \; < \; D_1 \;] \; E_1| \; E_2 \; < \; F_1.$$

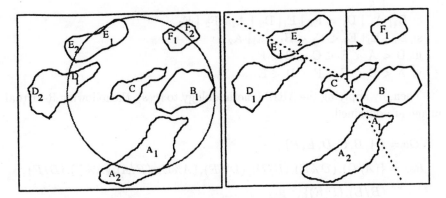

Fig. 11. A rotation of the picture in Fig. 10.

It is easily verified that this picture corresponds to a rotation of the picture of Fig. 10, since c and c' are identical while s' can be obtained by a rotation of s.

A further property of the complex iconic index (2R string, 2D string) is that the 2R string is defined in terms of objects and spatial relations as is the indexed 2D C-string, and in particular it exploits the same spatial operators by adapting their meanings to the polar system. Thus, since the AREM methodology does not depend on the fact that a Cartesian or polar system is used, the query definition introduced in [13] apply also in the case of the 2R string thereby enhancing the flexibility and usability of pictorial retrieval. The application of the AREM methodology to the 2R string generates a virtual image which is both reversion and rotation invariant.

Such virtual image is called *normalized virtual image* in the following.

4.2.1. *Definition*

The normalized virtual image can be defined as a pair (NOb, NRs) where

$NOb = \{ob_1, \ldots, ob_n\}$ is a set of entities,
$NRs = ((Rs_c, Rs_s), (u, v))$ where

$(NOb, (Rs_c, Rs_s))$ is the virtual image constructed by applying the AREM methodology to the 2R string, called R-virtual image, and (u, v) is the 2D string over the centroids.

As an example, let us consider the image in Fig. 10; its 2R string (c, s) and the 2D string (u, v) are

c: B_1] A_1] $D_1 = F_1$] E_1| D_2 [A_2 [F_2 [E_2
s: D_1] E_1| $E_2 < F_1 < B_1$] A_1| A_2
u: $D < A < E < C < B < F$
v: $A < B < C < F < D < E$

Then, by applying the AREM methodology to (c, s), the following R-virtual image are obtained:

$$NOb = \{A, B, C, D, E, F\},$$
$$Rs_c = \{(A/D), (D\%E), (B/D), (D\%F), (A\%E), (B/A), (A\%F), (B/F),$$
$$(B/E), (F]E)\},$$
$$Rs_s = \{(B/A), (D < A), (E < A), (F < A), (D < B), (E < B), (F < B),$$
$$(D < F), (D/E), (E < F)\}.$$

All the rotations of the image around the rotation center will have the same 2R string and then the same R-virtual image. The information regarding the original storing rotation is maintained by the 2D string so rendering possible approximated or precise queries.

The reconstructability of the normalized iconic index is driven by the reconstruction algorithm given for the 2D string [5].

5. Conclusion

The present work is part of a project aiming to define and implement a SQL-like query language for Image Databases. To this aim, the first issue to be faced is related to the definition of a good normalized image index, which does not depend on how the pictures are stored. In this chapter such an index has been proposed and its independence on rotation and reversing has been shown.

In the image database system we are considering storing images together with their iconic index (2R string, 2D string). Then, a query itself is formulated as an iconic index, which represent a comparison image. The rotation and reversing invariance guarantees that the solution to a query does not depend on how the pictures are stored in the database.

References

1. N. S. Chang and K. S. Fu, "Query-by-pictorial example", *IEEE Trans. on Softw. Eng.* **6** (Nov. 1980) pp. 519–524.

2. S.-K. Chang and A. Hsu, "Image information systems: where do we go from here?", *IEEE Trans. on Knowledge and Data Eng.* **TKDE-4**, 5 (October 1992) pp. 431–442.

3. S.-K. Chang and E. Jungert, "Pictorial data management based upon the theory of symbolic projections", *J. of Visual Languages and Comp.* **2**, 3 (Sept. 1991) pp. 195–215.

4. S.-K. Chang and S.-H. Liu, "Picture indexing and abstraction techniques for pictorial database", *IEEE Trans. Pattern Anal. Machine Intell.* **6**, 4 (Jul. 1984) pp. 475–484.

5. S.-K. Chang, Q. Y. Shi, and C. W. Yan, "Iconic indexing by 2D string", *IEEE Trans. Pattern Anal. Machine Intell.* **9**, 3 (May 1987) pp. 413–428.

6. S.-K Chang, C. W. Yan, D. C. Dimitroff, and T. Arndt, "An intelligent image database system", *IEEE Trans. on Softw. Eng.* **14** (May 1988) pp. 681–688.

7. G. Costagliola, G. Tortora, and T. Arndt, "A unifying approach to iconic indexing for 2D and 3D scenes", *IEEE Trans. on Knowledge and Data Eng.* **4** (June 1992) pp. 205–222.

8. E. Jungert, "Extended symbolic projection used in a knowledge structure for spatial reasoning", *4th BPRA Conf. on Pattern Recognition* (Springer, Cambridge, March 1988).

9. E. Jungert and S.-K. Chang, "An image algebra for pictorial data manipulation", *CVGIP: Image Understanding*, **58**, 2 (Sept. 1993) pp. 147–160.

10. S. Y. Lee and F. J. Hsu, "2D C-string: a new spatial knowledge representation for image database systems", *Pattern Recognition*, **23** (Oct. 1990) pp. 1077–1088.

11. S. Y. Lee and F. J. Hsu, "Picture algebra for spatial reasoning of iconic images represented in 2D C-string", *Pattern Recognition Letters*, **12** (July 1991) pp. 425–435.

12. S. Y. Lee and F. J. Hsu, "Spatial reasoning and similarity retrieval of images using 2D C-string knowledge representation", *Pattern Recognition*, **25** (March 1992) pp. 305–318.

13. G. Petraglia, M. Sebillo, M. Tucci, and G. Tortora, "Rotation invariant iconic indexing for image database retrieval", *Progress in Image Analysis and Processing III*, ed. S. Impedovo (World Scientific, 1994) pp. 271–278.

14. G. Petraglia, M. Sebillo, M. Tucci, and G. Tortora, "Towards normalized iconic indexing", *Proc. 1993 IEEE Symp. on Visual Language*, Bergen, Norway (Aug. 24–27, 1993) pp. 392–394.

15. C. Schlieder, "Ordering information and symbolic projection", this book.

16. H. Tamura and N. Yokoya, "Image database systems: a survey", *Pattern Recognition*, **17**, 1 (Oct. 1984) pp. 29–43.

17. S. L. Tanimoto, "An iconic symbolic data structuring scheme", *Pattern Recognition and Artificial Intelligence* (Academic Press, New York, 1976) pp. 452–471.

REPRESENTATION OF 3D SYMBOLIC AND BINARY PICTURES USING 3D STRINGS

S. K. CHANG and Y. LI

Department of Computer Science
University of Pittsburgh

A new way of representing three dimensional pictures, called 3D string, is defined in this chapter. The ambiguity of this representation is discussed with respect to the properties of pictures. Algorithms are presented for reconstructing a 3D binary picture from its 3D string. As an extension to Chang's earlier chapter about 2D string, a procedure is given in this chapter to calculate the number of binary 2D functions with a given 2D string as their 2D string. Picture matching can be carried out by means of 3D string matching, for which algorithms are presented. This representation is efficient and can be applied to construct iconic indexes for 3D pictures. However, problems about the ambiguity of 3D string remain to be solved.

1. Introduction

2D string has been proposed for representing symbolic pictures [4] and is shown to be an efficient approach in solving the problem of pictorial information retrieval and in constructing iconic indexes for pictures in an image database. In addition to its effectiveness, the idea of 2D string poses many interesting topics of further investigations, as discussed in [4]. Recently, we have extended 2D string to 2D H-string to represent 2D multi-resolution pictures [5], which is the result of our intention of generalizing 2D string representation through the combination of quadtrees [6], and 2D strings. Another intention is to expand 2D string approach to the 3D case, which becomes more important in many applications.

In this chapter, we will present an approach of representing 3D pictures, called 3D strings. We will first give the definitions in Sec. 2 along with some notations used in this chapter. The ambiguities of the representation will be thoroughly investigated in Sec. 3, which includes the results on the relation between the ambiguity of representation of a picture and the existence of switching components in the picture. For symbolic pictures, the ambiguity of a representation can be detected directly from the representation itself. However, necessary and sufficient conditions for a picture to be similar to another picture are left as conjectures. In Sec. 4, algorithms are presented for reconstructing 3D binary patterns from their 3-view orthogonal projections. As an extension to Chang's earlier paper about 2D string, a procedure is given for calculating the number of binary 2D functions with a given 2D string as their 2D string. Section 5 will address picture matching problem in terms of 3D string subsequence matching and the algorithms thereof are proposed. The final section will give a brief summary of the problems which need to be further investigated.

2. Notations and Definitions

Let V be a set of symbols. $M = \{1, 2, \ldots, n\}. A = \{:, =, <\}$.
A volumetric function f is a mapping from M^3 to 2^V.
A 3D string over V is defined as (u, v, w), in which

$$u = x_1 a_1 x_2 a_2 \cdots a_{n-1} x_n$$
$$v = x_{p(1)} b_1 x_{p(2)} b_2 \cdots b_{n-1} x_{p(n)}$$
$$w = x_{q(1)} c_1 x_{q(2)} c_2 \cdots c_{n-1} x_{q(n)}$$

Where $x_i \in V$, $a_j, b_j, c_j \in A$, $i = 1, 2, \ldots, n$, $j = 1, 2, \ldots, n-1$, p and q are permutations over M.

Notations.

$$f_x : M \to 2^V. \text{ For } i \in M, \ f_x(i) = \bigcup_{j=1}^{n} \bigcup_{k=1}^{n} f(i, j, k)$$

$$f_{xy} : M^2 \to 2^V. \text{ For } (i, j) \in M^2, f_{xy}(i, j) = \bigcup_{k-1}^{n} f(i, j, k)$$

For $i \in M, f_{x=i} : M^2 \to 2^V. \text{For} (j, k) \in M^2, f_{x=i}(j, k) = f(i, j, k).$

For $S \in 2^V, f^S : M^3 \to 2^V. \text{For}(i, j, k) \in M^3, f^S(i, j, k) = f(i, j, k) \bigcap S.$

Similarly, $f_y, f_z, f_{xz}, f_{yz}, f_{y=j}, f_{z=k}$ can be defined. If f is a binary picture, then in the definition $\cup$ means "sum of".

In terms of 2D or 3D string, symbols are arranged in strings. While in terms of volumetric function, symbols are arranged in sets. Here we take strings and sets as the same, which means a string can be regarded as a set and vice versa.

Definition 1. The 3D string of f is defined as (u, v, w), denoted as $s - 3d(f) = (u, v, w)$, where (u, v) is the 2D string of f_{xz} and (w, v) is the 2D string of f_{yz}.
Actually, $s - 3d(f)$ is

$$(f_x(1) < f_x(2) < \cdots < f_x(n), f_y(1) < f_y(2) < \cdots < f_y(n),$$
$$f_z(1) < f_z(2) < \cdots < f_x(n))$$

The reduced 3D string and the normal 3D string of picture f are defined in the same way as the reduced 2D string and the normal 2D string.

Suppose $u = u_1 < u_2 < \cdots < u_n$ such that there is no "$<$" in u_i, $i = 1, 2, \ldots, n$. Define $\text{subs}(i, u) = u_i$, called the ith local substring of u, for $i = 1, 2, \ldots, n$.

The *rank* of a symbol "a" in a string u, denoted by $r(a, u)$, is defined to be one plus the number of "$<$" preceding this symbol in u.

3. Ambiguities of 3D strings

3.1. *Ambiguities versus switching components*

Definition 2. A picture f is said to be ambiguous if there is a picture g such that $f \neq g$ and $s - 2d(f) = s - 2d(g)$ (or $s - 3d(f) = s - 3d(g)$).

Definition 3. f and g are said to be similar to each other if $f \neq g$ and $s - 2d(f) = s - 2d(g)$ (or $s - 3d(f) = s - 3d(g)$).

Theorem 1. *A 2D symbolic picture f without subpattern of the form*

$$
\begin{array}{ccc}
a & \cdots\cdots & a \\
\vdots & & \vdots \\
a & \cdots\cdots & a
\end{array}
$$

is ambiguous under the reduced 2D string if and only if its reduced 2D string contains the subsequence $(a < a, a < a)$, where "a" is some symbol in V.

Proof. Suppose f is ambiguous, then there exist g such that $f \neq g$ and $s - 2d(f) = s - 2d(g)$. We can find (i, j) such that $f(i, j) \neq g(i, j)$. Without loss of generality, suppose there is $a \in V$ such that $a \in f(i, j)$, but a is not in $g(i, j)$. Then $f^a(i, j) = a$, $g^a(i, j) = \varnothing$, while $f^a{}_x(i) = g^a{}_x(i)$, $f^a{}_y(j) = g^a{}_y(j)$, $i, j = 1, 2, \ldots, n$, because of $s - 2d(f) = s - 2d(g)$. By Chang [3], f^a has switching components. Thus $s - 2d(f)$ has $(a < a, a < a)$ as subsequence.

Suppose $s - 2d(f)$ has $(a < a, a < a)$ as a subsequence. There must be i_1, i_2, j_1, j_2 such that $i_1 \neq i_2$, $j_1 \neq j_2$, $a \in f(i_1, j_1)$, $a \in f(i_2, j_2)$. Let $g(i_1, j_1) = f(i_1, j_1) - \{a\}$, $g(i_2, j_2) = f(i_2, j_2) - \{a\}$, $g(i_1, j_2) = f(i_1, j_2) \cup \{a\}$, $g(i_2, j_1) = f(i_2, j_1) \cup \{a\}, g(i, j) = f(i, j)$ for other (i, j). Then $g \neq f$ but $s - 2d(g) = s - 2d(f)$. $\qquad\square$

Corollary 1. *If a picture f is ambiguous under normal 2D string, then $s - 2d(f)$ must contain $(a < a, a < a)$ as a subsequence.*

Corollary 2. *If $s - 2d(f)$ contains $(S < S, S < S)$ as a subsequence, then f must be ambiguous under normal 2D string, where S is a set in local substring.*

Theorem 2. *A 3D symbolic picture f without the subpattern of the form*

is ambiguous under the reduced 3D string if and only if its reduced 3D string contains the subsequence $(a < a, a < a, a < a)$ or $(a < a, a < a, aa)$ or $(a < a, aa, a < a)$ or $(aa, a < a, a < a)$, where "a" is some symbol in V.

Proof. Suppose f is ambiguous, i.e. there is g such that $f \neq g$ and $s - 3d(f) = s - 3d(g)$. If at least one of $f_{xy} \neq g_{xy}, f_{xz} \neq g_{xz}, f_{yz} \neq g_{yz}$ holds, without loss of generality supposing $f_{yz} \neq g_{yz}$, then f_{yz} is ambiguous under reduced 2D string, i.e. $s - 2d(f)$ has $(a < a, a < a)$ as subsequence. Hence $s - 3d(f_{yz})$ has $(aa, a < a, a < a)$ or $(a < a, a < a, a < a)$ as subsequence. Otherwise, we have $f_{xy} = g_{xy}, f_{xz} = g_{xz}, f_{yz} = g_{yz}$. There is (ii, jj, kk) such that $f(ii, jj, kk) \neq g(ii, jj, kk)$. Then $f_{x=ii} \neq g_{x=ii}$, while $f_{x=ii\ y}(j) = f_{xy}(ii, j) = g_{xy}(ii, j) = g_{x=ii\ y}(j); f_{x=ii\ z}(k) = f_{xz}(ii, k) = g_{xz}(ii, k) = g_{x=ii\ z}(k)$. This implies that $s - 2d(f_{x=ii})$ has $(a < a, a < a)$ as subsequence. Thus $s - 3d(f)$ has $(a < a, a < a, a < a)$ as subsequence.

The converse side of the theorem can be proven in the same way as in 2D case. $\qquad\square$

Definition 4. A binary picture f is said to have type-i switching component if there are indices $i_1, j_1, k_1, i_2, j_2, k_2, i_1 \neq i_2, j_1 \neq j_2, k_1 \neq k_2$ such that (type-1) $f(i_1, j_1, k_1) = f(i_1, j_2, k_2) = 1 - f(i_1, j_1, k_2) = 1 - f(i_1, j_2, k_1)$,

         also called yz — *plane* switching component.

(type-2) $f(i_1, j_1, k_1) = f(i_2, j_1, k_2) = 1 - f(i_1, j_1, k_2) = 1 - f(i_2, j_1, k_1)$,

         also called xz — *plane* switching component.

(type-3) $f(i_1, j_1, k_1) = f(i_2, j_2, k_1) = 1 - f(i_1, j_2, k_1) = 1 - f(i_2, j_1, k_1)$,

         also called xy — *plane* switching component.

(type-4) $f(i_1, j_1, k_1) = f(i_2, j_2, k_2) = 1 - f(i_2, j_1, k_1) = 1 - f(i_1, j_2, k_2)$,

         also called x — *direction* switching component.

(type-5) $f(i_1, j_1, k_1) = f(i_2, j_2, k_2) = 1 - f(i_1, j_2, k_1) = 1 - f(i_2, j_1, k_2)$,

         also called y — *direction* switching component.

(type-6) $f(i_1, j_1, k_1) = f(i_2, j_2, k_2) = 1 - f(i_1, j_1, k_2) = 1 - f(i_2, j_2, k_1)$,

         also called z — *direction* switching component.

Theorem 3. *If f and g are similar binary 3D pictures, and at least one of the equations $f_{xy} = g_{xy}, f_{xz} = g_{xz}, f_{yz} = g_{yz}$ holds, then f has a switching component. If a binary 3D picture f has a switching component, it must be ambiguous.*

Proof. Suppose f and g are similar. Then we have $f_x = g_x, f_y = g_y, f_z = g_z$, and there is (ii, jj, kk) such that $f(ii, jj, kk) \neq g(ii, jj, kk)$. Assume that f has no switching components and we will derive a contradiction.

Case 1. If just one of the three equations holds, suppose $f_{xy} = g_{xy}$. Assume that f has no switching components and we will derive a contradiction. Then by the same reasoning as in Chang [3] we have

$$f(i_1', j_1', k_1') = 1 \qquad g(i_1', j_1', k_1') = 0$$
$$f(i_2', j_2', k_1') = 0 \qquad g(i_2', j_2', k_1') = 1$$
$$f(i_2', j_2', k_2') = 1 \qquad g(i_2', j_2', k_2') = 0$$
$$f(i_3', j_3', k_2') = 0 \qquad g(i_3', j_3', k_2') = 1$$
$$f(i_3', j_3', k_3') = 1 \qquad g(i_3', j_3', k_3') = 0$$
$$\vdots \qquad\qquad\qquad \vdots$$
$$f(i_n', j_n', k_n') = 1 \qquad g(i_n', j_n', k_n') = 0$$
$$f(i_1', j_1', k_n') = 0 \qquad g(i_1', j_1', k_n') = 1$$

Since $f(i'_1, j'_1, k'_n) = 0$, $f(i'_n, j'_n, k'_n) = 1$, $f(i'_n, j'_n, k'_{n-1}) = 0$, we must have $f(i'_1, j'_1, k'_{n-1}) = 0$. Repeating the same process, we have $f(i'_1, j'_1, k'_{n-2}) = \cdots = f(i'_1, j'_1, k'_1) = 0$. This is contradictory to $f(i'_1, j'_1, k'_1) = 1$. Thus f must have a switching component. In this case, we can see that the switching component is a *direction* switching component.

Case 2. If at least two of the three equations hold, suppose $f_{xy} = g_{xy}, f_{xz} = g_{xz}$. Consider the 2D binary picture $f_{x=ii}$, we have $f_{x=ii} \neq g_{x=ii}$, while $f_{x=iiy}(j) = f_{xy}(ii, j) = g_{xy}(ii, j) = g_{x=iiy}(j), f_{x=iiz}(k) = f_{xz}(ii, k) = g_{xz}(ii, k) = g_{x=iiz}(k)$. By Chang [3], we know that $f_{x=ii}$ has a 2D switching component. Thus f has a 3D switching component, which must be a *plane* switching component.

The other part of the theorem is obviously correct. □

Definition 5. f is a 3D picture. Define a *x-plane switching operation* $S[x : i_1, i_2](f)$ on f, $i_1 \neq i_2$, to be a mapping from f to another 3D picture g such that for all j, k, $g(i_1, j, k) = f(i_2, j, k)$, $g(i_2, j, k) = f(i_1, j, k)$, and $g(i, j, k) = f(i, j, k)$, $i \neq i_1, i_2$.
Similarly, $S[y : j_1, j_2](f)$ and $S[z : k_1, k_2](f)$ can be defined.

Lemma. *f is a 3D binary picture, and g is the result of a series of plane switching operations on f, then f has switching components if and only if g has switching components.*

Definition 6. f is said to be equivalent to g under plane switching if it can be transformed to g by a series of plane switching operations.

Theorem 4. *3D binary picture g has no switching components if and only if g is equivalent to a picture f which has the following properties:*

$$f(i_1, j, k) \geq f(i_2, j, k) \text{ for all } (i_1, j, k) \text{ and } (i_2, j, k) \text{ with } i_1 < i_2$$

$$f(i, j_1, k) \geq f(i, j_2, k) \text{ for all } (i, j_1, k) \text{ and } (i, j_2, k) \text{ with } j_1 < j_2$$

$$f(i, j, k_1) \geq f(i, j, k_2) \text{ for all } (i, j, k_1) \text{ and } (i, j, k_2) \text{ with } k_1 < k_2$$

Proof. Suppose g has no switching components. We can find a series of plane switching operations $S = S_1 S_2 \cdots S_l$ on g to get f such that f_x, f_y, f_z decrease progressively.

If there are indices i_1, i_2, j, k, where $i_1 < i_2$ such that $f(i_1, j, k) < f(i_2, j, k)$, then since $f_x(i_1) \geq f_x(i_2)$ there must be (j_1, k_1) such that $f(i_1, j_1, k_1)$

$> f(i_2, j_1, k_1)$. Thus $(i_1, j, k), (i_2, j, k), (i_1, j_1, k_1), (i_2, j_1, k_1)$ form a switching component in f. Then g has a switching component, by Lemma 1. This contradicts to the premise. So f has the properties stated by the inequalities. The other part of the theorem is evidently true. □

Definition 7. If a picture f has the property stated by the above inequalities, f is called *straight convex*.

We have found a pair of functions which are straight convex and similar to each other. This indicates that there exist such functions that have no switching components but are ambiguous. Here are the examples:

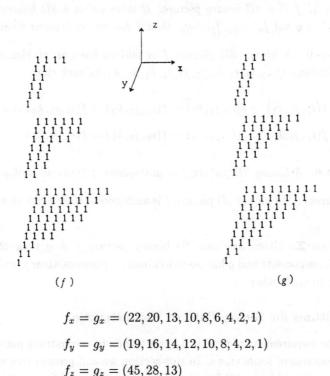

(f)
(g)

$$f_x = g_x = (22, 20, 13, 10, 8, 6, 4, 2, 1)$$

$$f_y = g_y = (19, 16, 14, 12, 10, 8, 4, 2, 1)$$

$$f_z = g_z = (45, 28, 13)$$

From these examples, we can see how tough the ambiguous characteristic problem is. Ambiguity has no relation with symmetry and is not directly related to the switching components defined early in these section. However, these examples give us a hint that the definition of switching components needs to be expanded to include slantwise switchings.

3.2. *Ambiguities versus ambiguous loops*

Definition 8. A binary 3D picture f is said to have an *ambiguous z-chain* if there are indices $i_1, i_2, j_1, j_2, k_1, k_2, k_3, k_4$ such that

$$f(i_1, j_1, k_1) = f(i_2, j_2, k_3) = 0$$

$$f(i_1, j_2, k_2) = f(i_2, j_1, k_4) = 1$$

Similarly, *ambiguous x-chain* and *ambiguous y-chain* can be defined.

Theorem 5. f *is a 3D binary picture. If there exists a 3D binary picture* g *such that* $f \neq g$ *but* $f_x = g_x, f_y = g_y$, *then* f *has an ambiguous z-chain.*

Definition 9. A binary 3D picture f is said to have an ambiguous loop if there are indices $i_1, i_2, i_3, i_4, j_1, j_2, j_3, j_4, k_1, k_2, k_3, k_4$ such that

$$f(i_1, j_1, k_1) = f(i_2, j_2, k_3) = f(i_3, j_4, k_2) = f(i_4, j_3, k_4) = 0$$

$$f(i_1, j_2, k_2) = f(i_2, j_1, k_4) = f(i_3, j_3, k_1) = f(i_4, j_4, k_3) = 1$$

Theorem 6. *A binary 3D picture* f *is ambiguous if* f *has an ambiguous loop.*

Conjecture 1. If a binary 3D picture f is ambiguous, then f has an ambiguous loop.

Conjecture 2. Given any two 3D binary picture $f \neq g$ such that f has switching components and g has no switching components, then f and g cannot be similar to each other.

4. Algorithms for Binary Pattern Reconstruction

It is the requirement of practical applications to reconstruct patterns from their projections of some views. In this section we will present two algorithms for constructing a binary 3D function f from its 3-view orthogonal projections f_x, f_y, f_z. However, the first question should be: given f_x, f_y, f_z, how many functions could be reconstructed? Let us denote the number of these functions by $\text{NC}(f_x, f_y, f_z)$. By now, we can give a procedural solution to this question in 2D case, i.e. a procedure can be provided to calculate $\text{NC}(f_x, f_y)$. Below gives the procedure for calculating $\text{NC}(f_x, f_y)$.

Procedure $Count(f_x, f_y)$

/*Given $f_x(i), f_y(j), f_x(i) \geq 0, f_y(j) \geq 0, \text{i,j} = 1, 2, \ldots, \text{N},$

and $\displaystyle\sum_{i=1}^{N} f_x(i) = \sum_{j=1}^{N} f_y(j)$

calculate $CN(f_x, f_y)$, the number of functions that have (f_x, f_y) as their projection. */

Begin

    For $v \in \{x,y\}$, let

        $N_v = |\{f_v(i) \neq 0, i = 1,2, \ldots, N\}|,$

        $C_v = \max\{f_v(i), i = 1,2, \ldots, N\},$

        I_V be the largest i such that $f_v(i) = C_v$.

    Let CN=0, CC=$\max(C_x, C_y)$.

    If $C_x \geq C_y$, let dir=x, dop=y;

    Otherwise, let dir=y, dop=x.

    If $CC = N_{dop}$

        begin

            Let $f'_{dir}(I_{dir}) = 0, f'_{dir}(i) = f_{dir}(i)$, for $i \neq I_{dir}$,

            Let $f'_{dop}(i) = \max(0, f_{dop}(i) - 1)$, for $i = 1,2, \ldots, N$.

            $CN = count(f'_x, f'_y)$.

        end

    else if $CC < N_{dop}$

        begin

            Let $S_{dop} = \{i | f_{dop}(i) \neq 0\}$

            For ever CC-combination $(I_1, I_2, \ldots, I_{CC})$ of S_{dop},

                begin

                    Let $f'_{dir}(I_{dir}) = 0, f'_{dir}(i) = f_{dir}(i)$, for $i \neq I_{dir}$.

                    Let $f'_{dop}(I_k) = \max(0, f_{dop}(I_k) - 1)$, for $k = 1,2, \ldots, CC$.

                    Let $f'_{dop}(i) = f_{dop}(i)$, for $i \neq I_1, I_2, \ldots, I_{CC}$.

                    $CN = CN + count(f'_x, f'_y)$.

                end

        end

    Return(CN).

End

As for 3D case, the problem is still under investigation. The following two algorithms are for reconstructing 3D functions from given projection (f_x, f_y, f_z).

Algorithm 1.

Define
$$h(i, j, k) = f_x(i) + f_y(j) + f_z(k).$$
Begin

   Set all points (i, j, k) to be qualified.

   Call Procedure *Select* repeatedly until no new points can be selected.

   Call Procedure *Select* with the modification that m is the smallest

         integer larger than or equal to $f_z(k)$ (or $f_x(i)$ or $f_y(j)$)

   Halt and exit with g as the reconstructed function.

End

Procedure *Select*

Begin

   For $k = 1, 2, \ldots,$ N, do

         begin

               Order all qualified points $(i, j, k), i, j=1,2,\ldots$,N, into a sequence
               $p_1 p_2 \cdots$ by their h-values such that $h(p_l) \geq h(p_{l+1})$. Select the
               first m points in this ordered sequence, where m is the largest
               integer such that $m \leq f_z(k)$ and $h(p_m) > h(p_{m+1})$.

               Let $gz(i, j, k)$=1 if (i, j, k) is selected. Otherwise let $gz(i, j, k)$=0.

         end

   Following the same principle of generating function gz, generate gy, gx.

   Let g=min(gx, gy, gz).

   For k=1,2,\ldots,N, if $g_z(k) = f_z(k)$ then on plane z=k, set all zero-points

   of gz to be not qualified.

   Do the same thing for plane x=i and y=j according to gx and gy.

End

This algorithm has been executed with the data exhausting all possible 3D pictures of size $3 \times 3 \times 3$. The running result of our program shows that in $3 \times 3 \times 3$ case the algorithm is capable of generating a function containing the original function if the original function is ambiguous, or reconstructing the original function if the original function is unambiguous. But a theoretical proof is hard to carry out.

By Lemma 2 of the preceding section, any function without switching components is equivalent to a straight convex function. Thus in reconstructing the unambiguous function, we can assume that the input projections f_x, f_y, and f_z decrease progressively. Next is an algorithm reconstructing all possible functions of the given projections by building the functions plane by plane.

Consider a plane, for example, $z = k$. We are required to construct a function $f_z = k$ which is straight convex. When all these functions $f_{z=k}, k = 1, 2, \ldots, KK$, are placed in 3D space layer by layer, they will yield a 3D straight convex function which has the given functions as its projections.

For plane $z = k$, k starts from 1 to KK, let $ny = \max\{i | f_x(i) > 0\}$, $nx = \max\{j | f_y(j) > 0\}$. Then the problem is turned into constructing a partition of $f_z(k)$ into ny parts with the largest part being nx. If we found a partition $\{n_i, i = 1, 2, \ldots, ny\}$, $n_i \geq n_{i+1} + 1, n_1 = nx$, then let $f(i, j, k) = 1$ for $i = 1, 2, \ldots, ny$, $j = 1, 2, \ldots, n_i$. For other (i, j) let $f(i, j, k)=0$; subtract the elements of $f(i, j, k)$ from f_x, f_y, f_z. Go on to $k = k + 1$ until $k = KK$. Below is the algorithm.

Algorithm 2.
Begin

    Set $a(i, j, k)=0$ for all (i, j, k), $1 \leq i \leq II, 1 \leq j \leq JJ, 1 \leq k \leq KK$.

    Let $\text{Top}_k = \max\{k | f_z(k) > 0\}$.

    Call Procedure A$(f_x, f_y, f_z, a, 1)$.

End

Procedure A$(f_x, f_y, f_z, a, \text{Current}_k)$
Begin

    Let $Ck^- = \text{Current}_k - 1$

    For $j = 1, 2, \ldots, JJ$, let $g_y(j) = f(j) - \sum_{i=1}^{II} \sum_{k=1}^{C_k^-} a(i, j, k)$.

    For $i = 1, 2, \ldots, II$, let $g_x(i) = f_x(i) - \sum_{j=1}^{JJ} \sum_{k=1}^{C_k^-} a(i, j, k)$.

    Let ny=$\max\{i\ |g_x(i) > 0\}$. Let nx=$\max\{j\ |g_y(j) > 0\}$. Let n=f_z
    (Current_k).

    Generate all the permutations of n into nx parts, p(1),p(2),...p(nx), such that p(1)=ny, p(l)≥p(l+1).

For each permutation p(1),p(2),...,p(nx), do

> begin
>> Let $a(i,j, \text{Current}_k) = 1$ for j=1,2,...,nx, i=1,2,...,p(j). If $\text{Current}_k = \text{Top}_k$
>>> check if a is a possible reconstruction or not, and report.
>> Else
>>> Call procedure A with $(f_x, f_y, f_z, a, \text{Current}_k + 1)$.
>>> Let $a(i,j,\text{Current}_k) = 0$ for $i = 1,2,\ldots,\text{II}, j = 1,2,\ldots,\text{JJ}$.
> end

End

Using the method in Beckenbach [1], we can orderly list, in procedure A, all partitions of n into nx parts $p(1)p(2)\cdots p(nx)$ such that $p(l) \geq p(l+1)$. This algorithm is implemented with some testing data, the result of which is exactly what we are seeking.

5. Picture Matching by 3D String Matching

In Chang [4], it has been shown that 2D string representation provides a simple approach to performing subpicture matching on 2D pictures, that is, a picture matching problem becomes a string matching problem. As for the string comparison problem, there have been quite a few approaches proposed by early researchers [2]. But our problem here is more complicated because 2D/3D strings have spatial information embedded which should not be ignored by considering only symbolic matching. Here we adopt the definition of Chang [4] about *type-i 1D* subsequences, while the definition of 2D subsequence is adapted to 3D case with a slight revision according to the type of 3D strings.

Definition 10. A string u' is said to be contained in a string u if u' is a subsequence of a permutation string of u, denoted as $u' \subset u$(or $u \supset u'$).

Definition 11. A string u' is a *type-i 1D subsequence* of string u if

1. u' is contained in u, and
2. if $a'wb'$ is a substring of u',a',b' match a,b in u respectively, then

$$(\text{type-0})r(b) - r(a) \geq r(b') - r(a') > 0 \text{ or}$$
$$r(b') - r(a') = 0$$

$$(\text{type-1})r(b) - r(a) \geq r(b') - r(a') > 0 \text{ or}$$

$$r(b) - r(a) = r(b') - r(a') = 0$$

$$(\text{type-2})r(b) - r(a) = r(b') - r(a')$$

Suppose $u' = u'_1 < u'_2 < \cdots < u'_m, u = u_1 < u_2 < \cdots < u_n$. It can be checked whether u' is a *type-0* 1D subsequence of u or not. Here we present an algorithm.

Definition 12. Let $u = u_1 < u_2 < \cdots < u_n$. The string consisting of the first l local substrings of u is denoted as $h(u, l)$; that is, $h(u, l) = u_1 < u_2 < \cdots < u_l$. The string formed by cutting off the first l local substrings is denoted as $cuth(u, l)$, that is, $cuth(u, l) = u_{l+1} < u_{l+2} < \cdots < u_n$.

Algorithm 1D match($u', u, 0$)
Begin
    Let $l_1 = \min \{l | h(u, l) | u'_1\}$;
    For i=1 to m-1
        begin
            If $\{l | h(cuth(u, l_i), l) \supset u'_{i+1}\} = \varnothing$, exit, and report "$u'$ is not a subsequence of u".
            Else, let $l_{i+1} = \min\{l | h(cuth(u, l_i), l) \supset u'_i\} + l_i$;
            Halt, report "u' is a type-0 subsequence of u".
        end
End

It is even easier to check whether u' is *type-1* and *type-2* 1D subsequence of u. Construct a $m \times n$ matrix $A_{m \times n}$ where $A(i, j) = 1$ if $u'_i \subset u_j$, $A(i, j) = 0$ otherwise. If there exists $j_0 \geq 0$ such that $A(i, j_0 + i) = 1$ for $i = 1, 2, \ldots, m$, then u' is a type-2 1D subsequence of u. If there are indices $j_1, j_2, \ldots, j_m$, where $j_1 < j_2 < \cdots < j_m$, such that $A(i, j_i) = 1$ for $i = 1, 2, \ldots, m$, then u' is a type-1 1D subsequence of u. Let's generalize the definition of A.

Definition 13. Suppose $u' = u'_1 < u'_2 < \cdots < u'_m, u = u_1 < u_2 < \cdots < u_n$. Define a matrix $A_{m \times n}$ where $A(i, j) = 1$ if $u'_i \subset u_j$, $A(i, j) = 0$ otherwise. A is called the *matching matrix* from u' to u, denoted as $M_-A(u', u)$.

Definition 14. In a matrix $A_{m \times n}$, if there is $j_0 \geq 0$ such that $A(i, j_0 + i) = 1$ for $i = 1, 2, \ldots, m$, then A is called a *type-2 matching matrix*. If there are indices $j_1, j_2, \cdots, j_m$, where $j_1 < j_2 < \cdots < j_m$, such that $A(i, j_i) = 1$, for $i = 1, 2, \ldots, m$, then A is called a *type-1 matching matrix*.

It can be seen that there are differences between augmented 2D string matching and reduced 2D string matching.

Definition 15. For reduced 3D strings, (u', v', w') is said to be a *type-i 3D subsequence* of (u, v, w) if $u', v',$ and w' are type-i 1D subsequence of $u, u,$ and w, respectively.

Definition 16. For augmented 3D strings, (u', v', w') is said to be a *type $- i$ 3D subsequence* of (u, v, w) if $u', v',$ and w' are type-i 1D subsequence of $u, u,$ and w, respectively, with the matchings from u' to u, from v' to v, and from w' to w being the same.

However, for the definition of subpicture we prefer that only *type-2* subsequences are considered as subpictures.

Definition 17. Let (u, v, w) and (u', v', w') be the 3D string representations of f and f' respectively. We say f' is a *subpicture* of f if (u', v', w') is a *type-2* 3D subsequence of (u, v, w).

Next, we will present an algorithm performing subpicture matching on augmented 3D strings.

Algorithm 3D subpicture matching

Begin

Call procedure Arrange((u, v, w), $\{u_i, n\}$, $\{v_{i,j}, n_i^1\}$, $\{w_{i,j,k}, n_{i,j}^2\}$) and call procedure Arrange((u', v', w'), $\{u_i', m\}$, $\{v_{i,j}', m_i^1\}$, $\{w_{i,j,k}', m_{i,j}^2\}$).

Construct matrices $AW_{i,j;ii,jj} = \mathrm{M}\ \_\mathrm{A}(v_{i,j}', v_{ii,jj})$, for $i = 1, 2, \ldots, m$, $j = 1, 2, \ldots, m_i^1$, and $ii = 1, 2, \ldots, n, jj = 1, 2, \ldots, n_{ii}^1$, where $v_{i,j}' = w_{i,j,1}' < w_{i,j,2}' < \cdots < w_{i,j,m_{i,j}^2}'$, and $v_{ii,jj} = w_{ii,jj,1} < w_{ii,jj,2} < \cdots < w_{ii,jj,n_{ii,jj}^2}$.

Construct matrices $AV_{i,ii}$ of dimension $m_i^1 \times n_{ii}^1$ as follows: for $j = 1, 2, \ldots, m_i^1$ and $jj = 1, 2, \ldots, n_{ii}^1$, if $AW_{i,j;ii,jj}$ is a type-2 matching matrix, let $AV_{i,ii}(j, jj) = 1$, otherwise let $AV_{i,ii}(j, jj) = 0$.

Construct matrices AU of dimension $m \times n$ as follows: for $i = 1, 2, \ldots, m$ and $ii = 1, 2, \ldots, n$, if $AV_{i,ii}$ is a type-2 matching matrix, let $AU(i, ii) = 1$, otherwise let $AU(i, ii) = 0$.

If AU is a type-2 matching matrix, report "(u', v', w') is a subpicture of

(u, v, w)". Otherwise, report "(u', v', w') is not a subpicture of (u, v, w)".
End

Procedure Arrange($(u, v, w), \{u_i, n\}, \{v_{i,j}, n_i^1\}, \{w_{i,j,k}, n_{i,j}^2\}$)
Begin

    Let r, s, and t be the rank functions of the symbols in (u, v, w), that is, for any $a \; \epsilon u, r(a) = r(a, u), s(a) = r(a, v)$, and $t(a) = r(a, w)$.

    Rearrange the symbols of u into local substrings $\{u_i\}, \{v_{i,j}\}, \{w_{i,j,k}\}$, that is,

$$u = u_1 < u_2 < u_2 < \cdots < u_n$$
$$u_i = v_{i,1} v_{i,2} \cdots v_{i,n_i^1}$$
$$v_{i,j} = w_{i,j,1} w_{i,j,2} \ldots w_{i,j,n_{i,j}^2}.$$

such that for any $a, b \in V$, $a \in w_{i,j,k}, b \in w_{ii,jj,kk}$, if $i < ii$, then $r(a) < r(b)$, if $i = ii$, then $r(a) = r(b)$; when $i = ii$, if $j < jj$, then $s(a) < s(b)$, if $j = jj$, then $s(a) = s(b)$; when $i = ii, j = jj$, if $k < kk$, then $t(a) < t(b)$, if $k = kk$, then $t(a) = t(b)$.

End

6. Further Investigations

It seems to us that the most interesting problem is to find out the properties of similar 3D pictures in terms of 3D string representation, although it is very difficult and is left as unsolved conjectures in this paper. Compared with the definition of other researchers who are working on representing 3D pictures in terms of projections, our representation is quite simple. Actually, our result about ambiguities implies their result. Of course, it is very far from completion. Another interesting problem could be stated as: given a 3D binary function, how can we know whether its 3D string representation is ambiguous or not? and Furthermore, given f_x, f_y, f_z, how can $\mathrm{CN}(f_x, f_y f_z)$ be calculated? In addition to the problems about ambiguity, spatial reasoning using 3D strings is also of interest to us. This may lead us to extend 3D string in order for it to be compatible with other picture operators and/or representations.

References

1. Edvin F. Beckenbach, ed., *Applied Combinatorial Mathematics* (John Wiley & Sons, Inc., 1964), p. 26.

2. Joseph B. Kruskal, ed., *Time Warp, String Edits, and Macromolecules: The Theory and Practice of String Comparison* (Addison-Wesley Publishing Company, Inc., 1983).
3. S. K. Chang, "*The reconstruction of binary patterns from their projections*", *Commun. ACM* **14**, 1 (1971) 21–25.
4. S. K. Chang, Q. Y. Shi, and C. W. Yan, "Iconic indexing by 2D string", IEEE *Trans. on Pattern Analysis and Machine Intelligence* **PAMI-9**, 3 (1987) 413–428.
5. S. K. Chang and Y. Li, "Representation of multi-resolution symbolic and binary pictures using 2D H-String", IEEE *Workshop Language for Automation* (1988) 190–195.
6. H. Samet, "The quadtree and related hierarchical data structure", *ACM Comput. Surv.* **16** (1984) 187–260.

SPATIAL KNOWLEDGE REPRESENTATION
FOR ICONIC IMAGE DATABASE

SUH-YIN LEE

Department of Computer Science and Information Engineering
National Chiao Tung University, Hsinchu, Taiwan, Republic of China

FANG-JUNG HSU

Computer and Communication Research Laboratories,
Industrial Technology Research Institute
Hsinchu, Taiwan, Republic of China

The preception of spatial relationships among objects in a picture is one important criterion to discriminate and retrieve images in an image database system. The data structure, called 2D string, to represent symbolic pictures was proposed by Chang *et al.* It allows a natural way of constructing iconic indexes for pictures. Jungert has extended 2D string to represent more types of spatial relationships, but the operators and the derived knowledge cannot be stored in a unified structure. Lee and Hsu proposed 2D C-string representation with a set of spatial operators and a more efficient cutting mechanism. 2D C-string is more characteristic of spatial knowledge and is more efficient in representation and manipulation of images. Since each symbolic picture can be represented by a 2D C-string, a picture query can also be specified by a 2D C-string. The problem of pictorial information retrieval then becomes the problem of 2D subsequence matching. Spatial relationship is a fuzzy concept. The capability of similarity retrieval for pictures is essential. Similarity measure and similarity retrieval of iconic images to different extents of precision is also presented.

Keywords: 2D C-string, spatial relationship, similarity retrieval, pictorial query, image database.

1. Introduction

In image information systems, one of the most important methods for discriminating the images is the perception of objects and the spatial relationships that exist among them in the desired images. Therefore, how images are stored and the capability of assembling queries on objects and their spatial relationships in a database are important issues of image database system design [1,2]. The data structure to represent the pictures should be object-oriented, and the spatial knowledge embedded in images should be preserved in the data structure [3,4,5]. So users can easily retrieve, visualize and manipulate objects in the image database systems [6].

Most systems of previous approaches provide search capability of simple table look up of image features and secondary information. The Intelligent Image Database System (IIDS) [6] provides high-level object-oriented search and supports spatial reasoning. The spatial reasoning is based on a data structure called 2D string [7,8] which preserves the objects' spatial knowledge embedded in images. The picture query can also be specified as a 2D string. The problem of pictorial information retrieval then becomes a problem of 2D string subsequence matching. This approach provides a natural way of constructing iconic indexes for pictures.

However, this representation is under challenge in solving the problems of spatial reasoning and planning in many applications. The spatial operators of 2D strings are not sufficient to give a complete description for a picture of arbitrary complexity. Jungert [9,10] introduced some local operators as compensation for handling more types of relations between pictorial objects in query reasoning. But these local operators and all the derived binary relations cannot be stored, in a unified structure with global operators, into a global 2D string. To overcome the problem, Chang et al. [11] introduced the generalized 2D string (2D G-string) with the cutting mechanism. The cuttings are performed at all extreme points of all the objects to segment the objects in the image. But it is not ideally economic for complex images in terms of storage space efficiency and navigation complexity in spatial reasoning.

Based on the above reasons, a set of spatial operators and a spatial knowledge representation 2D C-string were proposed [12]. All the spatial relations among objects with efficient segmentation are preserved with 2D C-string representation. It has been proved that this is more efficient than 2D G-string in storage space and in processing complexity. An algebraic point of view of 2D C-strings is presented in [13]. Transitive laws, distributive laws, and manipulation laws are discussed. From the 2D C-string representation of a symbolic picture, all the relationships among symbolic objects embedded in the picture can be derived. These laws form the theoretic basis for pictorial query inference and spatial reasoning.

To retrieve the images according to the spatial relationships, one problem may arise. Spatial relationship is a fuzzy concept and is thus often dependent on human interpretation. Also, the generation of 2D strings or 2D C-strings is sensitive to the shape, size and relative position of the objects in the images. Thus, similarity retrieval of images, which is one of the distinct functions different from a conventional database system, is essential.

In Sec. 2, a brief analysis of previous approaches is given. In Sec. 3, the spatial knowledge structure 2D C-string is introduced. The algebraic point of view of the 2D C-string is discussed in Sec. 4. The picture algebra provides the theoretic basis for spatial reasoning and pictorial query inference. In Sec. 5, we describe the spatial reasoning using 2D C-string and the powerful spatial 2D C-query. Similarity retrieval of images is discussed in Sec. 6. Conclusions and future works are summarized in the last section.

2. Spatial Query

Spatial relationship is a significant selection criterion when retrieving objects from an image. People often remember the relative spatial positions of the objects, rather than the absolute positions of the objects. The retrieval of an object by spatial relationship is called spatial query.

Spatial queries can be further classified into the following types:

(1) *Direction query.* Find the objects with directional relationship to the query objects. For example: "Find the hotels which are east of the city library and northeastern of the bus station."
(2) *Region query.* Find the objects with a regional relationship to the query objects. The regional relationships include covering, covered-by, intersection. For example: "Find the bridge which crosses the Mississippi River." or "Find the hotels which are located downtown."
(3) *Distance query.* Find the objects which are farthest from or nearest to the query objects. For example: "Find the hotels which are nearest to the bus station."

There exists two streams of approaches to process the spatial query. The first approach is based on the range query in conventional databases. The second approach is based on the iconic indexing technique of 2D string.

2.1. *Approaches of range queries*

The processing of the direction and the distance spatial query in the conventional database can be handled by the region query. For example, the spatial query to find the objects east of the house is to find the objects which are located in the eastern region of the house. Known methods for handling region queries of multi-dimensional objects are classified and briefly discussed below. Multi-dimensional objects include points, lines, rectangles, circles, or polygons, etc. Handling non-zero sized objects can be reduced to handling rectangles by finding the minimum bounding rectangle (MBR) of the given object. Two objects do not intersect if their corresponding MBRs do not intersect. This will reduce the cost of the potential intersection tests since the test on the intersection of two polygons or the intersection of a polygon and a sequence of line segments is more complicated than the test on the intersection of two rectangles.

The most common case of multi-dimensional data that has been studied in the past is points [3,14]. The main idea is to divide the whole space into disjoint subregions, usually in such a way that each subregion contains no more than C points. C is usually 1 if the data is stored in the core memory, or the capacity of a disk page, which is the number of data records one page can hold.

Insertions of new points may result in further partitioning of a region, known as a split. Split is performed by introducing one or more hyperplanes that partition a region further into disjoint subregions. The following attributes of a split help to classify the known methods:

1. *Position.* In fixed methods, the position of the splitting hyperplane is predetermined, e.g. the region is cut in half as in the grid file method. In adaptable methods, the position of the hyperplane is determined by the data points as in the k–d trees or the K–D–B-trees methods.
2. *Dimensionality.* In 1–d cut methods, the split is done with only one hyperplane. In k–d cut methods, the split is in all k dimensions with k hyperplanes, as the quad-trees and oct-trees do.
3. *Locality.* The splitting hyperplane splits not only the affected region, but all the regions in this direction, as in the grid file. We shall call these methods grid methods. The opposite way is to restrict the splitting hyperplane to extend solely inside the region to be split. These methods will be referred to as brickwall methods. The brickwall methods usually do a hierarchical decomposition of the space, requiring a tree structure. The grid methods use a multi-dimensional array.

Table 1 illustrates some of the most well-known methods and their attributes according to the above classification. Notice that methods based on binary trees or quad-trees cannot be easily extended to work in secondary

Table 1. Illustration of the classification of methods for range query.

Method	Position	Dimensions	Locality
point quad-tree	adaptable	$k-d$	brickwall
$k-d$ tree	adaptable	$k-d$	brickwall
grid file	fixed	$1-d$	grid
K–D–B tree	adaptable	$1-d$	grid

storage based systems. Since a disk page can hold pointers of the order of 50, trees with nodes of large fanout are more appropriate. Trees with two- or four-way nodes usually result in many (expensive) page faults.

There are other methods of range queries based on the handling of rectangles. The main classes of the methods are the following:

1. Methods that transform rectangles into points in a space of higher dimensionality: For example, a 2D rectangle (with sides-parallel to the axes) is characterized by four coordinates, and thus it can be considered as points in a 4D space. Therefore, one of the previously mentioned methods for storing points can be chosen.

2. Methods that use space-filling curves to map a $k-d$ space onto a $1-d$ space: Such a method, suitable for a paging environment, has been suggested, among others. The idea is to transform k-dimensional objects to line segments, using the so-called Z-transform. This transformation tries to preserve the distance, that is, points that are close in the $k-d$ space are likely to be close in the $1-d$ transformed space. Improved distance-preserving transformations have been proposed, which achieve better clustering of nearby points by using gray codes. The original Z-transform induces an ordering of the $k-d$ points, which is the very same one as the ordering that a (k-dimensional) quad-tree takes to scan pixels in a k-dimensional space. The transformation of a rectangle is a set of line segments, each corresponding to a quadrant that the rectangle completely covers.

3. Methods that divide the original space into appropriate sub-regions (overlapping or disjoint): If the regions are disjoint, any of the methods for points mentioned above can be used to decompose the space. The only complication to be handled is that a rectangle may intersect a splitting hyperplane. One solution is to cut the offending rectangle into two pieces and tag the pieces indicating that they belong to the same rectangle. Guttman [3] first proposed the use of overlapping subregions with R-trees. R-trees are an

extension of B-trees for multi-dimensional objects that are either points or regions. Like B-trees, they are balanced (in the sense that all leaf nodes appear on the same level, which is a desirable feature) and guarantee that the space utilization is at least 50%.

2.2. Approaches of iconic indexing

The approach of iconic indexing by 2D string for spatial reasoning was proposed by Chang et al. [8] to represent symbolic pictures. First, after preprocessing by applying the techniques of image processing and pattern recognition, the objects in the original image are recognized and the symbolic names can be obtained. Then each object is enclosed by a minimum bounding rectangle (MBR) with boundaries parallel to the horizontal (x-) and vertical (y-) axes. The basic idea for obtaining the relation between the objects is to regard one of the objects as a "point of view object" (PVO) and then view the other objects in four directions (north, east, south and west). The subobjects "seen" by PVO are called orthogonal relation objects of the original object. After all the objects have been processed, the objects can be segmented according to their orthogonal relation objects respectively. The reference points of the segmented objects which are the centroids of each orthogonal relation object thus dominate the spatial relations of objects and constitute the symbolic picture. At last, the symbolic picture which preserves the spatial relationships among objects of the original image is converted to a 2D string representation which is stored in the pictorial database as an iconic index for the picture. The problem of pictorial information retrieval then becomes the problem of 2D string subsequence matching. This approach thus allows a natural way to construct an iconic index for pictures.

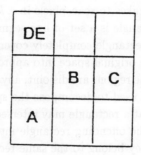

Fig. 1. A symbolic picture f.

Three spatial relation operators "$<$", "$=$" and "$:$" are employed in 2D strings. The symbol "$<$" denotes the left-right or below-above spatial relationship. The symbol "$=$" denotes the "at the same spatial location as" relation and the symbol "$:$" stands for "in the same set as" relation. The symbolic picture f in Fig. 1 may be represented as 2D string ($A = D{:}E < B < C$, $A < B = C < D{:}E$) or as ($A = DE < B < C$, $A < B = C < DE$) where the symbol "$:$" can be omitted and is omitted.

However, the spatial operators "$<$" and "$=$" are not sufficient to give a complete description of spatial knowledge for pictures of arbitrary complexity. For complex images with many objects the 2D string representation is difficult and the reference points of the relational objects which are the centroids of each subparts cannot truly reflect their spatial locations. For example, in Fig. 2, the picture is segmented into f' by using the orthogonal relations method. The centroid of A_{Cs} is west of E_{C_n}, but the relational object A_{Cs} is not west of the relational object E_{Cn} along x-direction. A_{Cs} means object A is segmented from the point of view of object C and s stands for A being south of C.

The 2D string representation of f' is listed below.

2D-u-string(f'): $D_{Cw} = D_{Ew} < D_{Fw} < A_{Bw} < D_{An} = A_{Ds} < D_{Es} <$
$E_{An} = A_{Es} < D_{Cn} < A_{Cs} = C_{An} < E_{Cn} < C_{Es} < C_{De} <$
$B_{Es} = E_{Bn} < E_{De} < B_{Cs} = C_{Bn} < B_{Ae} < B_{Fs} < F_{De}.$

2D-v-string(f'): $A_{Ds} = A_{Es} = A_{Cs} < A_{Bw} = B_{Ae} < B_{Es} = B_{Cs} = B_{Fs} <$
$D_{Cw} = C_{An} = C_{Es} = C_{De} = C_{Bn} < D_{Fw} = D_{An} = D_{Es} =$
$D_{Cn} = F_{De} < D_{Ew} = E_{An} = E_{Cn} = E_{Bn} = E_{De}.$

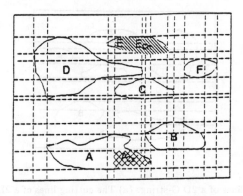

Fig. 2. The segmented picture f' using the orthogonal relations method.

To represent the spatial relationship between two non-zero sized objects, especially for the case of overlapping objects, Jungert [9,10] extended the operators of 2D strings as a global operator set and introduced a set of local operators to handle more types of spatial relationships among objects. These local operators can compensate 2D strings for more precise binary relations among objects, but they cannot be put unanimously as global operators into the global 2D string representation of symbolic pictures.

To overcome the problems in 2D strings and Jungert's work, Chang *et al.* [11] extended the concept of symbolic projection [7] and proposed generalized 2D string (2D G-string) representation with a cutting mechanism to describe the objects of an image. $G_{op} = \{$ "<", "=", "|" $\}$ is the set of generalized relational operators. "(,)" is a pair of separators used to describe a set of symbols as one local body and the content within which can be named and can always be regarded as first priority. It was pointed out that the edge to

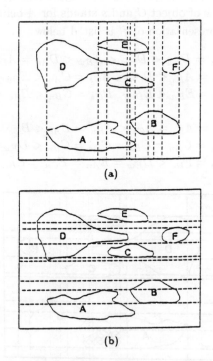

(a)

(b)

Fig. 3. The cutting lines of a 2D G-string. (a) The cutting lines of a 2D G-string along the *x*-axis direction. (b) The cutting lines of a 2D G-string along the y-axis direction.

edge relation operator "|" is useful to solve the problem of overlapping objects. Using symbolic projections, the cutting lines are performed at all the extreme points of each picture object in the image viewing from x- and y- projection, respectively. Then every object may be partitioned into many smaller subparts at the bounding lines of other overlapping objects. For the same picture in Fig. 2 the 2D G-string representation is listed below and is shown in Figs. 3(a) and (b).

2DG-u-string(f'): $D \mid A = D \mid A = D = E \mid A = C = D = E \mid A = C = E \mid$
$\qquad A = B = C = E \mid B = C = E \mid B = C \mid B \mid B = F \mid F.$

2DG-v-string(f'): $A \mid A = B \mid B < D \mid D = C \mid D = F \mid D \mid D = E.$

Although 2D G-strings can represent the spatial relationships among objects in pictures and spatial reasoning can be carried out on generalized 2D strings using a set of reasoning rules, there still exist some unsolved problems. The number of segmented subparts of an object is dependent on the number of bounding lines of other objects which completely or partly overlap this target object. For the cases of objects with overlapping, the storage space overhead is high and it is time consuming in spatial reasoning if pictures are represented in 2D G-strings. In the following, a more efficient and economic cutting mechanism by employing a sound and characteristic set of spatial operators is described.

3. 2D C-String Spatial Knowledge Representation

The formal definition of the set of spatial operators used in 2D C-string representation is illustrated in Table 2 [9,10,12]. The notation 'begin(A)' denotes the value of begin-bound of object A, and 'end(A)' denotes the value of the end-bound of object A. According to the begin-bound and end-bound of picture objects, spatial relationships between two enclosing rectangles can be categorized into 13 types, ignoring their length along the x-(or y-) coordinate axis as shown in Fig. 4. There are 169 types of spatial relationships between two rectangles in two-dimensional space as shown in Fig. 5. For example, $x : A\%B, y : B[\,A$ means

Table 2. The definition of characteristic spatial operators.

Notation	Condition	Meaning
$A < B$	$end(A) < begin(B)$	A disjoins B
$A = B$	$begin(A) = begin(B)$, $end(A) = end(B)$	A is the same as B
$A \mid B$	$end(A) = begin(B)$	A is edge to edge with B
$A \% B$	$begin(A) < begin(B)$, $end(A) > end(B)$	A contains B and they do not have the same bound
$A [B$	$begin(A) = begin(B)$, $end(A) > end(B)$	A contains B and they have the same begin-bound
$A] B$	$begin(A) < begin(B)$, $end(A) = end(B)$	A contains B and they have the same end-bound
A/B	$begin(A) < begin(B)$ $< end(A) < end(B)$	A is partly overlapping with B

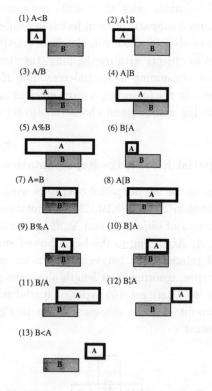

(1) A<B   (2) A|B

(3) A/B   (4) A]B

(5) A%B   (6) B[A

(7) A=B   (8) A[B

(9) B%A   (10) B]A

(11) B/A   (12) B|A

(13) B<A

Fig. 4. The 13 types of spatial relations in one dimension.

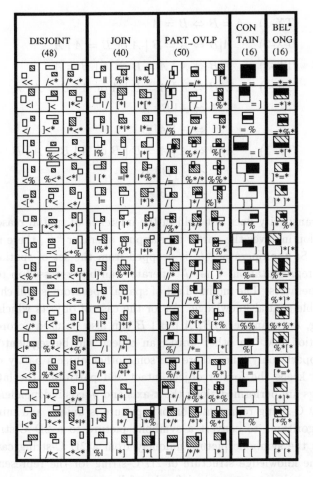

Fig. 5. The 169 types of spatial relations in two-dimensional space.

The seven operators in Table 2 are sufficient to describe precisely all the possible spatial relationships between any two MBRs in symbolic pictures.

For the characteristic spatial operators, considering x-axis or y-axis projection independently, five fundamental transformation laws can be observed as below. (TX-2), (TX-3), and (TX-4) are applied for the cases of completely overlapping objects and (TX-5) for the cases of partly overlapping objects. Thus, if the operators are fully utilized, no cutting or partitioning of objects into subparts is necessary.

(TX-1) $A = B \Leftrightarrow B = A$

(TX-2) $A[B \Leftrightarrow A = B \mid A \text{ or } B = A \mid A$

(TX-3) $A]B \Leftrightarrow A \mid A = B \text{ or } A \mid B = A$

(TX-4) $A\%B \Leftrightarrow A \mid A = B \mid A \text{ or } A \mid B = A \mid A$

$\quad\quad\quad \Leftrightarrow A]B \mid A$

$\quad\quad\quad \Leftrightarrow A \mid A[B$

(TX-5) $A/B \Leftrightarrow A \mid A = B \mid B \text{ or } A \mid B = A \mid B$

$\quad\quad\quad \Leftrightarrow A]B \mid B$

$\quad\quad\quad \Leftrightarrow A \mid B[A.$

Since transitivity does not hold in the inference of spatial reasoning when the derivation involves the partly overlapping operator "/", there might incur ambiguity. So the operator "/" is dropped from the set of spatial operators for unique representation. The "/" operator can be expressed in terms of the other six operators. The modified set of spatial operators is still characteristic of all possible spatial knowledge. As for the case of objects which are partly overlapping, for example A/B, $A \mid B \mid B$ can also be used according to the transformation law. In other words, an object will be segmented into two smaller subparts only when there are some other objects partly overlapping with it. It keeps the former object intact and partitions the latter object. The cuttings are performed along the x-axis and y-axis independently. In this way the 2D C-string representation of a picture is unique and minimal. The detailed algorithms to convert a symbolic picture to a 2D C-string and to reconstruct the symbolic picture uniquely from a 2D C-string can be found in [12]. The knowledge structure of 2D C-string for the representation and retrieval of symbolic pictures is defined as follows.

Definition 3.1. The knowledge structure of 2D C-string is a 5-tuple (S, C, R_g, R_l, "( )") where

1. S is the set of symbols in symbolic pictures of interest;
2. C is the cutting mechanism, which consists of cutting lines at the points with partial overlap from the x- and y-projection, respectively;
3. $R_g = \{$ "<", "|" $\}$ is the set of global relational operators;
4. $R_l = \{$ "=", "[", "]", "%" $\}$ is the set of local relational operators;
5. "()" is a pair of separators which is used to describe a set of symbols as one local body.

Basically, the cutting of 2D C-string is performed at the point of partial overlap. The former object is kept intact and the latter object is partitioned. The cutting mechanism is also suitable for pictures with many objects. Consider the example picture with three objects A, B and C. Only one cutting is performed at the end-bound of A and A is called dominating object. The other objects partly overlapping with the dominating object will be segmented. Then the picture is represented as $A]B]C \mid B[C$ compared to $A \mid A = B \mid A = B = C \mid B = C \mid B$ in 2D G-string with four cuttings at begin(B), begin(C), end(A) and end(C).

Furthermore, the end-bound point of a dominating object does not partition other objects which contain the dominating object. Consider another example picture   A   B C   . Object B is the dominating object, because it is

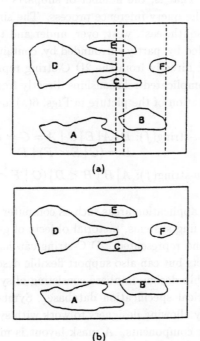

(a)

(b)

Fig. 6. The cutting lines of a 2D C-string. (a) The cutting lines of a 2D C-string along the x-direction. (b) The cutting lines of a 2D C-string along the y-direction.

the former object with partial overlap. Object C will be segmented by B, but not for object A. Thus the 2D C-string representation is $A\%(B\,]\,C\,|\,C)$. Actually, B and C constitute the local body of object A.

Less cuttings and no unnecessary cuttings in 2D C-strings will make the representation more efficient than 2D G-strings in the case of overlapping objects. Certainly, both mechanisms have the same result in the case of non-overlapping. It has been proved via simulation results that the number of segmented subparts of the 2D G-string is approximately $\log_2 N$ times that of the 2D C-string, where N is the number of objects in the image. The 2D C-string representation is more efficient in storage complexity at the expense of a little additional computation complexity only in the stage of converting a symbolic picture to a 2D G- or 2D C-string representation. For 2D G-string, it is more time consuming in the manipulation and integration of many partitioned subparts in order to derive the integral spatial relationship between objects in a picture. That is, the number of subparts directly influences the spatial reasoning in the query inference process. The simple spatial relationships such as north, south, east, west, over, under and the more complicated ones such as surrounded by, partly surrounded by, contain, belong, etc. can be derived naturally and directly from the 2D C-string representation. It is difficult to derive the complicated relationships directly from 2D G-strings. The 2D C-string representation of the picture in Figs. 6(a) and (b) is listed below.

$$2\text{D C-}u\text{-string}(f)\colon D\,]\,A\,]\,E\,]\,C\,|\,A = C = E\,]\,B\,|$$
$$B = (C\,[\,E < F)\,|\,F\,.$$

$$2\text{D C-}v\text{-string}(f)\colon A\,]\,B\,|\,B < D\,]\,(C\,|\,F < E)\,.$$

In some advanced application areas such as computer aided design systems and image understanding systems, pictorial objects of great complexity must be integrally stored and represented. 2D C-string can handle not only spatial relations among objects but can also support flexible description of compound objects. Consider a chip design database consisting of symbolic layout, masking layout and electrical specification database. Symbolic layout simplifies layout specification by allowing designers to work with symbols that represent primitive elements or components. A mask layout is made from a symbolic layout by expanding each symbol into the rectangles that form it, using coordinates of the symbols to guide the placement of rectangles. An 8 : 1 ratio inverter mask expressed in 2D C-string can be found in [12]. This description of a compound object is rather useful for image understanding as in automatic layout testing. We can retrieve the images under some constraints using the appropriate pictorial queries. For example, "Retrieve all chips that contain a-device and replace them with b-device".

4. Algebraic Point of View of 2D C-Strings

From the algebraic point of view of 2D C-strings, three kinds of fundamental laws, transitive laws, distributive laws, and manipulation laws are derived [13]. For pictorial query inference and spatial reasoning, all spatial relationships among objects can be derived based on these laws.

4.1. *Transitive laws*

Suppose that a 2D C-string is expressed as

$$s_1 r_{12} s_2 r_{23} \cdots r_{(i-1)i} s_i \cdots r_{(n-1)n} s_n$$

where $s_1, \ldots, s_i, \ldots, s_n \in S$, $r_{(i-1)i} \in R_g \cup R_l$, and $i \in [2, n]$.

Can all the spatial relationships between any two objects, s_i and s_j, $i \neq j$, be derived from a 2D C-string? In other words, is the 2D C-string a characteristic representation of the spatial knowledge contained in a picture? The answer is yes and this is proved through the following derivations. First, we probe a 3-symbol string,

$$s_1 r_{12} s_2 r_{23} s_3 .$$

It is easy to derive three binary relations among s_1, s_2, and s_3:

1. $s_1 r'_{12} s_2$,
2. $s_2 r'_{23} s_3$, and
3. $s_1 r'_{13} s_3$.

The three derived binary relational operators are shown in Table 3. For the example string $A \ [\ B \ | \ C$, we can get (1) $A \ [\ B$, (2) $B < C$, and (3) $A \ | \ C$.

From Table 3, three facts can be observed:

1. r'_{12} is always the same as r_{12}.
2. r'_{23} is the same as r_{23}, except for r_{23} being '|' and r_{12} being '[' or '%'.
3. r'_{13} is the same as r_{23} when $r_{12} \in R_l$ and $r_{23} \in R_g$.

Table 3. The derivation table of a 3-symbol string.

(a)

r'_{12}	r_{23}					
	<	|	=	[	]	%
<	<	<	<	<	<	<
|	|	|	|	|	|	|
=	=	=	=	=	=	=
[	[	[	[	[	[	]
]	]	]	]	]	]	]
%	%	%	%	%	%	%

(column header r_{12} at left of rows)

(b)

r'_{23}	r_{23}					
	<	|	=	[	]	%
<	<	|	=	[	]	%
|	<	<	=	[	]	%
=	<	<	=	[	]	%
[	<	<	=	[	]	%
]	<	<	=	[	]	%
%	<	<	=	[	]	%

(column header r_{12} at left of rows)

(c)

r'_{13}	r_{23}					
	<	|	=	[	]	%
<	<	<	<	<	<	<
|	<	<	|	|	<	<
=	<	<	=	[	]	%
[	<	|	[	[	%	%
]	<	|	]	%	]	%
%	<	|	%	%	%	%

(column header r_{12} at left of rows)

Any binary relationships among three symbols can be derived without difficulty. Based on the basic results, five transitive laws are presented in [13].

4.2. Distributive law

In Definition 3.1, we have defined the knowledge structure of 2D C-strings. Included in the knowledge structure is a pair of separators '( )' which is used to describe some set of symbols as a local body. First we probe a three-symbol string with the separators, $s_1 r_{12}(s_2 r_{23} s_3)$, where $r_{12} \in R_l$ and $r_{23} \in R_g$, to illustrate the basis of the distributive law. It is easy to derive the following three binary relationships among s_1, s_2, and s_3.

1. $s_1 r'_{12} s_2$,
2. $s_2 r'_{23} s_3$, and
3. $s_1 r'_{13} s_3$.

Table 4. The distributive derivation table of 3-symbol string.

(a)

r'_{12}		r_{23}	
		<	|
	=	[	[
	[	[	[
r_{12}	]	%	%
	%	%	%

(b)

r'_{23}		r_{23}	
		<	|
	=	<	|
	[	<	|
r_{12}	]	<	|
	%	<	|

(c)

r'_{13}		r_{23}	
		<	|
	=	]	]
	[	%	%
r_{12}	]	]	]
	%	%	%

The three derived binary relational operators are shown in Table 4. For the example $A \mid (B \mid C)$, we can get (1) $A \% B$, (2) $B \mid C$, and (3) $A \mid C$. Based on the above results, two distributive laws are presented in [13].

Based on transitive laws and distributive laws, all the binary spatial relationships among symbols in a 2D C-string can be derived. It means that the spatial relational operators of 2D C-strings preserve complete spatial knowledge of pictorial objects embedded in symbolic pictures. 2D C-strings are more efficient in the representation of spatial relationships than other knowledge structures in earlier approaches because of less cuttings.

4.3. *Manipulation laws*

In the case of objects with partial overlap, a pictorial object must be cut to some segmented subparts at the bounding lines of other subjects partly overlap with it. It is necessary to integrate and manipulate these smaller subparts for the inference of spatial reasoning in pictorial query. The manipulation laws are for the inference of the segmented objects treating their relationships integrally [13].

The manipulation laws are simple and it is easy to manipulate the segmented subparts of objects. For example, objects A and B are partitioned relative to other objects in a symbolic picture and are represented as the 2D C-string shown below. It can be simplified by employing the manipulation laws. For example,

$$A \mid A \mid A] B \mid A = B \mid A = B \mid B [A \mid B$$

$$\Rightarrow A \mid A] B \mid A = B \mid A = B \mid B [A \mid B$$
$$\Rightarrow A] B \mid A = B \mid A = B \mid B [A \mid B$$
$$\Rightarrow A] B \mid A = B \mid B [A \mid B$$
$$\Rightarrow A] B \mid B [A \mid B$$
$$\Rightarrow A] B \mid B [A$$
$$\Rightarrow A/B .$$

The final relationship between A and B is A/B. This gives demonstration and support for the theoretical basis for spatial reasoning.

5. Spatial Reasoning

Spatial reasoning means the inference of a consistent set of spatial relationships among the objects in an image. It is important in computer vision and robotics as well as in image database applications. When retrieving images from a database, one of the most powerful methods for discriminating images is the perception of spatial relationships that exist among objects in the desired image. The capability of making queries based on spatial relationships plays an important role in image database systems. A simple tabular account of these relationships soon overwhelms the system due to their combinatorial nature. Also, the addition of new facts may require a major reconfiguration of the database. For these reasons, a more practical approach is to store the information as facts from which these relations can be derived following a set of rules when they are needed.

However, the primary direction relationships are not sufficient for pictorial queries of various complex cases of objects with overlap in two-dimensional space. According to the characteristics of spatial knowledge in two-dimensional space, all the spatial relationships between two non-zero sized objects, as shown in Fig. 5, can be categorized into five categories of relations. Suppose that two pictorial objects A and B are enclosed by minimum bounding rectangles. Then we have the five categories of relations below.

1. A disjoins B. All parts of A are separated from all parts of B.
2. A is edge to edge with B. The bound of A is edge to edge with the bound of B, and no part of A is overlapping with any part of B.
3. A contains B. All parts of B are completely overlapping with some parts of A.
4. A belongs to B. All parts of A are completely overlapping with some parts of B.
5. A is partly overlapping with B.

The 2D C-string is characteristic of spatial knowledge and is complete in the sense that every spatial relation is derivable from the representation. Based on the transitive laws, distributive laws, and manipulation laws of picture algebra [13], it has been proved that all the binary relationships among objects in an image can be derived from a 2D C-string.

The problem of how to infer the spatial relations between two pictorial objects from a given 2D C-string representation in spatial reasoning is solved [15] by using the ranking mechanism, in which the ranks of pictorial objects in a 2D C-string can be defined. The rank values of objects stand for the relative sequencing in the u- or v-string representing the relative spatial positioning of the original symbolic picture along the x- and y-projection respectively.

The rank plays an important role in 2D string subsequence matching [8]. The spatial knowledge is embedded in the ranks of the pictorial objects. In fact, the ranks become representative of the spatial knowledge of the pictorial objects in an image. The spatial relations between two symbols can be identified by their ranks according to the rules.

Because the spatial operators of 2D C-strings can directly support a richer spatial knowledge of images, the abundant pictorial query, called 2D C-query, is constructed by employing the set of operators [15]. The fundamentals of 2D C-query are based on the inference of spatial relationships among pictorial objects in a 2D C-string.

The objects may be divided into some subparts with the cutting mechanism. If the predicate (west, A, B) is true, it means there exist some subparts of A west of all subparts of B. But the converse predicate (east, B, A) cannot be established because there does not exist any subpart of B east of all subparts of A. It is useful to add an operator "*", name "reverse", for the purpose of spatial reasoning. $A <^* B$ means $B < A$. The fundamental direction relationships for each spatial operator have been reconsidered and are listed in Table 5. r^u_{AB} indicates the relationship between A and B along the x-direction. The relational operators r^v_{AB} of the v-string along the y-direction are analogously defined as r^u_{AB}.

As shown in Table 5, the primitive direction relationships can be inferred from the spatial operators of 2D C-strings. The following basic orthogonal directional aggregates are the main body of the 2D C-query.

1. u: $Ar^u_{AB}B$, $r^u_{AB} \in \{<^*, |^*, [, \%, /^*\}$ iff (east, A, B)
2. v: $Ar^v_{AB}B$, $r^v_{AB} \in \{<^*, |^*, [, \%, /^*\}$ iff (north, A, B)
3. u: $Ar^u_{AB}B$, $r^u_{AB} \in \{<, |,], \%, /\}$ iff (west, A, B)
4. v: $Ar^v_{AB}B$, $r^v_{AB} \in \{<, |,], \%, /\}$ iff (south, A, B).

Table 5. The direction predicates of spatial operators.

Predicate r^U_{AB}	<	|	=	[	]	%	/	<*	|*	=*	[*	]*	%*	/*
(west, A, B)	✓	✓			✓	✓	✓							
(east, B, A)	✓	✓		✓			✓						✓	
(east, A, B)				✓		✓		✓	✓					✓
(west, B, A)								✓	✓			✓	✓	✓

The pictorial queries in 2D C-query can be summarized and classified into seven classes in the form of (RELATION, ?which_object, X) or (?which_relation, A, B).

1. *Orthogonal direction object query.* The primary orthogonal direction aggregates can be combined to derive more direction aggregates. For example, from 2D C-string u: $A] B$ and v: A/B, three aggregates are inferred (west, A, B), (south, A, B), and (north, B, A). Then the relationship between A and B are (south-west, A, B) and (north, B, A). For the orthogonal directions in two-dimensional space, there are 15 spatial queries about the orthogonal direction between two objects in the first class of 2D C-query.
2. *Category relation object query.* The characteristic spatial operators are sufficient to describe the relationships among the non-zero sized objects. From the definition of the operators, there are twelve 1D relation aggregates along the x-direction or y-direction. Based on these relation aggregates, there are five queries of category relation, DISJOIN, EDGE, CONTAIN, BELONG, and PARTOVLP, in the second class of 2D C-query.
3. *Auxiliary relation object query.* The relations of "same", "surround","partly surround", "surrounded" and "partly surrounded" are important and useful in pictorial query.

The definitions are given below.

1. A is the same as B, if A is at the same location as B along the western, eastern, southern, and northern directions.
2. A surrounds B, if A contains B and A completely surrounds B along four orthogonal directions.
3. A partly surrounds B, if A contains B and A surrounds B along two or three orthogonal directions.

The relations "surround" and "partly surround" are with respect to "contain". The relations "surrounded" and "partly surrounded" are with respect to "belong".

4. *Icon relation object query.* The fourth kind of 2D C-query is simple and natural. The query spatial relation can be specified by using an icon or a symbol. These queries are in the form of (rel_icon, ?object, X).

The above four classes of 2D C-query, allow the users to retrieve all objects with a specified orthogonal direction or category relation or auxiliary relation or icon-relation in an image. There are three types of pictorial queries to examine the spatial relation between two specified objects in a given image. (?icon, A, B), (?category, A, B), and (?direction, A, B) stand for icon relation, category relation, and orthogonal direction query.

6. Similarity Retrieval

Similarity retrieval is one of the distinct functions of the image database systems. The target is to retrieve the images that are similar to the query image. The similarity between two patterns or pictures can be measured on the basis of the maximum-likelihood or minimum-distance criterion. The similarity between 1D strings based upon the minimum-distance criterion has been developed in the techniques of pattern recognition [16]. The distance between two strings is defined in terms of the minimum number of error transformation used to derive one from the other. The alternative approach based on the maximum likelihood criterion is defined in terms of the longest common subsequence between two strings. Adopting the maximum likelihood approach, the similarity retrieval of images represented in 2D C-strings is our concern.

Chang *et al.* [8] defined type-0, type-1, and type-2 2D subsequences to provide a simple approach to perform subpicture matching on 2D strings. Lee *et al.* [17] proposed a similarity retrieval algorithm, called 2D-string-LCS, to retrieve the most similar picture whose type-i similarity is the longest common subsequence among all the pictures stored in the image database. For representing the spatial relationships efficiently, 2D C-string is proposed and is applied to develop the pictorial query. Similarity retrieval based on 2D C-string is developed in [15].

Definition 6.1. Picture f' is a type-i unit picture of f, if

(1) f' is a picture containing the two objects A and B, represented as u: $A\, r_{AB}^{u'} B$, v: $A\, r_{AB}^{v'} B$,
(2) A and B are also contained in f,
(3) the relations between A and B in f are represented as u: $A r_{AB}^{u} B$, v: $A r_{AB}^{v} B$,

then

$$(\text{type-0}): \ \text{Category}(r^u_{AB}, r^v_{AB}) = \text{Category}(r^{u'}_{AB}, r^{v'}_{AB});$$
$$(\text{type-1}): \ (\text{type-0}) \ \text{and}(r^u_{AB} = r^{u'}_{AB} \ \text{or} \ r^v_{AB} = r^{v'}_{AB});$$
$$(\text{type-2}): \ r^u_{AB} = r^{u'}_{AB} \ \text{and} \ r^v_{AB} = r^{v'}_{AB},$$

where Category (r^u, r^v) denotes the relation category of the spatial relationships as shown in Fig. 5. The pair (A, B) is called a type-i similar pair.

Take the pictures f_1 and f_2 in Figs. 7(a) and (b) as an example. There are eight pictorial objects in these two pictures. The 2D C-string representations of the pictures are as below.

f_1 : u-string: $\ A](B]E = H \mid E = H \mid C) < F]G \mid D[G,$
$\quad\ \,$ v-string: $\ A](D[C[B \mid E) \mid E \mid F]G \mid H[G.$

f_2 : u-string: $\ G]H]A \mid A](B]E \mid E) \mid E < C \mid D]F \mid F,$
$\quad\ \,$ v-string: $\ H = C < F]A = B = D]G \mid A = (D[G \mid E) \mid E.$

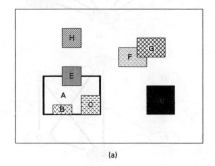

(a)

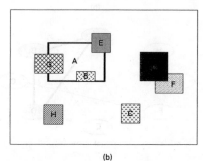

(b)

Fig. 7. An example of similarity retrieval. (a) An example of similarity retrieval (f_1). (b) An example of similarity retrieval (f_2).

By applying the reasoning rules, the spatial relationships among objects can be inferred by the ranks of symbols.

According to the definition of type-i similar picture in 2D C-string, we have the set of type-i similar pairs of pictures f_1 and f_2:

type-0: $(A, B), (A, D), (A, E), (A, F), (A, H),$
$(B, C), (B, D), (B, E), (B, F), (B, G),$
$(B, H), (C, D), (C, E), (C, F), (C, G),$
$(C, H), (D, E), (D, G), (D, H), (E, F),$
$(E, G), (E, H), (F, H), (G, H).$

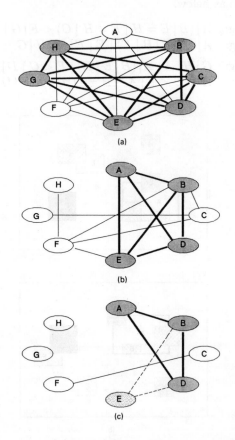

(a)

(b)

(c)

Fig. 8. Similar pairs between f_1 and f_2. (a) Type-0 similar pairs between f_1 and f_2. (b) Type-1 similar pairs between f_1 and f_2. (c) Type-2 similar pairs between f_1 and f_2.

type-1: (A, B), (A, D), (A, E), (B, C), (B, D),
$\quad\quad$ (B, E), (B, F), (C, F), (C, G), (D, E),
$\quad\quad$ (E, F), (F, H).

type-2: (A, B), (A, D), (B, D), (B, E), (C, F),
$\quad\quad$ (D, E).

As shown in Figs. 8(a), (b), and (c), the maximal complete subgraphs of type-0, type-1, and type-2 are found respectively. The corresponding type-i longest common subpictures of f_1 and f_2 are constructed from the following object sets:

type-0: $\{B, C, D, E, G, H\}$,
type-1: $\{A, B, D, E\}$,
type-2: $\{A, B, D\}$ *or* $\{B, D, E\}$.

In this example, f_1 is type-0, type-1, type-2 similar to f_2 with similar degree of 6, 4, and 3, respectively.

7. Conclusion

The approach of 2D strings opens a new area for iconic picture indexing and retrieval. Previous approaches of 2D strings were not powerful enough to give a complete description of spatial knowledge for pictures of arbitrary complexity. The spatial knowledge representation 2D C-string with a more efficient cutting mechanism is proposed to overcome the deficiencies. This representation supports flexible description and retrieval of compound objects or images with great complexity.

An algebraic point of view of 2D C-string is presented. Transitive laws, distributive laws, and manipulation laws are discussed. From the 2D C-string representation of symbolic pictures, all the spatial relationships among symbolic objects embedded in the pictures can be derived. These laws form the theoretic basis for pictorial query inference and spatial reasoning. The inference of spatial reasoning in 2D C-string by using the ranking mechanism is described. The powerful pictorial query 2D C-query is summarized. The similarity retrieval based on 2D C-string is also discussed.

The topic of how to detect picture objects which have similar shapes but different sizes needs further investigation. The extension of 2D C-string to 3D object representation, which is useful to object understanding and retrieval, is worth further study.

References

1. H. Tamura and N. Yokoya, "Image database systems: A survey", *Pattern Recogn.* **17**, 1 (1984) 29–43.
2. S. K. Chang, *Principles of Pictorial Information Systems Design* (Prentice-Hall, Englewood Cliffs, NJ, 1989).
3. A. Guttman, "R-trees: A dynamic index structure for spatial searching", *Proc. ACM-SIGMOD 1984 Int. Conf. on Management of Data* (June 1984), pp. 47–57.
4. N. Roussopoulos and D. Leifker, "Direct spatial search on pictorial database using packed R-tree", *Proc. ACM-SIGMOD 1985 Int. Conf. on Management of Data*, (May 1985), pp. 17–31.
5. S. K. Chang and S. H. Liu, "Picture indexing and abstraction techniques for pictorial databases", *IEEE Trans. Pattern Anal. Mach. Intell.* **6**, 4 (1984) 475–484.
6. S. K. Chang, C. W. Yan, D. C. Dimitrof, and T. Arndt, "Intelligent image database system", *IEEE Trans. Softw. Eng.* **14**, 5 (1988) 681–688.
7. S. K. Chang and E. Jungert, "A spatial knowledge structure for image information systems using symbolic projections", *Proc. Fall Joint Computer Conf.*, Dallas, TX, (November 1986), pp. 79–86.
8. S. K. Chang, Q. Y. Shi, and C. W. Yan, "Iconic indexing by 2D strings", *IEEE Trans. Pattern Anal. Mach. Intell.* **9**, 3 (1987) 413–428.
9. E. Jungert, "Extended symbolic projection used in a knowledge structure for spatial reasoning", *Proc. 4th BPRA Conf. on Pattern Recognition* (Springer Verlag, 1988).
10. E. Jungert and S. K. Chang, "An algebra for symbolic image manipulation and transformation", Ed. T. S. Kunii, *Visual Database Systems* (North-Holland, 1989), pp. 301–317.
11. S. K. Chang, E. Jungert, and Y. Li, "Representation and retrieval of symbolic pictures using generalized 2D strings", *SPIE Proc. on Visual Communications and Image Processing* Philadelphia, (November 1989), pp. 1360–1372.
12. S. Y. Lee and F. J. Hsu, 2D C-string: "A new spatial knowledge representation for image database systems", *Pattern Recogn.* **23**, 10 (1990) 1077–1087.
13. S. Y. Lee and F. J. Hsu, "Picture algebra for spatial reasoning of iconic images represented in 2D C-string", *Pattern Recogn. Lett.* **12**, 7 (1991) 425–435.
14. T. Sellis, N. Rousspoulous, and C. Faloutsos, "The R+ tree: A dynamic index structure for multi-dimensional objects", *Proc. 13th VLDB Conf.* (1987), pp. 507–518.
15. S. Y. Lee and F. J. Hsu, "Spatial reasoning and similarity retrieval of images using 2D C-string knowledge representation", *Pattern Recogn.* **25**, 3 (1992) 305–318.

16. K. S. Fu, *Syntactic Pattern Recognition and Applications*, Prentice Hall, Englewood Cliffs, NJ (1982).
17. S. Y. Lee, M. K. Shan, and W. P. Yang, "Similarity retrieval of iconic image database", *Pattern Recogn.* **22**, 6 (1989) 675–682.

ORDERING INFORMATION AND SYMBOLIC PROJECTION

CHRISTOPH SCHLIEDER

University of Freiburg, Institute of Computer Science and Social Reserch
Friedrichstrasse 50, 79098 Freiburg, Germany

Two types of ordering information about a finite set of points are studied in discrete and computational geometry. Some properties of ordering information are reviewed which help to analyze the symbolic projection approach to spatial reasoning. Then the problem of rotation invariance is addressed. Bounds are given on the number of different symbolic projections that may arise from rotating a configuration of n points. Consequences of this result on the design of rotation-invariant extensions of symbolic projection are discussed. Finally the panorama is introduced as a representation of ordering information which can be used as an rotation invariant index to symbolic descriptions of point configurations.

1. The Representation of Ordering Information

Representing the position of an object for the purpose of spatial reasoning becomes a problem whenever the object position is not completely determined. Indeterminacy, fuzzyness, and sometimes even inconsistency of spatial information pose a challenge to applications such as visual scene analysis and sensor-based robot navigation. Research on spatial reasoning has provided some solutions to this problem and it has shown that spatial information which is not completely determined can nevertheless be efficiently used (Kak [12], Chen [2], McDermott [15]). Several representational and inferential formalisms have been proposed for qualitative reasoning about object location. In a recent survey Freksa & Röhrig [4] reviewed nine approaches, analyzing the type of spatial information that is represented. Besides topological relations ("X touches Y", "X is connected") also genuine geometric relations ("X lies to the left of Y", "X is convex") are found. Many of the latter relate to a topic that has been studied extensively in discrete and computational geometry, namely order relations for points.

In the first section of this chapter we will present two types of information about the 2-dimensional order of a configuration of points, both frequently

115

used in discrete geometry, the configuration's triangle orientations and its permutation sequence. A well-known result states that the permutation sequence carries more information than the triangle orientations. On the base of this result we will show in the second section that symbolic projection encodes a subset of the ordering information conveyed by the permuation sequence. All this serves as a preparation to address the problem of rotation invariance in the third section. Rotating a configuration of points generally changes its symbolic projection. Since a rotation invariant indexing scheme is preferable for some applications it has been proposed to state case-by-case rules that identify symbolic projections belonging to rotated images of the same configuration. How many cases are to be handled? In other words, how many different symbolic projections are generated by rotating the configuration? Lower and upper bounds for this number are given. These bounds do suggest not to try to solve the problem of rotation invariance by stating case-by-case rules. In the last section an alternative solution is proposed which makes use of the configuration's triangle orientations, that is, of the type of ordering information which is less closely related to symbolic projection.

1.1. *Qualitative landmark navigation*

Before being more precise on the notion of ordering information we will take a brief look at an application problem in which this kind of information plays a prominent role. A mobile robot equipped with a visual sensor can identify surrounding landmarks and this will provide information about the robots position. The angle under which two landmarks are seen constrains the position to lie on a certain arc of circle. Even if due to measurement errors the metric information is unreliable the order in which the landmarks appear from left to right can in many cases still be determined. This kind of qualitative information is used in the scenario for qualitative landmark navigation set up by Levitt & Lawton [14]. In their QUALNAV system a special representational layer exists which organizes information about the visual order of landmarks. A qualitative navigation strategy uses the information to plan a path from the robot's present position to a given goal position. Qualitative navigation is less intended to be used as a stand-alone strategy than to serve as a reliable supplement to metric navigation strategies.

At the level of qualitative navigation landmarks are conceived as points making the additional assumption that every landmark can be seen and identified from any observer position. Two classes of positions with respect to two

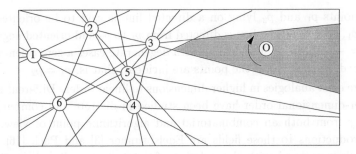

Fig. 1. Qualitative positions of an observer relative to two landmarks.

landmarks 1 and 2 are distinguished: positions from which 1 is seen to the left of 2 and positions from which 1 is seen to the right of 2. The two classes of positions are separated by the line connecting 1 and 2. Figure 1 shows a configuration of landmarks together with the lines defined by them. The lines decompose the plane into regions, the outer regions being unbounded. Depending on the region the observer is positioned, the landmarks will appear in a certain visual order. For the position O the following left-to-right order is found: $4 > 6 > 5 > 1 > 3 > 2$. Note that projecting the landmarks orthogonally onto the y-axis results in the same order. In fact, there is a one-to-one correspondence between the different orthogonal projections of the landmarks and the unbounded regions, in the sense that by choosing the viewpoint in a region the landmarks will appear in the same order as in the corresponding projection.

The qualitative navigation problem now consists in devising an algorithm that finds a path between a start and a goal region, both described by the visual order of landmarks. The QUALNAV system simply uses the circular order in which the landmarks appear. As detailed in Schlieder [17] not all "ordering information" involved in the problem is encoded that way. A more efficient path finding algorithm can only be formulated after a representation which is able to capture the missing information introduced: the panorama. We will use (and define) the panorama in the last section where it serves us to give a solution to the problem of rotation invariant indexing.

1.2. *Two types of ordering information*

Representational formalisms for qualitative spatial information frequently provide some means to encode the linear order of points on a line. A pair of two points p_1 and p_2 lying on a directed line is said to be oriented positively, $[p_1, p_2] = +$, if the line is directed from p_1 to p_2 and oriented negatively, $[p_1, p_2] = -$, otherwise. For dealing with degenerate cases a zero orientation is introduced, $[p_1, p_2] = 0$, if the points are incident, that is, $p_1 = p_2$.

There exist analogies in higher dimensions to linear order. Different notions of higher-dimensional order have been studied in discrete and computational geometry from both an combinatorial and algorithmic point of view. General introductions to these fields are Edelsbrunner [3] and Pach [16]. More specifically concerned with the ordering of points in two dimensions is a series of works by Jacob Goodman and Richard Pollack. Especially interesting for an application to spatial reasoning are Goodman & Pollack [5], [6] and [7]. In a recent survey article their results are summarized and related to other topics in discrete geometry (Goodman & Pollack [8]). Since the work on higher-dimensional point order is not well known within the spatial reasoning community it seems appropriate to give the basic definitions for two notions of order and discuss briefly how they compare. The following account is restricted to two-dimensional order, since this is the most important case for qualitative navigation as well as for iconic indexing.

The orientation of a triple of points lying in an oriented plane is said to be positive if visiting the points in the order p_1, p_2 and p_3 yields a counterclockwise turn, we then write $[p_1 p_2 p_3] = +$. If the turn is in clockwise sense, then the orientation is said to be negative, $[p_1 p_2 p_3] = -$. For collinear points the orientation is defined to be zero, $[p_1 p_2 p_3]$ which includes all cases with incidences such as $p_1 = p_2 = p_3$. Note that the orientation $[p_1 p_2 p_3]$ determines the orientation for any permutation of the points:

$$[p_1 p_2 p_3] = + \Leftrightarrow [p_2 p_1 p_3] = - \Leftrightarrow [p_2 p_3 p_1] = + \Leftrightarrow$$
$$[p_3 p_2 p_1] = - \Leftrightarrow [p_3 p_1 p_2] = + \Leftrightarrow [p_1 p_3 p_2] = - p_1, p_2 \text{ and } p_3$$

A set $P = \{p_1, \ldots, p_n\}$ of points in the plane is often called a *configuration*. The *triangles* of the configuration are the subsets constituted of three points. There are thus $\binom{n}{3}$ triangles for a configuration of n points. A first type of planar ordering information is defined in terms of the triangles.

Definition 1. Let $P = \{p_1, \ldots, p_n\}$ be a configuration then the *triangle orientations* of P are given by $\{[p_i p_j p_k] | p_i p_j p_k$ is a triangle of $P\}$.

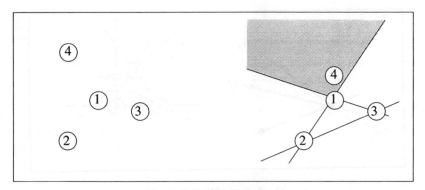

Fig. 2. Triangle orientations.

For an example of how the triangle orientations describe a configuration see Fig. 2. The configuration shown to the left consist of 4 points and has 4 triangles for which the following orientations are found

$$[123] = + \quad [124] = - \quad [134] = + \quad [234] = +$$

A simple way to visualize how the triangle orientations constrain the relative positions of a point consists in looking at the lines defined by the points. $[124] = -$ may be interpreted as stating that 4 lies in the halfplane on the right side of the directed line from 1 to 2. The point 4 also appears in two other triangles, $[134] = +$ and $[234] = +$. The intersection of the halfplanes determined by the three triangle orientations is marked in the configuration shown to the right in Fig. 2. Moving the point 4 within the marked area does not change the triangle orientations.

The set of triangle orientations defines what Goodman and Pollack call the *order type* of the configuration. Both configurations shown in Fig. 2 are said to be of the same order type in the sense that there is a one-to-one correspondence between the points of the configurations which preserves the orientation of the triangles. Several geometric definitions exist for order types and it is not always trivial to see their equivalence — the interested reader is referred to Goodman and Pollack [7].

Another notion of planar point ordering, not equivalent to the triangle orientations, is given by the permutation sequence. The permutation sequence is a structure that records all different orthogonal projections of the configuration. First, a directed line l_1 is chosen which is not orthogonal to any *connecting line*, that is, a line defined by two points of the configuration $P = \{p_1, \ldots, p_n\}$. The

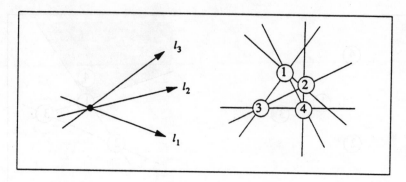

Fig. 3. Permutation sequence.

orthogonal projection of P onto l_1 determines the first permutation of P in the sense that the linear order of the images on the line is encoded as a *permutation of P*. Figure 3 illustrates a possible choice for l_1, the corresponding orthogonal projection of P onto l_1 is described by the permutation 3124. By rotating the line counterclockwise the permutation will eventually change. This happens whenever the line passes through a slope that is orthogonal to a connecting line. In the example the permutation changes to 3142 when the line moves across the horizontal direction, because that is the orthogonal to the line connecting the points 2 and 4. The new line position l_2 defines the second permutation of the sequence. If the number of different slopes of the connecting lines is k then this is also the number of different orthogonal projections (permutations) that will be found during a 360° rotation of the line.

Definition 2. Let $P = \{p_1, \ldots, p_n\}$ be a configuration and l_1 a line not orthogonal to the k different slopes of the connecting lines, then the *permutation sequence* of P is $(\pi_1, \ldots, \pi_k, \pi_{k+1}, \ldots, \pi_{2k})$ where π_i is the ith permutation of P arising from rotating l_1 counterclockwise and projecting P orthogonally onto it.

The permutation sequence has a periodic structure which is due to the fact that after a 180° rotation the line coincides with itself being directed in the opposite direction. Therefore the permutations in the second *half period* of the sequence repeat those from the first half period in reversed form. It is the circular order in which the permutations appear in the sequence that encodes the configuration; the choice of the first permutation does not give any further information. Two permutation sequences are *equivalent* if the permutations appear in the same circular order. All configurations that can be described by equivalent permutation sequences are said to be of the same *combinatorial type*. We will later see how this differs from classifying the configurations according to order type. What has been said about the periodic structure can be verified for the permutation sequence of the configuration from Fig. 3:

$$
\begin{array}{llll}
& \times & & \times \\
\pi_1 & 3\ 1\ 2\ 4 & \pi_7 & 4\ 2\ 1\ 3 \\
& \times & & \times \\
\pi_2 & 3\ 1\ 4\ 2 & \pi_8 & 2\ 4\ 1\ 3 \\
& \times & & \times \\
\pi_3 & 3\ 4\ 1\ 2 & \pi_9 & 2\ 1\ 4\ 3 \\
& \times & & \times \\
\pi_4 & 3\ 4\ 2\ 1 & \pi_{10} & 1\ 2\ 4\ 3 \\
& \times & & \times \\
\pi_5 & 4\ 3\ 2\ 1 & \pi_{11} & 1\ 2\ 3\ 4 \\
& \times & & \times \\
\pi_6 & 4\ 2\ 3\ 1 & \pi_{12} & 1\ 3\ 2\ 4 \\
& \times & & \times
\end{array}
$$

Between two successive permutations, *switches* of points occur. They are marked in the above listing by a cross. Although we see in the example only a single switch between two points at each step, we will find in general more complex switches. If there is a line connecting several points of the configuration, then all these points will switch in a single step. Furthermore, if there are parallel lines among the connecting lines, then this will produce several simultaneous switches in one step, one for each parallel.

1.3. *Triangle orientations and permutation sequence*

Permutation sequences have been used to solve different problems in discrete geometry and they enjoy popularity as a data structure in computational geometry. Sometimes they are also referred to as circular sequences or allowable sequences. The latter name derives from a combinatorial characterization of the type of switches that may appear in a permutation sequence. Any sequence of permutations satisfying this characterization is an "allowed" sequence. It turns out however, that there are allowable sequences for which no configuration has as permutation sequence. Actually it is a computationally hard problem to determine whether an allowable sequence is the sequence of some

122   *C. Schlieder*

configuration. Details concerning the *realization problem* and references to the rich literature on this topic are given by Goodman and Pollack [8]. For most spatial reasoning applications one does not have to worry about realization since the permutation sequence or triangle orientations come from configurations which are realized in the physical space as for example the configuration of landmarks in qualitative navigation.

Several of the representations commonly used in spatial reasoning systems relate to the permutation sequence or the triangle relations — though this fact has not been much exploited. We will say that a representation encodes *ordering information* about a configuration if it can be constructed given the permutation sequence or the triangle orientations. As evidenced by the solution to the qualitative navigation problem given in Schlieder [17], the analysis of the ordering information involved in a spatial reasoning task can give a hint on how to efficiently solve it. In introducing the notion of ordering information, both permutation sequences and triangle orientations, were mentioned. This is not really necessary, since it is a well-known fact (see Goodman and Pollack, [5], [7]) that the ordering information given by the permutation sequence is richer than that given by the triangle orientations. This holds in a strict sense, that is to say:

Observation 1. The triangle orientations are determined by the permutation sequence, but generally the inverse is not the case.

The triangle orientations can be recovered from the permutation sequence by looking at the switches. Consider the example given in Fig. 4. The order in

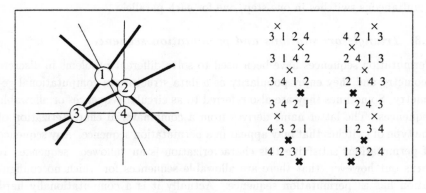

Fig. 4. Determining triangle orientations from the permutation sequence.

which the switches appear in the sequence reflects the counterclockwise order of the slopes of the connecting lines: the directed line 24 precedes the directed line 14, that precedes 12, and so on. A triangle of the configuration defines 6 directed lines and knowing the cyclical order of these lines one knows the orientation of the triangle. For the triangle 123 the cyclical order of the lines is $12 > \cdots > 32 > \cdots > 31$ and thus the orientation is $[123] = -$.

The general rule for translating the order of switches into triangle orientations is

$[p_1 p_2 p_3] = +$ iff the switches are ordered $p_1 p_2 > \cdots > p_3 p_2 > \cdots > p_3 p_1$

$[p_1 p_2 p_3] = 0$ iff the switches occur simultaneously

$[p_1 p_2 p_3] = -$ iff the switches are ordered $p_3 p_1 > \cdots > p_3 p_2 > \cdots > p_1 p_2$

It remains to provide an counter-example showing that the permutation sequence cannot generally be reconstructed from the triangle orientations. See Fig. 5 for two configurations which have the same triangle orientations but different permutation sequences. Only the half periods of the sequences are given — they differ in the permutation π_4.

left configuration	right configuration
$[123] = -$	$[123] = -$
$[124] = -$	$[124] = -$
$[134] = +$	$[134] = +$
$[234] = +$	$[234] = +$

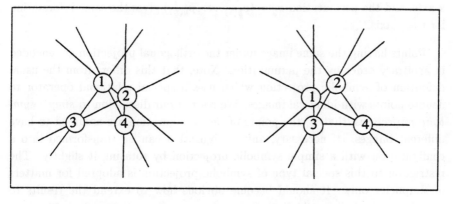

Fig. 5. Same orientation relations, but different permutation sequences.

$$
\begin{array}{llll}
\pi_1 & 3\ 1\ 2\ 4 & \quad \pi_1 & 3\ 1\ 2\ 4 \\
\pi_2 & 3\ 1\ 4\ 2 & \quad \pi_2 & 3\ 1\ 4\ 2 \\
\pi_3 & 3\ 4\ 1\ 2 & \quad \pi_3 & 3\ 4\ 1\ 2 \\
\pi_4 & 3\ 4\ 2\ 1 & \quad \pi_4 & 4\ 3\ 1\ 2 \\
\pi_5 & 4\ 3\ 2\ 1 & \quad \pi_5 & 4\ 3\ 2\ 1 \\
\pi_6 & 4\ 2\ 3\ 1 & \quad \pi_6 & 4\ 2\ 3\ 1
\end{array}
$$

2. Ordering Information Encoded by Symbolic Projection

Since Chang, Shi & Yan [1] introduced symbolic projections as a method for iconic indexing several modifications of the original definition have been proposed, among others by Lee & Tsu [13] and Holmes & Jungert [9]. We are going to discuss symbolic projection only in its most elementary form omitting any extensions. In particular, the analysis of the slope projection method proposed by Jungert [10] perhaps the extension of symbolic projection that comes closest to permutation sequences — will have to be postponed to a forthcoming paper. In the following we continue to use the terminology that was introduced for ordering information. As a consequence permutations will appear in the definition of symbolic projection instead of the strings commonly found in the literature. This notation, although unfamiliar, has the advantage to facilitate the task of comparison.

Definition 3. The *symbolic projection* of a configuration $P = \{p_1, \ldots, p_n\}$ is as a pair (π_x, π_y) of permutations of P. The permutation $\pi_x = (p_{x(1)}, \ldots, p_{x(n)})$ specifies the linear order of the image of P under orthogonal projection onto the x-axis, and the permutation $\pi_y = (p_{y(1)}, \ldots, p_{y(n)})$ gives the same information for the y-axis.

Points having the same image under the orthogonal projection are encoded in arbitrary order by the permutation. Note, that this differs from the usual definition of symbolic projection which uses a special relational operator to denote points with identical images. We restrict our discussion to *simple symbolic projections*, that is, the points of the configuration are assumed to have different images. If necessary, any configuration can be transformed into a configuration with a simple symbolic projection by rotating it slightly. The restriction to this special type of symbolic projection is adopted for matters of simplicity only. It should become obvious how to extend the results to non-simple symbolic projections.

2.1. *Determining the symbolic projection from the permutation sequence*

Definition 3 bears some resemblance to that of the permutation sequence because orthogonal projection plays a prominent role. The first question that arises is: to what extent does the permutation sequence determine the symbolic projection of that configuration? The symbolic projection encodes two specific orthogonal projections while the permutation sequence takes all possible orthogonal projections into account. We can however not conclude from this fact that strictly less information is given by the symbolic projection. Since the symbolic projection depends on the choice of the coordinate system it is in that respect more specific and more informative than the permutation sequence. To get a quantitative picture of the specificity of this information we will ask for the number of different symbolic projections that can be obtained from the set of configurations described by a given permutation sequence.

This is equivalent to asking for the number of ways in which (π_x, π_y) can be chosen among the permutations of the sequence $(\pi_1, \ldots, \pi_k, \pi_{k+1}, \ldots, \pi_{2k})$. Without caring about the geometrical background of the problem which might prohibit certain choices, there are $2k$ ways to choose π_x. For the subsequent choice of π_y we find that there are geometrical examples for which $\pi_y = \pi_x$, so this will be allowed. There is however an restriction on choosing π_y which has to do with the fact that oriented angles between directed lines are measured. The 90° angle between the coordinate axes is $\angle(\vec{x}, \vec{y})$, the angle from the unit vector of the directed x-axis to the unit vector of the directed y-axis; $\angle(\vec{y}, \vec{x})$ instead, is the complement of that angle, it measures 270°. Let $\vec{v}_i$ and $\vec{v}_j$ be the unit vectors of two directed lines that produce the permutations π_i and π_j under orthogonal projection. The angle $\angle(\vec{v}_i, \vec{v}_j)$ is greater than 180° when $i - j \, mod(2k) > k$. As we do not want to worry about complementing angles, it will be assumed that $i - j \, mod(2k) \leq k$. When this condition is given π_i and π_j are said to *appear in increasing order* in the sequence. Since the angle between the axes is 90° (not 270°), we obtain the constraint that π_y has to be chosen in such manner that π_x and π_y appear in increasing order. Having chosen π_x this leaves us thus with $k + 1$ choices for π_y.

Now we take the geometrical aspect of the problem into account. By rotating the configuration the symbolic projection changes but the permutation sequence stays invariant. In the course of a 360° rotation π_x successively takes all values of the permutation sequence $(\pi_1, \ldots, \pi_k, \pi_{k+1}, \ldots, \pi_{2k})$. Therefore, all $2k$ choices for π_x are geometrically possible. This could be different for

π_y insofar as choosing π_x restricts the geometric possibilities to choose π_y. Knowing that the angle between the axes is 90° one might for instance look for a criterion that puts some constraints on the distance at which π_x may appear from π_y in the sequence. The following observation implies that no such criterion can be found.

Observation 2. For the permutation sequence $(\pi_1, \ldots, \pi_k, \pi_{k+1}, \ldots, \pi_{2k})$ of any configuration P and any two permutations, π_i and π_j, which appear in increasing order in the sequence, a configuration $f(P)$ can be found with the same permutation sequence and the symbolic projection π_i, π_j.

Consider $\vec{n}_i$ and $\vec{n}_j$ the unit normal vectors of two directed lines that produce the permutations π_i and π_j under orthogonal projection and $\vec{n}_x = (0, 1), \vec{n}_y = (-1, 0)$ the unit normals of the coordinate axes. Now simply take $f(P)$ to be the image of P under the affine transformation f: $\vec{n}_i \to \vec{n}_x, \vec{n}_j \to \vec{n}_y$. The symbolic projection of $f(P)$ is then (π_i, π_j) and since affine transformations preserve ordering information $f(P)$ has the same permutation sequence as P.

See Fig. 6 for a concrete example of how by transforming a configuration we can force two orthogonal projections to become the symbolic projection. Note, that the normal vector designates the direction into which to project, whereas the direction of the line onto which is projected is orthogonal to that. For both configurations we find $\pi_i = 4132$ and $\pi_j = 4312$. It is because of this invariance under affine transformations that the permutation sequence does not convey any metric information such as distances or angles. Used as a

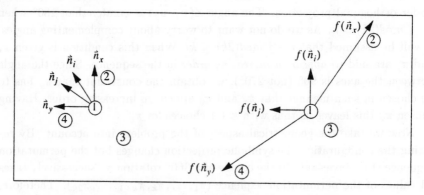

Fig. 6. Transforming two orthogonal projections into the symbolic projection.

representation it is, so to say, more qualitative than the symbolic projection which implicitly specifies the angle between the coordinate axes — a metric property.

To sum up the above discussion, there are $2k$ ways to choose π_x, and $k+1$ ways for a subsequent choice of π_y thereafter which leads to the following

Observation 3. The number of different symbolic projections that can be obtained from the set of configurations described by a given permutation sequence is $2k(k+1)$.

This observation is a more precise way to state that the symbolic projection cannot be recovered from the permutation sequence. It also answers to what extent the permutation sequence determines the symbolic projection, which was the very first question raised. Note, that $2k(k+1)$ is not the number of symbolic projections that are obtained by rotating a configuration. This number is smaller and depends on the configuration. Later bounds on this number will be given.

2.2. *Determining the permutation sequence from the symbolic projection*

The second question that is interesting is the reverse of the first: to what extend does the symbolic projection determine ordering information? On the one hand the symbolic projection only specifies two permutations (one permutation for $\pi_x = \pi_y$), and the permutation sequence could very well be a redundant way to define ordering information. We know that there are cases in which the whole sequence can be reconstructed from some of its permutations.

Given a symbolic projection (π_x, π_y) then according to observation 2 the only fact known about the permutation sequence is that it contains π_x and π_y in increasing order. As can be expected two permutations in increasing order do not generally determine the sequence. We will provide an example showing more, namely that there are configurations with permutation sequences that differ only in very few permutations. This has as a consequence that by not knowing these permutations it makes the reconstruction of the sequence impossible. An example of two configurations with permutations sequences that differ only in such *essential permutations* can easily be constructed starting with an appropriate configuration and moving some critical point across to yield the second configuration.

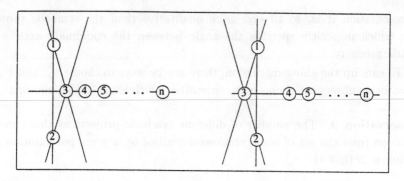

Fig. 7. Configurations for which the permutation sequences differ little.

Observation 4. There exist two families of configurations, $\mathbf{P} = \{p_n | n > 3\}$ and $\mathbf{Q} = \{Q_n | n > 3\}$ where each P_n and Q_n consists of n points and the half periods of the permutation sequences for P_n and Q_n only differ in two permutations.

Figure 7 shows P_n on the left side and Q_n on the right side. A half period of the permutation sequences reads as follows:

permutation	sequence for P_n	sequence for Q_n
π_1	1 3 4 ... n 2	1 3 4 ... n 2
π_2	1 3 4 ... 2 n	1 3 4 ... 2 n
...	...	...
π_{n-3}	1 3 4 2 ... n	1 3 4 2 ... n
π_{n-2}	1 3 2 4 ... n	1 3 2 4 ... n
π_{n-1}	1 2 3 4 ... n	3 1 2 4 ... n
π_n	2 1 3 4 ... n	3 2 1 4 ... n
π_{n+1}	2 3 1 4 ... n	2 3 1 4 ... n
...	...	...
π_{2n-3}	2 3 4 ... 1 n	2 3 4 ... 1 n
π_{2n-2}	2 3 4 ... n 1	2 3 4 ... n 1

As can be seen, only the permutations π_n and π_{n-1} are different.

As a consequence of observation 4 the reconstruction of a sequence, depends not just on the number but also on the choice of the permutations.

Knowing $2n - 4$ of the permutations, namely all but π_2 and π_3, it is possible to uniquely reconstruct the sequence. On the other hand, also knowing $2n - 4$ of the permutations, all but π_n and π_{n-1}, allows for two different reconstructions, whereas the number of symbolic projections corresponding to a given permutation sequence, is already determined by the length of the sequence the number of permutation sequences corresponding to a given symbolic projection is determined by what permutations the symbolic projection gives. Since there can be more and less informative symbolic projections there is no direct equivalent to observation 3.

For several applications it would be interesting to know how to solve the *reconstruction problem*: that is, to have an algorithm which gives some permutations (in arbitrary order) that efficiently constructs the set of compatible permutation sequences. This problem arises for instance in the context of qualitative navigation where one wants to integrate views showing landmarks in linear order (i.e. permutations) into a qualitative picture of the configuration of landmarks (i.e. a permutation sequence). Maybe the problem has already been solved in combinatorics without that this has become known to the spatial reasoning community — in that case a reference would be very much appreciated by the author.

3. The Problem of Rotation Invariance

Absolute location with respect to an external frame of reference is not relevant to every application dealing with point data. In qualitative landmark navigation for instance it is only the position of the observer relative to the landmarks that matters, not the absolute position of the landmarks themselves. Of course it depends much on the problem context of which configuration points are to be considered equivalent, or in other words, which group of transformations is expected to leave the representation invariant. For problems where distance information is available subgroups of the isometries play an important role as invariant groups.

Ordering information is invariant under translation and so is the symbolic projection. A reflection inverts all triangle orientations and the permutation sequence — independent of the mirror axis chosen. Representations of ordering information thus change in a way that is easy to predict: there is one representation for the configuration and one corresponding representation for its mirror image. Both can be identified with the help of a single equivalence rule. But often invariance with respect to reflection is not desired, as in qualitative navigation where one wants to distinguish between a configuration of landmarks and its mirror image. Although ordering information is invariant under rotation, the symbolic projection is not. That becomes a problem when the application domain does not provide a normal form with respect to rotation (e.g. y-axis = geographic north) into which configurations can be transformed.

3.1. *Symbolic projections of rotated configurations*

One way to achieve rotation invariance is to state a rule that generates from a symbolic projection all other projections that arise by rotating the configuration. For the special case of 90° rotations a set of such transformation rules has been stated by Jungert [11]. Each transformation rule describes the effect of one specific rotation on the symbolic projection. Can the general rotation invariance problem be approached by such case-by-case rules? In order to answer this question it is helpful to know how many different symbolic projections can be obtained by rotation. The following bounds are found for the number of symbolic projections of rotated configurations:

Observation 5. If P is a configuration such that the lines defined by the points have k different slopes then rotating P will produce a minimum of $2k$ and maximum of $4k$ different symbolic projections.

Without loss of generality it can be assumed that the permutation sequence $(\pi_1, \ldots, \pi_k, \pi_{k+1}, \ldots, \pi_{2k})$ describing P is numbered in such a way that the symbolic projection of P has the form (π_1, π_v) where π_v is a permutation from $\pi_1, \ldots, \pi_k$. If the the angle α of an rotation r_α is measured in clockwise orientation the following equivalence describes how the symbolic projection proj_α of $r_\alpha(P)$ determines the symbolic projection $\text{proj}_{\alpha+90}$ of $r_{\alpha+90}(P)$

$$\text{proj}_\alpha = (\pi_i, \pi_j) \Leftrightarrow \text{proj}_{\alpha+90} = (\pi_j, \pi_{i+k})$$

Thus, the same number p of symbolic projections is going to be found for $0 \leq \alpha < 90$ as for α lying in any of the other three quadrants. This gives a total of $4p$ symbolic projections produced by a 360° rotation of P — with an unknown p. Numbering the symbolic projections in the order they appear during a 360° rotation of P : $\text{proj}_1, \ldots, \text{proj}_{4p}$ translates the equivalence given above into

$$\text{proj}_r = (\pi_i, \pi_j) \Leftrightarrow \text{proj}_{r+p} = (\pi_j, \pi_{i+k}).$$

Lower and upper bounds for p are found by considering the first $2p$ symbolic projections:

$$
\begin{aligned}
\text{proj}_1 &= (\pi_1, \pi_v) \\
\cdots & \qquad \cdots \\
\text{proj}_p &= (\pi_u, \pi_k) \\
\text{proj}_{p+1} &= (\pi_v, \pi_{1+k}) \\
\cdots & \qquad \cdots \\
\text{proj}_{2p} &= (\pi_k, \pi_{u+k})
\end{aligned}
$$

The $2p$ permutations $\pi_1, \ldots, \pi_u, \pi_v, \ldots, \pi_k$ are the values that the x-projection successively assumes during rotation. Note that generally the x-projection does not change from one symbolic projection to the next. In the first $2p$ symbolic projections the x-projection takes k different values because all permutations from $\pi_1, \pi_2, \ldots, \pi_k$ become the x-projection for at least one symbolic projection. This gives a lower bound of $2p \geq k$. For even k the minimum $p = k/2$ is attained when P is chosen to consist of the k vertices of a regular polygon. In this case the k slopes will have angular increments of $180°k$ as shown by the left diagram in Fig. 8. The $2k$ different symbolic projections obtained by a $360°$ rotation are for this type of configuration:

$$
\begin{aligned}
\text{proj}_1 &= (\pi_1, \pi_{k-1}) \\
\text{proj}_2 &= (\pi_2, \pi_k) \\
\cdots & \qquad \cdots \\
\text{proj}_{2k} &= (\pi_{2k}, \pi_{k-2})
\end{aligned}
$$

An upper bound for p derives from the fact that two successive symbolic projections have to differ in at least the x- or the y-projection. As was observed, the x-projection changes $k - 1$ times in the first $2p$ symbolic projections. At the same time the y-projection changes a maximum of k times because it takes as value every permutation from $\pi_v, \pi_{v+1}, \ldots, \pi_{u+k}$ at least in one symbolic projection. Thus, a total of $2k$ symbolic projections can be obtained this way, in other words $p \leq 2k$. This upper bound is attained by configurations which define k slopes such that there are two consecutive slopes forming an obtuse angle (see right diagram in Fig. 8). Note, that any P defining k slopes can be transformed into a configuration meeting this requirement by applying an appropriate affine transformation (cf. observation 2). The $4k$ different symbolic projections obtained by a $360°$ rotation of a configuration of this type are:

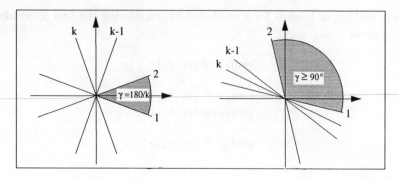

Fig. 8. Slopes that yield a minimal and a maximal number of symbolic projections.

$$\text{proj}_1 = (\pi_1, \pi_1)$$
$$\text{proj}_2 = (\pi_1, \pi_2)$$
$$\cdots \qquad \cdots$$
$$\text{proj}_k = (\pi_1, \pi_k)$$
$$\text{proj}_{k+1} = (\pi_1, \pi_{1+k})$$
$$\text{proj}_{k+2} = (\pi_2, \pi_{1+k})$$
$$\cdots \qquad \cdots$$
$$\text{proj}_{2k} = (\pi_k, \pi_{1+k})$$
$$\cdots \qquad \cdots$$
$$\text{proj}_{4k} = (\pi_{2k}, \pi_1)$$

3.2. *Adding the Solution of the Slope Problem*

Observation 5 can be used to derive bounds on the number of symbolic projections that arise in an application problem. In order to do so one needs to know the number of slopes defined by the problem configuration. Frequently, this number is difficult to determine because the number of points is the parameter that one actually controls. This happens in the qualitative navigation scenario where information about the number of landmarks is available and where the computational costs for finding an optimal path depend on this number. Lower and upper bounds on the number of symbolic projections stated in terms of the number of points of the configuration would be useful in this and similar cases.

The maximum number of slopes determined by n points in general position occurs when no lines are parallel, because then all $\binom{n}{2}$ lines correspond to a different slope. We have seen that the maximum of $4k$ symbolic projections is obtained by any configuration defining k slopes such that there are two consecutive slopes forming an obtuse angle. Since any configuration can be transformed by an appropriate affine transformation into a configuration with slopes meeting the requirement we find the maximum number of symbolic projections with $k = \binom{n}{2}$.

Bounding the minimum number of slopes is immediate only for the trivial case of all n points lying on a line. This case is not likely to be of practical importance and it is more interesting to ask for the minimum number of slopes that is determined by n points not all on one line. That question is much more difficult and a number of papers in discrete geometry has been devoted to this *slope problem* (a survey of results is given by Goodman & Pollack, [8]. Ungar [18] finally settled the issue by showing that the minimum is $2\lfloor n/2 \rfloor$, that is $2n$ for even n and $2(n-1)$ for odd n. This bound is realized by configurations that consist of the vertices of the regular n-gon if n is even and the vertices of the regular $(n\text{-}1)$-gon together with its center if n is odd. As we have seen such configurations define k slopes which yield the minimum number of $2k$ symbolic projections. In terms of n the minimum is thus obtained for $k = 2\lfloor n/2 \rfloor$. To sum up we formulate the following observation (reminding that the hard part is not observation 4 but the solution to the slope problem).

Observation 6. If P is a configuration of n points not all on one line then rotating P will produce a minimum of $4\lfloor n/2 \rfloor$ and maximum of $4 \binom{n}{2}$ different symbolic projections.

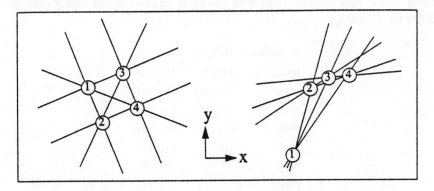

Fig. 9. Configurations with minimal and maximal number of symbolic projections.

According to this result there is quite a gap between the minimum number of symbolic projections which is linear in n and the maximum number which is quadratic in n. An example will illustrate this effect for $n = 4$. Figure 9 shows on the left side a configuration P and on the right side a configuration Q. While P defines the minimum number of 4 slopes that is possible for 4 points, Q defines the maximum number possible, namely 6. Therefore the permutation sequence for P is of length 8 and the one for Q is of length 12. Given below is the halfperiod of each sequence:

permutation	sequence for P	sequence for Q
π_1	1 2 3 4	1 2 3 4
π_2	2 1 4 3	1 2 4 3
π_3	2 4 1 3	1 4 2 3
π_4	4 2 3 1	1 4 3 2
π_5	$\cdots$	4 1 3 2
π_6		4 3 1 2

P defines a slope pattern that yields a minimum number of different symbolic projections when the configuration is rotated. The 4 slopes allow for 8 symbolic projections which is the number given by observations 5 and 6. Q defines in contrast to this a slope pattern that yields a maximum number of symbolic projections. It allows for 24 symbolic projections which is in accordance with observations 5 and 6. In the following one fourth of the symbolic projections is given for P and Q which as we have seen determines the rest of them. Note, that permutations with the same number in the listing generally differ for P and Q.

projection	for $r(P)$	for $r(Q)$
proj_1	(π_1, π_3)	(π_1, π_1)
proj_2	(π_2, π_4)	(π_1, π_2)
proj_3	(π_3, π_5)	(π_1, π_3)
proj_4	(π_4, π_6)	(π_1, π_4)
proj_5	$\cdots$	(π_1, π_5)
proj_6		(π_1, π_6)
proj_7		(π_1, π_7)
proj_8		(π_1, π_8)

4. The Panorama Representation of Ordering Information

The discussion sofar has shown that the symbolic projection of a configuration encodes the ordering information partially for which reason it is not invariant under rotation. There are two obvious ways to achieve rotation invariance. The first consists in stating an equivalence rule which identifies the symbolic projections of rotated configurations. It cannot be expected however to find strong general constraints on what the symbolic projections of the rotated configuration may be. Examples of configurations P_1, P_2, ... with different permutation sequences but the same symbolic projection (π_x, π_y) are not difficult to construct. Rotating any such P_i generates symbolic projections equivalent to (π_x, π_y). The equivalence classes will thus in general encompass more symbolic projections than just the ones obtained by rotating a single P_i, the number of which is bounded by observation 5. Such a coarse notion of equivalence is not likely to satisfy the demands of every application. Qualitative navigation for instance requires one to be able to distinguish between the $P_1, P_2 \cdots$.

A second way to achieve rotation invariance consists in encoding additional information, more precisely, the complete ordering information. Devising a data structure that encodes the permutation sequence is straightforward. Care has to be taken only to ensure that the retrieval of the successor of a permutation and the retrieval of the switches between permutations are computationally cheap operations. Another solution along this line is to represent the other type of ordering information, namely the triangle orientations. The panorama representation described below shows how to compactly encode this information. Which of the solutions is judged more adequate for solving the rotation invariance problem, representation with equivalence rule or representation of complete ordering information, will very much depend on the application.

4.1. *The panorama of a point*

The definition of the panorama that will be given is restricted to configurations of points in general position, i.e. no more than two points lie on a line. It is not difficult however to extend both the definition and the observations following it to configurations in special position. The panorama is defined for each point of the configuration and gives information about the point's location relative to the other points. It was introduced as a representation which supports an efficient algorithmic solution of the qualitative navigation problem mentioned in the introduction. Consider Fig. 11 showing the relative angles under which five reference points $1, 2, 3, 4$ and 5 are seen from a point 0. In a clockwise turn the arrow pointing to 2 is preceded by the tail of the arrow pointing to 4 and succeeded by the tail of the arrow pointing to 5. Recording only the circular order 12345 means loosing this information. The distinction made between the head and the tail of an arrow is captured in the panorama by taking for each reference point two directed lines into account: the lines directed towards and from the reference point.

Definition 6. Let $\mathbf{P} = \{p_1, \ldots, p_2\}$ be a configuration, $p_i \in P$ a point, and $L_i = \{l_{i1}, l_{1i}, \ldots, l_{in}, l_{ni}\}$ the arrangement of the $n - 1$ directed lines incident with p_i and another point of P, then the clockwise oriented cyclical order of L_i is called the *panorama* of p_i.

For the purpose of encoding the panorama of a point p_i we introduce a shorthand notation for the two directed lines incident with p_i and a reference point p_j. The line l_{ij} directed from p_i to p_j is denoted by the index j only and the line l_{ji} directed in opposite direction is denoted by $\bar{j}$ — the context will make clear which point p_i is referred to. Using this notational convention the panorama can be written in form of a diagram as in Fig. 10 or in form of a string, $1\bar{3}42\bar{5}1\bar{3}4\bar{2}5$. Because of the periodic structure of the panorama it can be encoded by giving any n consecutive elements of it, e.g. $1\bar{3}4\bar{2}5$ or $\bar{4}2\bar{5}1\bar{3}$.

Note, that the panorama encodes more information than just the circular ordering of the points. In this it differs from both the viewframes of Levitt & Lawton [14] and the polar symbolic projection of Jungert [10]. We will briefly state some other properties of the panorama representation. From definition 4 it is clear that the panorama is invariant under translation and rotation of the

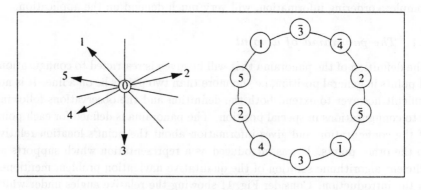

Fig. 10. The panorama of a point.

configuration. By a reflection the ordering in every panorama is inverted. A simple equivalence rule which reverses the encoding string can thus identify mirror images. For a configuration of n points the panorama of each point is given by a string of length n (or length $2n$ when the whole period is encoded). The whole panorama representation therefore consists of n strings of length n. Compared to the symbolic projection which uses 2 strings of length n this is a noticeable increase in storage requirement. Applications for which storage is a real problem are however difficult to imagine since in the case of qualitative navigation $n < 20$.

Usually the panorama representation is computed directly from the coordinate representation of the points, but as will be shown later it also can be determined from the triangle orientations. An convenient method (which is not claimed to be computationally optimal) to build the panorama representation proceeds as follows:

> step 1: Sort all the directed lines $l_{12}, l_{21}, \ldots, l_{nn-1}, l_{n-1n}$ defined by
> two points of the configuration in order of increasing slope into
> a list S.
>
> step 2: for $i = 1 \cdots n$
> Determine P_i as the ordered sublist of S whose elements
> are of the form l_{ij} or l_{ji} with $j \in \{1 \cdots n\} - \{i\}$.
>
> step 3: Return the panorama representation $P_1, \ldots, P_n$.

Now it needs to be verified that the panorama encodes the same information as the triangle orientations. A simple equivalence which directly follows from definition 4 is helpful for the conversion between both representations.

Observation 7. $[p_i p_j p_k] = +$ if and only if the clockwise circular order of lines in the panorama of p_i is, $\ldots, l_{ij}, \ldots, l_{ik}, \ldots, l_{ji}, \ldots, l_{ki}, \ldots$

Making use of the observation we can immediately read off the triangle orientations from the panorama representation. As an example consider the panorama shown in Fig. 10 which shows the clockwise circular order $\cdots 3 \cdots 1 \cdots \bar{3} \cdots \bar{1} \cdots$ implying $[031] = +$. In that way all orientations of triangles having the form $[0ij]$ can be recovered from the panorama of 0. Observation 7 is also the base for determining the panorama given the triangle orientations. The computation of panorama of a point p_i takes the triangles into account in which p_i appears. Any of these triangles determines the circular order of two pairs of directed lines in the panorama. The panorama is obtained by starting with an arbitrary order of lines which is then sorting according to circular order.

4.2. *The panorama of a region*

Originally, the panorama was conceived for representing the position of an observer relative to some landmarks. Since landmarks are considered to be points in qualitative navigation it poses no problem to apply the representational scheme to other domains with point data. In virtue of being invariant to rotation the panorama representation could very well find a use as index for retrieval in an image information system. It seems however necessary to test different modifications of the panorama representation to yield an optimum result. A modification that seems particularly promising consists in integrating metric information into this pure framework of ordering information. Remember that it is because the symbolic projection implicitly encodes some metric information about the angle formed by the coordinate axes that it cannot be fully recovered from the permutation sequence.

In place of an overview of possible modifications of panorama representation a brief sketch of one such extension will be given, the extension to region data. First, some characteristic point is identified for each region, e.g. the center of gravity under a uniform mass distribution. This point is used to construct the panorama for the region, for an example see point C in Fig. 11. The panorama is found by sweeping a directed line around C and the order in which it hits the

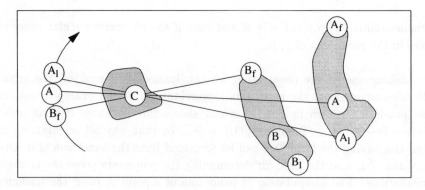

Fig. 11. The panorama for a region.

characteristic points A and B of the other regions is recorded. Other points of interest are the first and last point of a region that are encountered by the rotating line. In Fig. 11 we find $B_f > A > A_l$. The order of these points in the panorama gives information about the occlusion or visibility of the regions.

It should be observed, that the additional points A_f, A_l, B_f and B_l appear only in the panorama of the region C. From a different viewpoint these points are not going to be seen as extremal points of their region. In other words, the extension of the panorama representation to regions is achieved by making reference to points for which position is not completely determined with respect to ordering information. All suggestions for extension of the original representation will have to deal with the problem that two regions do not define a line — maybe this is part of the reason why the semantics of the concepts "left" and "right" which we use currently in everyday life is so difficult to define in precise terms. Regions introduce some kind of fuzzyness into the neat world of incident points and lines. On one hand there is a price to pay for this, it is the loss of the algebraic properties that allow for highly constrained inferences, on the other hand there is something to be gained and that is a more realistic modelling of the domain dependent constraints.

References

1. S. Chang, Q. Shi, & C. Yan, "Iconic indexing by 2D strings", *IEEE Transactions on Pattern Analysis and Machine Intelligence,* **9** (1987) 413–428.
2. S. Chen ed., *Advances in Spatial Reasoning* (Ablex Publishing Co., Norwood, NJ, 1990).
3. H. Edelsbrunner, *Algorithms in Combinatorial Geometry*, (Springer, Berlin, 1987).
4. C. Freksa and R. Röhrig, "Dimensions of qualitative spatial reasoning", in *Qualitative Reasoning and Decision Technologies*, eds. N. Piera Carreté and M. Singh, (Barcelona: CIMNE, 1993) pp. 483-492.
5. J. Goodman and R. Pollack, "On the combinatorial classification of nondegenerate configurations in the plane", *Journal of Combinatorial Theory* **A29** (1980) 220–235.
6. J. Goodman and R. Pollack, "A theorem of ordered duality", *Geometriae Dedicata* **12** (1982) 63–74.
7. J. Goodman and R. Pollack, "Multidimensional sorting", *SIAM J. Comput.* **12** (1983) 484–507.
8. J. Goodman and R. Pollack, "Allowable sequences and order types in discrete and computational geometry", in *New Trends in Discrete and Computational Geometry*, ed. J. Pach, (Springer, Berlin, 1993) pp. 103–134.

9. P. Holmes and E. Jungert, "Symbolic and geometric connectivity graph methods for route planning in digitized maps", *IEEE Transactions on Pattern Analysis and Machine Intelligence* **14** (1992) 549–565.

10. E. Jungert, "The observers point of view: An extension of symbolic projections", eds. A. Frank, I. Campari and U. Formentini, in *Theories and Methods of Spatio-Temporal Reasoning in Geographic Space* (Springer, Berlin, 1992) pp. 179-195.

11. E. Jungert, "Rotation invariance in symbolic projections as a means for determination of binary object relations", eds. N. Piera Carrete & M. Singh, *Qualitative Reasoning and Decision Technologies* (Barcelona: CIMNE., 1993) 503–512.

12. A. Kak, ed., "Spatial reasoning [special issue]", *AI Magazine*, **9**, 1988.

13. S. Lee and F. Tsu, "Picture algebra for spatial reasoning of iconic images represented in 2D C-string", *Pattern Recognition Letters* **12** (1991) 425–435.

14. T. Levitt and D. Lawton, "Qualitative navigation for mobile robots", *Artificial Intelligence* **44** (1990) 305–360.

15. D. McDermott, "Reasoning, spatial", in *Encyclopedia of Artificial Intelligence* ed. S. Shapiro (Wiley, New York, 1992) pp. 1322–1334.

16. J. Pach, ed., *New Trends in Discrete and Computational Geometry* (Springer, Berlin, 1993).

17. C. Schlieder, "Representing visible locations for qualitative navigation", eds. N. Piera Carrete and M. Singh, *Qualitative Reasoning and Decision Technologies*, CIMNE Barcelona: 1993) pp. 523–532.

18. P. Ungar, "2N noncollinear points determine at least 2N directions", *Journal of Combinatorial Theory* **A33**, (1982) 343–347.

DETERMINATION OF THE VIEWS OF A MOVING AGENT BY MEANS OF SYMBOLIC PROJECTION

ERLAND JUNGERT

FOA (Swedish Defence Research Establishment)
Box 1165, Linköping, Sweden
E-mail:jungert@lin.foa.se

In this chapter, two approaches concerned with object relations seen from a moving object (agent) that is moving in a space of fixed landmarks, will be discussed. Both approaches are complementary to each other from certain aspects. In the first approach the agent itself is of no concern when reasoning about the view as it is seen by the agent. Furthermore, in this approach only some simple aspects of symbolic projection are used, while most other aspects are based on novel concepts. The second approach, on the other hand, is entirely based on symbolic slope projection which is a generalization of the original approach to symbolic projection. Contrary to the first approach, the landmark-agent relations play a more fundamental role since they can easily be determined. Common to both approaches are that they are based on qualitative reasoning techniques.

1. Introduction

Qualitative spatial reasoning is presently subject to strong research efforts of which most are concerned with a single global perspective for which various kinds of binary or topological relations can be determined, e.g. [1], [2] and [3] where the last work was also concerned with temporal aspects. However, another type of problem that needs to be studied as well is concerned with the determination of object relations as they are seen from a particular place and direction by a free or autonomous agent. An attempt in this direction has been made by Freksa [4], who showed a method where the later part of the track of a moving object can be related to earlier parts. Another work by Schlieder [5], which is discussed in Chapter 5 of this book is very much related to the work in this chapter, considers the more general view by taking the full scene of all surrounding landmarks into account. At this point, this chapter does not take moving objects into account but the foundation for such an extension is present. In all, the efforts of reasoning on views seen from moving objects must be brought further, since there is a large group of applications that requires this kind of reasoning. Examples of such application areas are mobile robots, GIS and other applications that are concerned with sensor data fusion.

The work that will be discussed in this chapter is based on symbolic projection, which is a reasoning technique originally suggested by Chang *et al.*[6]. This method has later been subjected to considerable extension. Two such extensions, made more or less in parallel, are of particular interest. Lee [7] showed how rotations of symbolic projection strings can be made through a technique that is closely related to coordinate transformations. Jungert [8] developed a technique, called slope projection, which goes much further than Lee's work in that it can be shown that slope projection is a generalization of the original projection method. That is, the perpendicular projections of the original method are just special cases of the slope projection technique. The use of slope projection will be discussed further subsequently in Sec. 4.

The problem discussed here is quite complex, and efficient methods are required. Two fairly different approaches, which to some degree are complementary, will be discussed and compared. It turns out that both methods suffer in different ways. The first one is incomplete since not all relations can be derived while the second is less efficient than the first. For this reason it would be of interest to merge the two approaches, but at this point no such solution is known. The first approach uses a set of matrices and is therefore called the matrix approach. The second method uses slope projection for determination of the views. The motivation for considering the two approaches is primarily due to the fact that the matrix method does not take the relationships between the landmarks and the agent into account.

2. The Main Objective

The objective of this chapter is to determine the view of an agent that is primarily moving in a two-dimensional world. The objects that will be part of this view are just landmarks or point objects with known positions. An agent can be considered as any type of vehicle that uses a set of sensors to get the necessary information for the determination of the position of its surrounding landmarks. The position of the agent for which the views should be determined is known as well. In a real situation the path of the agent should be subject to investigation but path determination is not part of this chapter and will not be discussed. An illustration of the problem can be seen in Fig. 1 where the path of the agent is described by the coordinates (x_1, y_1) through (x_3, y_3). The

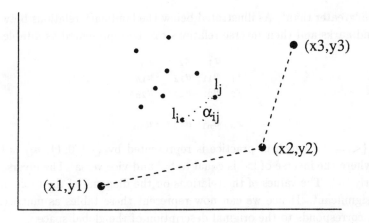

Fig. 1. An illustration of the basic problem of the moving agent.

landmarks are pairwise associated with a slope angle e.g. in Fig. 1 the angle α_{ij} corresponds to the slope angle of the landmarks l_i and l_j.

The objective can hence be formulated in a more formal way: given an agent moving in a free space of landmarks the problem is to generate a description of the space at every position as it is seen from the agent. The agent can have an arbitrary orientation in the space which may influence the description of its view of the space. The description of the space should be made in qualitative terms so that it can serve as a means for reasoning about the view and also for determining various existing object relations.

3. The Matrix Approach

3.1. *Basic structures*

As can be seen in Fig. 1, the relations between the agent and the landmarks are changing as the agent moves along its path. These relations also change when the agent changes its orientation, that is, the view of the landmarks will change if the agent turns in different directions. For instance, a certain landmark may be to the left of another in a particular orientation while it may be to the right in another orientation. For this reason, the angles between the landmarks are of importance when this type of relation is determined. Furthermore, information necessary when determining the various object relations is the basic relations that are used in symbolic projection, that is, 'less than' and 'equal to'. However, in this approach it turns out that it is necessary to also

include 'greater than'. As illustrated below the landmark relations between all
the landmarks and their inverse relations can be represented as a table.

$$
\begin{array}{cccc}
 & x_1 & x_2 & \cdots x_n \\
x_1 & u_{11} & u_{12} & \cdots u_{1n} \\
x_2 & u_{21} & u_{22} & \cdots u_{2n} \\
\cdots & \cdots & & \\
x_n & u_{n1} & u_{n2} & \cdots u_{nn}
\end{array}
$$

$u_{ij} \in \{<, =, >\}$ which in practice is represented by $\{-1, 0, 1\}$, $u_{ij} =$ inverse
(u_{ji}) where the inverse of '>' is equal to '<' and vice versa. The inverse of '='
is clearly '='. The values of the relations on the diagonal of the table, i.e. u_{ii},
are insignificant. Hence we can now represent these tables as matrices. U_0,
below, corresponds to the original description of the global space.

$$
U_0 = \begin{bmatrix}
u_{11} & u_{12} \cdots u_{1n} \\
u_{21} & u_{22} \cdots u_{2n} \\
\cdots & \cdots \cdots \cdots \\
u_{n1} & u_{n2} \cdots u_{nn}
\end{bmatrix}
$$

The U_0-matrix corresponds to the relations as they are projected down to
the x-axis as in the original approach of the symbolic projection. The only
exception is that the inverses of '<' are included as well. Consequently there is
also a V matrix needed that corresponds to the projected relations along the
y-axis. For the global orientation this matrix is called V_0.

$$
V_0 = \begin{bmatrix}
\nu_{11} & \nu_{12} \cdots \nu_{1n} \\
\nu_{21} & \nu_{22} \cdots \nu_{2n} \\
\cdots & \cdots \cdots \cdots \\
\nu_{n1} & \nu_{n2} \cdots \nu_{nn}
\end{bmatrix}
$$

However, from the discussion above it is clear that the angles between the
landmarks must also be available, these angles are available in the A_0 matrix
below which concludes the set of pre-calculated, basic and global matrices.

$$
A_0 = \begin{bmatrix}
\alpha_{11} & \alpha_{12} \cdots \alpha_{1n} \\
\alpha_{21} & \alpha_{22} \cdots \alpha_{2n} \\
\cdots & \cdots \cdots \cdots \\
\alpha_{n1} & \alpha_{n2} \cdots \alpha_{nn}
\end{bmatrix}
$$

Evidently, the following relationships and constraints exist between the angles
of A_0 : $\alpha_{ij} = \pi + \alpha_{ji}$, and here as well the values of the diagonal elements, α_{ii}
are insignificant.

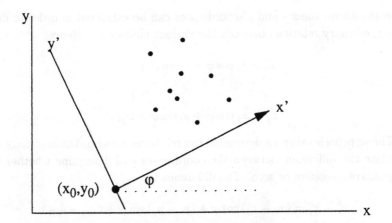

Fig. 2. The new coordinate system from which U_φ and V_φ should be determined.

Besides the above, the rotation angle φ must be available. This angle is defined as illustrated in Fig. 2, that is, the angle between the x'-axis and the x-axis where x', y' is the new coordinate system. The agent is moving in a certain direction, called the facing direction, that is equivalent to the direction of the x'-axis which in Fig. 2 is indicated with an arrow.

3.2. *The principles of the matrix approach*

As can be seen in Fig. 2 a new coordinate system is introduced whose origin corresponds to the position of the agent. The approach taken is to generate the agent's view by a regular coordinate transformation:

$$X_i' = \Phi X_i + \Omega$$

where

$$X_i' = \begin{bmatrix} x_i' \\ y_i' \end{bmatrix}$$

$$X_i = \begin{bmatrix} x_i \\ y_i \end{bmatrix}$$

$$\Phi = \begin{bmatrix} \cos\varphi & \sin\varphi \\ -\sin\varphi & \cos\varphi \end{bmatrix}$$

and

$$\Omega = \begin{bmatrix} \omega_{i1} \\ \omega_{i2} \end{bmatrix} .$$

From the above the x'- and y'-coordinates can be extracted in order to determine the binary relations between the various landmarks. Hence

$$x_i' = x_i \cos\varphi + y_i \sin\varphi + \omega_{i1} ,$$

and

$$x_j' = x_j \cos\varphi + y_j \sin\varphi + \omega_{j1} .$$

The approach taken to determine the relations between the landmark is to calculate the difference between the coordinates and determine whether they are positive, negative or zero. The difference is

$$x_i' - x_j' = (x_i - x_j) \cos\varphi + (y_i - y_j) \sin\varphi + (\omega_{i1} - \omega_{j1})$$

and since

$$\Omega_i = \Omega_j ,$$

the expression can directly be simplified into

$$x_i' - x_j' = (x_i - x_j) \cos\varphi + (y_i - y_j) \sin\varphi .$$

The above expression is generally established by using the observation that

$$\tan\alpha_{ij} = \frac{y_i - y_j}{x_i - x_j} .$$

A further simplification can thus be made, which leads to

$$x_i' - x_j' = \frac{(x_i - x_j)\cos(\varphi - \alpha_{ij})}{\cos\alpha_{ij}} , \quad \alpha_{ij} \neq \frac{\pi}{2}, \quad \alpha_{ij} \neq \frac{3\pi}{2} ,$$

where $(x_i - x_j)/\cos\alpha_{ij}$ can be pre-calculated. For $\pi/2$ and $3\pi/2$ the following expression can be determined:

$$x_i' - x_j' = (y_i - y_j)\sin\varphi = \text{const} \cdot \sin\varphi, \quad \alpha_{ij} = \frac{\pi}{2}, \quad \alpha_{ij} = \frac{3\pi}{2} .$$

Analogous to the above, we can now determine the corresponding difference between the y-coordinates in the new coordinate system, i.e:

$$y_i' - y_j' = \frac{(x_j - x_i)\sin(\varphi - \alpha_{ij})}{\cos\alpha_{ij}} , \quad \alpha_{ij} \neq \frac{\pi}{2}, \quad \alpha_{ij} \neq \frac{3\pi}{2} ,$$

and

$$y'_i - y'_j = (y_i - y_j) \cos \varphi = \text{const} \cdot \cos \varphi, \quad \alpha_{ij} = \frac{\pi}{2}, \quad \alpha_{ij} = \frac{3\pi}{2}.$$

The determination of the projected relations can now be made by looking at the right-hand side of the expressions, that is, to analyse the function:

$$x'_i - x'_j = F_{xij}(\varphi, \alpha_{ij})$$

where

$$F_{xij}(\varphi, \alpha_{ij}) = 0 \implies x'_i = x'_j,$$

$$F_{xij}(\varphi, \alpha_{ij}) > 0 \implies x'_i > x'_j.$$

Since the constant part can be pre-calculated, $x'_i < x'_j$ otherwise it is simple to build up the following matrix containing all this information:

$$C_x = \begin{bmatrix} c_{x11} & c_{x12} & \cdots & c_{x1n} \\ x_{x21} & c_{x2n} & \cdots & c_{x2n} \\ \cdots & \cdots & \cdots & \cdots \\ c_{xn1} & c_{xn2} & \cdots & c_{xnn} \end{bmatrix}.$$

The components of the C_x-matrix are $c_{xij} = \text{sign}((x_i - x_j)/\cos(\alpha_{ij}))$ for $\alpha_{ij} \neq \pi/2$ and $\alpha_{ij} \neq 3\pi/2$ and $c_{xij} = \text{sign}(y_i - y_j)$ for $\alpha_{ij} = \pi/2$ and $\alpha_{ij} = 3\pi/2$. Since $c_{xij} \in \{-1, 0, 1\}$ it is clear that $c_{xij} = -c_{xji}$, while the values on the diagonal are insignificant. The rules for determination of F_{xij} are thus:

$$F_{xij}(\varphi, \alpha_{ij}) = c_{xij} \, \text{sign}(\cos(\varphi - \alpha_{ij})) \quad \text{for } \alpha_{ij} \neq \pi/2 \text{ and } \alpha_{ij} \neq 3\pi/2,$$

$$F_{xij}(\varphi, \alpha_{ij}) = c_{xij} \, \text{sign}(\sin \varphi) \quad \text{for } \alpha_{ij} = \pi/2 \text{ and } \alpha_{ij} = 3\pi/2.$$

It is easy to show that

$$\cos(\varphi - \alpha_{ij}) > 0 \quad \text{for } 0 \leq \varphi - \alpha_{ij} < \pi/2 \quad \text{and} \quad 3\pi/2 < \varphi - \alpha_{ij} \leq 2\pi,$$

$$\cos(\varphi - \alpha_{ij}) = 0 \quad \text{for } \varphi - \alpha_{ij} = \pi/2 \quad \text{and} \quad \varphi - \alpha_{ij} = 3\pi/2.$$

For this reason all the relations, that is the U_φ-matrix, can be determined from the following rules:

if $\alpha_{ij} = \pi/2$ or $\alpha_{ij} = 3\pi/2$ then

(if $c_{ij} = 0$ or $\varphi = 0$ or $\varphi = \pi$ then $F_{xij}(\varphi, \alpha_{ij}) = 0 \Rightarrow x_i = x_j \Rightarrow u_{\varphi ij} = 0$,

if $c_{ij} = 1$ and $\varphi > 0$ and $\varphi < \pi$ then $F_{xij}(\varphi, \alpha_{ij}) = 1 \Rightarrow x_i > x_j \Rightarrow u_{\varphi ij} = 1$,

if $c_{ij} = -1$ and $\varphi > \pi$ and $\varphi < 2\pi$ then $F_{xij}(\varphi, \alpha_{ij}) = 1 \Rightarrow x_i > x_j \Rightarrow u_{\varphi ij} = 1$,

otherwise $F_{xij}(\varphi, \alpha_{ij}) = -1 \Rightarrow x_i < x_j \Rightarrow u_{\varphi ij} = -1$);

if $\alpha_{ij} \neq \pi/2$ and $\alpha_{ij} \neq 3\pi/2$ then,

(if $c_{xij} = 0$ or $\varphi - \alpha_{ij} = \pi/2$ or $\varphi - \alpha_{ij} = 3\pi/2 \Rightarrow F_{xij}(\varphi, \alpha_{ij}) = 0 \Rightarrow x_i = x_j \Rightarrow u_{\varphi ij} = 0$,

if $c_{xij} = 1$ and $((\varphi - \alpha_{ij} \geq 0$ and $\varphi - \alpha_{ij} < \pi/2)$ or $(\varphi - \alpha_{ij} > 3\pi/2$ and $\varphi - \alpha_{ij} \leq 2\pi)) \Rightarrow F_{xij}(\varphi, \alpha_{ij}) = 1 \Rightarrow x_i > x_j \Rightarrow u_{\varphi ij} = 1$,

if $c_{xij} = -1$ and $(\varphi - \alpha_{ij}) > \pi/2$ and $(\varphi - \alpha_{ij}) < 3\pi/2 \Rightarrow F_{xij}(\varphi, \alpha_{ij}) = 1 \Rightarrow x_i > x_j \Rightarrow u_{\varphi ij} = 1$,

otherwise $F_{xij}(\varphi, \alpha_{ij}) = -1 \Rightarrow x_i < x_j \Rightarrow u_{\varphi ij} = -1$).

The corresponding V_φ-matrix can be determined in an analogous way by first determining the C_y-matrix and then applying the corresponding rules.

A conclusion of this approach is that it does not require any form of heavy computation to determinate the relations between the landmarks. Simply expressed, the tests in the above rules are the only required computations. Since not all elements in the U_φ and V_φ matrices need to be directly calculated, that is, since $u_{ij} = -u_{ji}$, the method can be considered as being very efficient.

Single rows (or columns) of U_φ corresponds to relations between landmark l_j and all other landmarks in the space. For all '<' relations occurring in the set, the corresponding landmarks are to the right of lj while for '>' relations the landmarks are to the left of l_j. For the rows and columns in V_φ the corresponding relations becomes 'behind' and 'in-front-of'.

3.3. *A simple example of the matrix approach*

The example given here is the simplest possible but it cannot be considered too simple since it includes all aspects of the approach. Hence, only two landmarks are present in this example.

The basic rotation angles are $\varphi = \pi/4$, $2\pi/3$ and $5\pi/6$ and the basic projection strings are $U : x_1 < x_2$ and $V : y_1 < y_2$, as can be seen in Fig. 3. The angles between the landmarks are available in the A_U matrix:

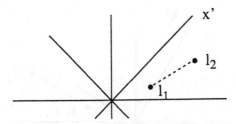

Fig. 3. A simple example with two landmarks where $\varphi = \pi/4$, $\alpha_{12} = \pi/6$ and $\alpha_{21} = 5\pi/6$.

$$A_0 = \begin{bmatrix} 0 & \frac{\pi}{6} \\ \frac{5\pi}{6} & 0 \end{bmatrix} .$$

From the above the U_0 and V_0 matrices can be determined:

$$U_0 = \begin{bmatrix} 0 & -1 \\ 1 & 0 \end{bmatrix} ,$$

$$V_0 = \begin{bmatrix} 0 & -1 \\ 1 & 0 \end{bmatrix} .$$

The C matrix which also can be pre-calculated becomes:

$$C_x = \begin{bmatrix} 0 & -1 \\ 1 & 0 \end{bmatrix} .$$

Furthermore, since the translation of the new coordinate system is independent of the actual position of the agent, we are just dealing with rotations around the origin of the x, y-coordinate system as can be seen in Figs. 3 through 5. For the rotation angle $\varphi = \pi/4$ the U_φ-matrix becomes:

$$U_{\frac{\pi}{4}} = \begin{bmatrix} 0 & -1 \\ 1 & 0 \end{bmatrix} .$$

From this matrix the following relation can be extracted and described in terms of a symbolic projection string:

$$U : x_1 < x_2 .$$

For this rotation angle the string is unchanged. If however, the rotation angle is increased to $2\pi/3$, the result becomes somewhat different which is illustrated in Fig. 4.

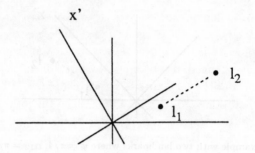

Fig. 4. Two landmarks where $\varphi = 2\pi/3$, $\alpha_{12} = \pi/6$ and $\alpha_{21} = 5\pi/6$.

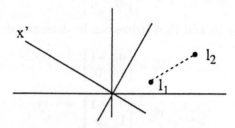

Fig. 5. Two landmarks where $\varphi = 5\pi/6$, $\alpha_{12} = \pi/6$ and $\alpha_{21} = 5\pi/6$.

For this angle the U_φ-matrix becomes:

$$U_{\frac{2\pi}{3}} = \begin{bmatrix} 0 & 0 \\ 0 & 0 \end{bmatrix}.$$

This corresponds to the following U-string:

$$U : x_1 = x_2.$$

The final rotation which corresponds to $\varphi = 5\pi/6$ is even larger than the two earlier examples, see Fig. 5.

This gives the following U_φ-matrix

$$U_{\frac{5\pi}{6}} = \begin{bmatrix} 0 & 1 \\ -1 & 0 \end{bmatrix}$$

from which the U-string

$$U : x_1 > x_2,$$

can be generated.

From these three demonstrated cases it is easy to see how the relations between the landmarks change as the rotation angle φ increases. The disadvantage of this approach is that although we can see how the relations between the landmarks have changed, it is computationally difficult to see the relations between the agent and the landmarks. These relations can be calculated but quite heavy computations are then required. Since this can be done more efficiently with slope projection, an approach based on that method has been developed. This approach including the slope projection itself will be discussed more thoroughly in the forthcoming sections.

4. The Slope Projection Approach

Symbolic projection is a qualitative reasoning technique which originally suffered from a number of basic problems. A solution to one of those problems led to an extension of symbolic projection that will be discussed here since it forms the basis for the second approach to the problem discussed in this chapter. This solution is called symbolic slope projection and can among other things, be used to determine directions, distances, and other object relations seen from the observer's perspective, i.e. the projections are in the majority of cases concerned with a singular point. It can also be demonstrated that slope projection is a generalization of the original approach to symbolic projection. Symbolic slope projection is discussed more deeply in [8] and [9]. Here we are just dealing with those aspects that are of concern for the method that is discussed in this chapter.

4.1. *Some aspects of generalized symbolic slope projection*

Symbolic projection is basically a method where objects in an image is projected to the x- and y-coordinate axes in the 2D case. The 3D case is a generalization of the 2D case. As a result, two strings can be created, one along each coordinate axis, which shows the relative position of the objects. These projection strings can be used for qualitative spatial reasoning. In the original work by Chang *et al.* [6], these strings described the relative positions along each axes by means of an operator set including just two relational operators, i.e. $\{<, =\}$. Later Jungert [10] introduced the edge-to-edge operator. As a consequence, a minimal operator set could be defined, i.e. $\{<, =, |\}$, which can be used for description of any image by means of symbolic projection. However, in the method of symbolic projection some fundamental problems

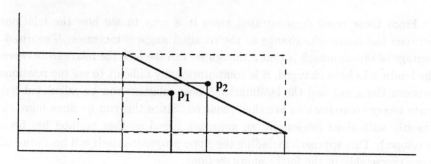

Fig. 6. An illustration of the fundamental problem in symbolic projection.

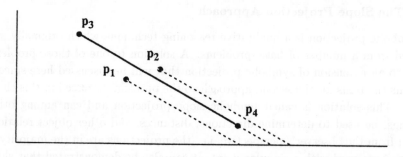

Fig. 7. The solution to the fundamental problem in symbolic projection.

exist, among which the most important one is illustrated in Fig. 6. Briefly, the problem can be stated as follows: Using symbolic projection, there is no way to infer on which side of the line 'l' the two point objects p_1 and p_2 lies, if they are situated inside the rectangle spanned up by 'l'.

This problem is due to the fact that lines that are neither horizontal nor vertical cannot be represented such that the knowledge of their slope is preserved in the strings. However, there is quite a simple solution to this problem, which is illustrated in Fig. 7.

As can be seen, the point objects and the line object are all projected in the direction of the slope of the line object, i.e. they are projected parallel to the line. These projections can either be made down to the x-axis or the y-axis. It is not necessary to have both cases since either alternative contains all necessary information. The result of this slope-projection, u_l, is:

$$u_l : x_{p_1} < x_l < x_{p_2} \, ,$$

where

$$x_{p_1} = x_1 - \frac{y_1}{k},$$

$$x_{p_2} = x_2 - \frac{y_2}{k},$$

$$x_l = x_3 - \frac{y_3}{k},$$

and k is the slope coefficient of the line object, that is:

$$k = \frac{y_3 - y_4}{x_3 - x_4}.$$

Two extreme cases, for $k = 0$ and $k = \infty$ exist, which will be discussed further. Evidently, k can take any value besides the two extreme cases. The method also works for several lines at different orientations, in which case there must be separate slope projections for each line.

Basically three further projections also exist besides the above. That is, a point can be projected along a "slope" to both the x- and y-axes and perpendicular to that slope. Projections perpendicular to a line are simple to identify because of the well-known relationship between slope coefficients corresponding to two perpendicular lines:

$$k' = -\frac{1}{k}.$$

Hence, the y-projection perpendicular to a given line, for instance, point p_1 in Fig. 6 then becomes:

$$y_{p_1} = y_1 + \frac{x_1}{k},$$

the other two projections are:

$$x'_{p_1} = x_1 + ky_1,$$

and

$$y'_{p_1} = y_1 - kx_1.$$

By looking at the first pair from a general view we can identify the following projections:

$$U : x_i - \frac{y_i}{k},$$

$$V : y_i + \frac{x_i}{k}.$$

From this pair (U, V), it is now simple to see that for $k = \infty$ the projections become:

$$U : x_i \,,$$

$$V : y_i \,,$$

which correspond to the original projection method according to the definition given by Chang *et al.* [6]. The same is also true for the $k = 0$ in the second U, V-pair, subsequently called (U', V'). For $k = 0$ in the first pair and for $k = \infty$ in the second the projections are corrupted and are hence not useful any longer.

A further observation that can be made is that when k is close to or equal to zero, the (U, V) projections can be substituted with the (U', V') pair and the other way around when k is close to ∞ for (U', V'). This can be expressed in terms of the following two rules:

if k is close to or equal to zero then (U', V') ,

if k is very large then (U, V) .

Subsequently these rules are used even when this is not explicitly expressed. An observation that needs to be pointed out, however, is that if we use (U, V) for lines with moderate coefficients and if suddenly a line appears with a slope coefficient that is equal to zero then there is a switch of focus if (U', V') is used instead of (U, V). Hence, the projections can no longer be directly compared. For this reason we need a symbolic representation of the $k = 0$ projection. This is possible because the projection strings are of qualitative type and do not necessarily represent infinity in a quantitative way. This can be illustrated in the following way:

$$U : A_{k=0} < B_{k=1} < C_{k=\infty} \,.$$

However, this case may not be typical.

A consequence of the discussion above is that the original approach is just a special case of slope projection. Therefore, the slope projection method is a generalization of the original one. Slope projection also includes a second pair of projection strings which can be combined with the first. Hence, further object information or knowledge can be inferred and are explicitly available.

The idea with the projections along the slope of a line can be expanded further as can be seen in Fig. 8, which illustrates how qualitative reasoning on line segments can be performed in order to identify relations like 'crossing', 'not crossing' and 'parallel to'. The non-crossing case is illustrated in Fig. 8(a)

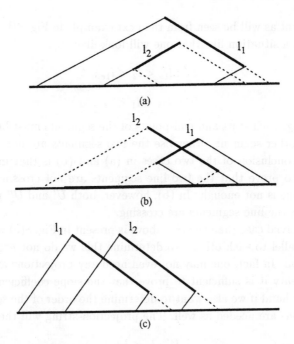

Fig. 8. Examples of slope-projection applied line segments that are (a) not crossing, (b) crossing and (c) in parallel.

where two slope-strings can be created by projecting along each of the two line segments down to the x-axis. The segments can be projected to the y-axis as well, but it is sufficient to apply the projections to just one coordinate axis. The two projection strings in Fig. 8(a) are:

$$U' : l_{2s} < l_{2e} < l_1,$$

$$U'' : l_{1s} < l_2 < l_{1e},$$

where line segments containing 's' and 'e' correspond to the start and end of the segments respectively.

Here the U' string corresponds to the projections with dashed lines, while U'' corresponds to the projection with the thin solid beams. In this particular case we do not need both cases to prove that the line-segments l_1 and l_2 are not crossing, just U' is sufficient, because both ends of l_2 are situated on the same side, in this case to the left side of the line-segment l_1. However, in order to determine that two segments are crossing each other, one projection is not sufficient as will be seen from the next example in Fig. 8(b). The strings created from a situation like that one will look like:

$$U' : l_{1s} < l_2 < l_{1e} ,$$

$$U'' : l_{2s} < l_1 < l_{2e} .$$

In both strings each start and end-points of the segments must be on opposite sides of the other segment, otherwise the two segments are not crossing each other. The conclusion of the two cases in (a) and (b) is that in (a), just U' is sufficient to prove that the two line segments are not crossing each other, while U'' alone is not enough. In (b), however, both U' and U'' are necessary to prove that the line segments are crossing.

A more trivial case than the two above is present in Fig. 8(c) where the two lines are parallel to each other. To determine this we do not need more than one projection. In fact, one may not even need any projections at all, since to check parallelity it is sufficient to prove that the slope coefficients are equal. On the other hand if we also want to determine the order of the segments then the projections are needed as well. The projection-string will then look like:

$$U' : l_1 < l_2 .$$

Furthermore, if the relative occurrence of the segments are of interest then the perpendicular projection of U'' is needed as well, i.e. the particular example in Fig. 8(c) will then look like:

$$U'' : l_{1s} < l_{2s} < l_{1e} < l_{2e} .$$

From this it can, depending on which direction we are going, be concluded that l_1 starts a little bit before l_2 and that it also ends before l_2, and finally that l_1 is to the left of l_2. Clearly, several other alternatives may occur.

A new way of projecting the symbolic objects was demonstrated above, which, contrary to the technique used so far, is not perpendicular to the co-ordinate axes. It was demonstrated that the projections could be made in arbitrary directions. This is a solution to a fundamental problem in symbolic projection. However, the approach can be applied to other problems as well, of which a few more will be discussed here.

Slope projection can be used for determination of directions as well. This is particularly useful in reasoning about geographical directions like north, west and north-east, etc. In such a directional system 8 directions are of

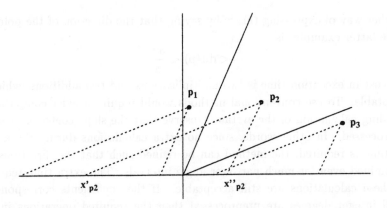

Fig. 9. Determination of directions using symbolic slope projection.

particular interest, that is {N, NE, E, SE, S, SW, W, NW}. To illustrate this, only the 3 directions of the first quadrant are considered here. However, it is a simple task to generalize the technique into the full space. The first quadrant is thus split into three parts as illustrated in Fig. 9. The angle between the two dividing lines is $\pi/4$ and the angles between the dividing lines and the coordinate axes is consequently $\pi/8$. The sector between the dividing lines indicates the northeastern direction while the area between a dividing line and a coordinate axis corresponds to half the cone in the northern and eastern directions respectively. The example in Fig. 9 shows the method for the determination of the direction of the points. The points are projected parallel to the edges of the sector. The result of these projections is, for point p_1, where both projections hit the x-axis to the left of the "origin", subsequently called the observer's position since it does not necessarily have to correspond to the origin, p_2 on the other hand lies in the north-eastern sector and the observer's position is in-between the projected points. The following rules for deduction of the directions can hence be identified:

$$U_0 : x' < x'' < O \Rightarrow \text{north}(p, O).$$

If the two projections of point p on the x-axis, i.e. x' and x'', are less than the observer's position (O) in the U_0-string, then the direction of p is north of O (as seen in the first quadrant). Similarly

$$U_0 : x' < O < x'' \Rightarrow \text{north} - \text{east}(p, O).$$

Another way of expressing this is by saying that the direction of the point p_2 in the latter examples is:

$$\frac{\pi}{8} < \text{dir}(p) < \frac{3\pi}{8}.$$

The cost in execution time is two multiplications and two additions, which is acceptable. To use conventional methods would require heavier computation including calculation of the arctan. Observe that the slope coefficient can be preprocessed. In other words, since no extra calculations during the actual run time is required, the method can be refined such that the directions are determined even for much narrower angle intervals. The extra time required for these calculations are still acceptable. If the coefficients corresponding to all integer degrees are preprocessed then the required operations in the first quadrant are at most 6 multiplications and 6 additions if binary search is applied. For intervals of 10 degrees, the operations are at most 4 multiplications and 4 additions. The above can now be formulated more generally as follows:

$$\text{for all } p_i, \text{ where } i = 1, 2, \ldots \quad \text{if } x_{p_i}^{(\alpha)} < O < x_{p_i}^{(\beta)} \Rightarrow p_i \in [\alpha, \beta].$$

Finally, it can also be seen that for $x_{p_i}^{(\alpha)} < O$, the angle of p_i is greater than α and for $x_{p_i}^{(\alpha)} > O$ the angle of p_i is less than α.

4.2. *Slope projection applied to the moving agent problem*

The slope projections are a means for determining the projection strings of the landmarks, which may include a potential observer as well. The required slope projection points are associated with arbitrarily located points in the space. To make this possible a translated and rotated coordinate system is introduced. In those cases where an observer is present, the position of the observer corresponds to the origin of the local coordinate system. The projections in the local coordinate system correspond to the original perpendicular projection type. Generation of these projection strings is described below. The approach taken is to create them from the global system which then are transformed into the strings of the local coordinate system.

In Fig. 10 the coordinate points in the local coordinate system are denoted (x_i', y_i'), while the projection points in the global system are denoted by x_i and y_i respectively. The observer, if present, is ω, and φ is the rotation angle of the local coordinate system relative to the global. The projection string labels U_φ and V_φ corresponds to the strings along the x'- and y'- axes, i.e. the local system where the subscript φ corresponds to the actual rotation angle. Further

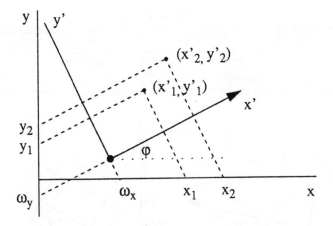

Fig. 10. Using slope projection to represent the agent's relations to the landmarks considering the facing direction of the agent as well.

information about the slopes between all landmarks may be needed. Here that information is represented as the angles denoted with α_{jk} between landmarks i and k.

To get the projection strings of the local coordinate system the strings of the global system must be identified and transformed into strings corresponding to the local ones. The opposite operation can be performed analogously as well. A problem in the projection composition occurs for rotation angles equal to $\pi/2$ and $3\pi/2$. The solution to this problem is to change projection directions, that is, x-components are projected on the y-axis while y-components are projected on the x-axis. A second problem, which has quite a simple solution, is that for the rotation angle interval $[\pi/2, 3\pi/2]$ the projected strings must be reversed to get the correct projection strings of the local coordinate system. The slope projection strings, U_φ and V_φ, for different rotation angle intervals is found in Table 1 where *rev* means reverse and indicates cases for which the projected strings should be taken in reversed order. U_p^G and V_p^G are the labels of the global strings.

As can be seen, this requires an extra multiplication in each direction for each point. This can for most cases be considered acceptable. In this particular approach $2(n+1)$ multiplications are required for n landmarks and a single agent.

Table 1.

	$0 \leq \varphi < \pi/2$	$\varphi = \pi/2$	$\pi/2 < \varphi < 3\pi/2$	$\varphi = 3\pi/2$	$3\pi/2 < \varphi \leq 2\pi$
U_φ	U_p^G	V_p^G	$\mathrm{rev}(U_p^G)$	$\mathrm{rev}(V_p^G)$	U_p^G
V_φ	V_p^G	$\mathrm{rev}(U_p^G)$	$\mathrm{rev}(V_p^G)$	U_p^G	V_p^G

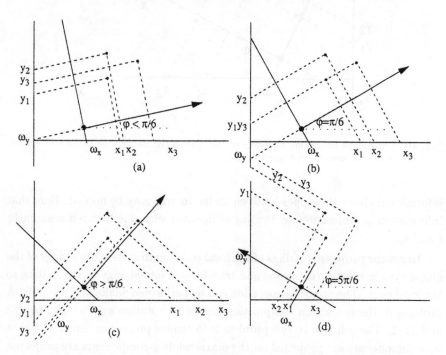

Fig. 11. An agent whose directional orientation is gradually increasing.

4.3. *An illustration of the slope projection approach*

The examples given here correspond to a space containing three landmarks. For simplification the agent here is not moving, only the rotation angle is gradually increasing from an angle that is somewhat smaller than $\pi/6$ up to $5\pi/6$. These examples can be seen in Figs. 11(a) through (d). The global orientation, that is $\varphi = 0$, gives us the following projections:

$$U_0^G : \omega_x < x_1 < x_2 < x_3,$$

$$V_0^G : \omega_y < y_1 < y_3 < y_2.$$

In Fig. 11(a) a rotation with an angle less than $\pi/6$ can be seen. Slope projections as demonstrated in the figure give us the following projection strings, which are unchanged compared to the starting situation:

$$U^G_{p<\pi/6} = U_{\varphi<\pi/6} : \omega_x < x_1 < x_2 < x_3 ,$$

$$V^G_{p<\pi/6} = V_{\varphi<\pi/6} : \omega_y < y_1 < y_3 < y_2 .$$

The next case, Fig. 11(b), for which $\varphi = \pi/6$ shows a situation where in the V-string, y_1 has become equal to y_3. The U-string is still unchanged. The conclusion is thus that y_3 has begun to propagate towards the left in the projection string.

$$U^G_{\pi/6} = U_{\pi/6} : \omega_x < x_1 < x_2 < x_3 ,$$

$$V^G_{\pi/6} = V_{\pi/6} : \omega_y < y_1 y_3 < y_2 .$$

The third case, Fig. 11(c), demonstrates further propagation of y_3 and where y_3 has become less than y_1. The reason for this is, of course, that φ has become larger than α_{13}. The U-string has, however, not yet changed position compared to the original expression:

$$U_{\varphi<\pi/6} : \omega_x < x_1 < x_2 < x_3 ,$$

$$V_{\varphi>\pi/6} : \omega_y < y_3 < y_1 < y_2 .$$

Finally, in the last case, the rotation angle is $5\pi/6$, see Fig. 11(d). In this particular case the situation has changed radically, and now the three landmarks have become situated to the right of the agent. Since the rotation angle is larger than $\pi/2$ the projected strings must be taken in the reversed order.

$$U_{5\pi/6} : \mathrm{rev}(x_2 < x_1 < \omega_x < x_3) \Rightarrow U_{5\pi/6} : x_3 < \omega_x < x_1 < x_2 ,$$

$$V_{5\pi/6} : \mathrm{rev}(\omega_y < y_1 < y_2 < y_3) \Rightarrow V_{5\pi/6} : y_3 < y_2 < y_1 < \omega_y .$$

In this approach it is easy to determine whether a certain landmark is to the left or right of the agent but also whether it is in front or behind. All these four relations can easily be determined from the projection strings. Another type of relation that can be determined is whether the agent when taking a certain path will have to pass in-between certain landmarks.

In the above examples, only slope projections are used. An alternative technique to determine the relational projection strings is to start with the original slope projection strings and then compare the rotation angle with the angles in the A_0 matrix. This approach would give the same result as the pure projection method. A disadvantage with this method is that the relations between the agent and the landmarks are lost, and we are therefore back to the situation in the matrix approach. Furthermore, it is also probable that this later method is less efficient than the matrix approach. Another aspect is that when starting with the projection strings it is probably difficult to find all the changes in the strings since the landmarks are propagating back and forth. This becomes especially complicated when the number of landmarks is large.

5. Conclusions

In this chapter, two different approaches to the problem of qualitative reasoning about what happens when a free agent is moving in a space of landmarks have been discussed. The main difference between the two approaches is that in the former, i.e. the matrix approach, the agent is not part of the spatial description, while in the second approach this is the case. The matrix approach does not require any heavy computations; it is just a question of simple rule-testing. The slope projection method, on the other hand, requires two multiplications for each projection required for determination of the relative position of each landmark. This cannot be considered as heavy from a general computational point of view but nevertheless, this second approach is somewhat heavier to deal with compared to the first approach.

In neither of the two given approaches reasoning along the track of the agent has been introduced as has been done by Freksa [4], who refers the latest position of the agent to earlier. This is probably not a serious problem and the solution is most likely to give old positions of the agent the same status as the landmarks.

If the agent corresponds to some type of vehicle where the landmarks have to be sensed by a type of sensor, then most likely the positions of both vehicle and landmarks must be represented with some kind of uncertainty. It is quite clear that this problem can be dealt with in terms of symbolic projection. This will, however, be subject to future research. Other problems that must be studied further concerns types of objects other than just landmarks, that is objects of extended or linear types may have to be considered as well. Another problem of interest is how to deal with time in more elaborate ways than was done here. In this chapter just a few time stamps of the agent's positions are dealt with. In more complicated cases, other types of moving objects, i.e. multiples of moving objects must be considered as well.

References

1. T. Smith and K. K. Park, "Algebraic approach to spatial reasoning", *Int. J. Geographical Information Systems* **6**, 3 (1992) 177–192.
2. S. Y. Lee and F. J. Hsu, "Picture algebra for spatial reasoning of iconic images represented in 2D C-string", *Pattern Recognition Letters* **12** (1991) 425–435.
3. M. J. Egenhofer and K. Al-Taha, "Reasoning about gradual changes of topological relationships", in *Theories and Methods of Spatio-Temporal Reasoning in Geographic Space*, eds. A. U. Frank, I. Campari and U. Formentini (Springer, 1992) pp. 196–219.
4. Ch. Freksa, "Using orientation information for qualitative spatial reasoning", in *Theories and Methods of Spatio-Temporal Reasoning in Geographic Space*, eds. A. U. Frank, I. Campari and U. Formentini (Springer, 1992) pp. 162–178.
5. Ch. Schlieder, "Representing visible locations for qualitative navigation", in *Qualitative Reasoning and Decision Technologies, CIMNE*, eds. N. Piera Carreté and M. G. Singh (Barcelona, 1993) pp. 523–532.
6. S.-K. Chang, O. Y. Shi and C. W. Yan, "Iconic indexing by 2D strings", *IEEE Trans. on Pattern Anal. and Machine Intell. (PAMI)* **9**, 3 (1987) 413–428.
7. C. M. Lee, "The unification of the 2D string and spatial query processing", Dissertation Thesis, Graduate College of the Knowledge Systems Institute, Skokie Illinois (1992).
8. E. Jungert, "The observer's point of view: An extension of symbolic projections", in *Theories and Methods of Spatio-Temporal Reasoning in Geographic Space*, eds. A. U. Frank, I. Campari and U. Formentini (Springer, 1992) pp. 179–195.
9. E. Jungert, "Qualitative spatial reasoning from the observer's point of view — Towards a generalization of symbolic projection", *J. Pattern Recognition* **27**, 6 (1994) 801–813.
10. E. Jungert, "Extended symbolic projection used in a knowledge structure for spatial reasoning", *Proc. 4th BPRA Conf. on Pattern Recognition* (Springer Verlag, Cambridge, March 28–30, 1988).

A LOGICAL FRAMEWORK FOR SPATIO
TEMPORAL INDEXING OF IMAGE SEQUENCES

A. DEL BIMBO and E. VICARIO

Dipartimento Sistemi e Informatica, Università di Firenze
*3, via santa Marta, 50139, Firenze, Italy**

The joint representation of spatial and temporal phenomena is relevant in many research areas, including spatio-temporal reasoning, video sequence representation and querying by-contents. In this chapter, an original language for the symbolic representation of the contents of dynamic scenes is presented. This language incorporates and extends concepts of Temporal Logic to deal in an uniform way with both time and space, and supports metric qualifiers for distance and speed.

1. Introduction

The joint representation of time and space is a research subject of growing relevance due to the large number of applications that it involves. These include the description of evolutionary spatial phenomena in GIS, their analysis and retrieval, qualitative reasoning about time and space for autonomous navigation systems, agent animation in virtual environments, content-based image sequence indexing, and query by-content in video databases.

In this chapter, we will present a new language which provides a homogeneous framework for the symbolic representation of spatial and temporal object relationships, both qualitative and with metric conditions. This framework is intended to support both spatio-temporal reasoning and flexible image sequence indexing for querying by-content. Evolutionary phenomena are described through symbolic representation structures which include two nested static and dynamic levels. At the static level, frame assertions provide an explicit representation of spatial relationships between objects. At the dynamic level, frame assertions are used as predicates within Temporal Logic [20] assertions. To treat distances and speeds, spatial relations are derived through

*This work was partially supported by MURST under project 40%.

the use of marked object reference points without necessarily referring to rectangular objects.

In the past years, few investigations addressed the subject of defining frameworks for the joint representation of space and time. Most of researches concentrated on efficient knowledge structures for the symbolic representation of spatial relationships, as well as for the symbolic representation of metric spaces such as distances and orientations.

In particular, the *symbolic projection* technique, first proposed in [3], is an effective approach for the indexing of image contents based on spatial relationships. They are represented through a *2D string* [4] which encodes the ordering relationships between the projections of the objects on two reference coordinate axes. Symbolic projection and 2D strings are also an ideal approach to represent visual iconic queries based on spatial relationships [5]. Icons on the screen are projected on the two coordinate axes, and a 2D string is again derived as the output of a spatial analyzer. Retrieval is thus reduced to the comparison of two symbolic strings.

The incompleteness of the earlier formulation of the 2D string representation was pointed out by several authors, and a number of extensions and developments were proposed in [6, 7, 8, 10, 15, 16, 17, 18, 19, 21, 22, 23]. In [6], local operators were introduced for handling multiple types of relationships between objects. *Generalized 2D strings* with cutting mechanism were introduced, where the cuttings are performed at the extreme points of the objects and the tiles in the image are determined: objects may be partitioned in subparts and effective spatial reasoning may be performed. *2D C-strings* were presented in [17] which support a complete representation of image contents with the minimum number of cuttings, thus promising to be more effective in the presence of very complex images, but do not maintain information about the distinct subparts in which objects are subdivided. *Indexed 2D C-strings* proposed in [21] appear to overcome this latter limitation and can be used to provide rotation invariant representations [22].

Extensions of 2D string to 3D scene descriptions have been expounded in [7] and [8]. In [7], projections of a three-dimensional symbolic scene in two and three directions are derived with the analysis of ambiguity conditions; a new linear representation named Gen-string for the representation of three and higher dimensional scenes is proposed which exhibits appealing properties of the 2D string representation. In [8], image indexing with symbolic strings is considered in the realm of image retrieval. It is discussed that image descriptions according to symbolic projection must be expressed referring to the original imaged scene to avoid any ambiguity in the representation of contents. This requires that the dimensionality of the representation must follow that of the original scene. Images of 3D scenes require 3D scene-based descriptions.

Symbolic representation of distances and orientations supports qualitative reasoning when precise information is not available [13]. In [24], directional orientations of points in a two-dimensional space is regarded as a one-dimensional feature which is determined as an oriented line. Properties of these features are analyzed with the objective of reconstructing the two-dimensional scene from a set of 1D projections. In [14], spatial knowledge is structured according to *conceptual neighborhoods* of spatial relations between points. Two relations in a representation are conceptual neighbors when an operation can result in a transition from one relation to the other. This knowledge structure is demonstrated to support orientation-based spatial inferences and to be especially suited to dealing with incomplete knowledge and uncertainty. Extensions of symbolic projection with metric properties such as distances have been proposed in [15], where polar projections are also discussed.

Symbolic projection technique and 2D strings are effective also to represent contents of image sequences [2]. 2D strings may be used to represent spatial relationships between objects in individual frames and time tags may be employed to index changes in 2D strings through the sequence. For each frame, objects having the same relationship in the 2D string are grouped in sets, and changes between subsequent frames are expressed through set operations such as addition/deletion or merging/splitting.

Although the 2D string representation supports a representation at a very fine level of detail, nevertheless, it does not provide a sufficient flexibility and expressivity in the representation of spatio-temporal relationships, as needed, for instance, in spatio-temporal reasoning, or in image sequence querying.

Spatio-Temporal Logic (STL) has been proposed in [9] as a language to support symbolic descriptions of sequence contents at different levels of abstraction, which is especially useful for image sequence querying. STL provides a unified formalism to deal with space and time, defined by extending concepts of Temporal Logic. Individual frame descriptions in STL are obtained according to symbolic projection, considering the projections of the objects on the axes of a reference system [10].

The new representation language discussed in this chapter extends STL with metric description capability, supporting the notions of distance (both in space and time) and speed. The language is referred to as *eXtended Spatio Temporal Logic (XSTL)*. Different from STL, spatial relationships are not derived according to the symbolic projection paradigm, but employing space *walkthroughs* between points of different objects. The language was initially conceived in the realm of image sequence symbolic indexing and iconic querying by contents; dynamic scenes are indexed by considering the spatial relationships between the imaged objects and their changes through time. It was subsequently found suitable also to model spatio-temporal relationships occurring in a virtual space to support reasoning by virtual agents acting in that space.

The chapter is organized as follows. In Sec. 2, issues related to the representation of dynamic scenes are discussed and the *walkthrough paradigm* which XSTL relies on is introduced with simple examples. XSTL is formally expounded in Sec. 3 and its expressivity in the representation of some usual spatio-temporal conditions is discussed in Sec. 4. Finally, a brief review of some major applications of XSTL is given in Sec. 5, and conclusions are drawn in Sec. 6.

2. Description of Dynamic Scenes

In order to capture situations that are significant in dynamic scenes, the expressivity of the language used for specification of *spatio-temporal* relationships must match the natural perceptual process of real-life objects. This implies some major requirements for the specification language itself:

- The language must be oriented towards the expression of *qualitative* spatial and temporal relationships so as to match the incomplete and imprecise knowledge which pervades the perception of the environment in real-life entities; besides, the language must also incorporate some form of *smooth quantity* to permit the expression of *qualitative metric relationships* about distances between entities (such as *near* and *far*) and time intervals between subsequent conditions (such as *soon* and *late*);
- The language must encompass both spatial and temporal phenomena within a cohesive and homogenous framework;
- The language must support both 2D and 3D scene descriptions [8].

Most of these requirements are satisfied by Spatio Temporal Logic (STL).

This logic, which is derived from the basic concepts of *conventional* Temporal Logic [20], was originally proposed in [9] for the representation of spatio-temporal relationships based on symbolic projection, and was used for indexing digital video sequences in a retrieval-by-content system. Unfortunately, while largely supporting the *qualitative* representation of ordering relationships, STL does not permit the expression of *metric relationships* in spatio-temporal phenomena. Qualitative distances have been discussed in [13] for the case of point-like objects, and have been extended in [15] to the case of objects represented by their bounding rectangles in static images.

Combining the concepts proposed in those papers with the approach used to augment conventional Temporal Logic with metric expressivity, spatio-temporal relationships are specified through an extended version of STL, referred to as eXtended Spatio Temporal Logic (XSTL). XSTL captures the evolution over time of spatial relationships with metric qualifiers between entities in a scene through assertions that can be regarded as structured in two nested *static* and *dynamic* levels.

At the static level, *frame assertions* capture ordering relationships between the entities within a single frame of the sequence. These relationships are expressed through the use of spatial operators such as *eventually in the space* ($\Diamond_{e\pm}$), *always in the space* ($\Box_{e\pm}$) and *until in the space* ($unt_{e\pm}$) which transpose the semantics of the usual operators of Temporal Logic so as to deal with the spatial axis e_i rather than with the axis of time. For instance, referring to a bi-dimensional scene S^1, if r is a point, p is an object, and e_1 is a reference axis for the scene S (see Fig. 1(a)), the assertion

$$(r) \models_s \Diamond_{e_1^+} p$$

expresses that, starting from the point r and moving along the positive direction of the coordinate axis e_1, there is a point which is part of the object p.

At the dynamic level, static *frame assertions* can be composed through the temporal operators of conventional Temporal Logic such as *eventually* ($\Diamond_t$), *always* ($\Box_t$) and *until* (unt_t) so as to form *sequence assertions* capturing the evolution over time of the spatial relationships expressed as frame assertions.

---

[1] For the sake of simplicity, the examples in our discussion will be limited to the case of 2D scenes. While reducing the complexity of notation, this limitation does not change the essence of the treatment with respect to the 3D case.

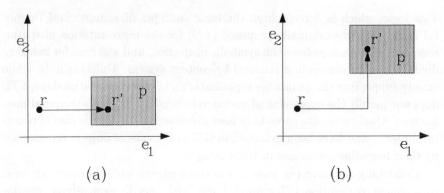

Fig. 1. Meaning of assertions $(r) \models_s \Diamond_{e_1+} p$ (a) and $(r) \models_s v_r.[\Diamond_{e_1+}\Diamond_{e_2+} v_{r'}.[p]]$ (b).

For instance, if σ is a sequence of frames, j is a frame index and ϕ is a frame assertion,

$$(j) \models_t \Diamond_t \phi$$

means that, along the sequence σ, after the jth frame, there is a frame in which the frame assertion ϕ holds.

Following the approach proposed in [1], qualitative metric relations are added both in frame and sequence assertions through the use of spatial and temporal *freeze variables*.

- On the one hand, spatial freeze variables are used to mark points on the objects, and to track their subsequent positions in the evolution of the sequence. For instance, the frame assertion

$$(r) \models_s v_r.[\phi]$$

means that $(r) \models_s \phi$ is satisfied if the position of point r in the current frame is assigned to the freeze variable v_r. After this freezing operation, the variable v_r cannot be used in any other freezing operation but it can be used to refer to the position taken by the point r along the subsequent frames of the sequence.

Positional values assigned to spatial freeze variables may be used to express metric relationships regarding the *distance* between the points that they track. For instance, the frame assertion

$$(r) \models_s v_r.[\Diamond_{e_1+}\Diamond_{e_2+} v_{r'}.[p]]$$

means that (see Fig. 1(b)) starting from point r, whose position is freezed in the variable v_r, and moving along the positive direction of the axis e_1 and along the positive direction of the axis e_2, a point is reached, whose position is freezed in the variable $v_{r'}$, which is part of the object p. This assertion can be refined through metric conditions on the distance between the positions freezed in the variables v_r and $v_{r'}$:

$$(r) \models_s \quad v_r.[\Diamond_{e_1^+} \Diamond_{e_2^+} v_{r'}.[p]] \quad \wedge \quad \|v_r - v_{r'}\| = \text{NEAR}$$

specifies that the positions freezed in v_r and $v_{r'}$ are *near* (i.e. their distance is lower than a certain threshold defining the range of *near*).

- On the other hand, temporal freeze variables are used to retain the indexes of frames in which certain conditions hold and to express metric relationships among these indexes. For instance, the sequence assertion

$$(j) \models_t t_a.[\Diamond_t t_b.[\theta]] \quad \wedge \quad |t_a - t_b| = \text{SOON}$$

expresses that, after the jth frame of the sequence, a frame will be encountered *soon* (i.e. within a time interval which can be characterized by the *SOON* qualifier) in which the assertion θ holds.

Temporal freeze variables can be used to state qualitative temporal distances between frames in which different spatial conditions hold. By combination of spatial and temporal metric relationships, considerations about the relative speed of the objects are possible.

As suggested by the interpretation of the previous examples, by composing multiple spatial operators, frame assertions define spatial *walkthroughs* between couple of points. In these walkthroughs, intermediate and extreme points may be freezed so as to permit the expression of metric relationships between their mutual distances. In this perspective, the spatial relationship of an object p with respect to a point r can be represented through the set of the possible walkthroughs leading from r to any of the points in p. The *walkthrough paradigm* does not refers to projections on coordinate axes, thus basically differentiating frame assertions of XSTL from previous approaches based on symbolic projection [2, 10]. This new paradigm supports an effective definition of spatial positioning and naturally encompasses the concept of distance as measured between the extreme points of the walkthrough.

Walkthroughs are expressed considering paths parallel to the coordinate axes of an underlying reference system which can be either *observer-centered* or *object-centered*. Observer-centered scene descriptions are based on the position of the observer's point of view and thus spatial relationships are referred to the Cartesian coordinate system of the camera (the x-y axes of the image plane for 2D scenes). Object-centered scene descriptions are independent of the observer's point of view. Each object is provided with its individual reference coordinate system, and the overall description of the scene is given by a set of descriptions, each capturing how one object *sees* the other objects with respect to its own reference coordinate system.

3. eXtended Spatio Temporal Logic

XSTL captures spatio-temporal phenomena by taking spatial assertions as atomic propositions within temporal statements. According to this, for the sake of presentation, XSTL assertions can be structured in two nested *static* and *dynamic* levels.

3.1. *Sequence assertions*

A *sequence assertion* Θ on a sequence σ is expressed in the form

$$\Theta = (j) \models_t \theta$$

where j denotes the index of a frame in σ, and θ is a *sequence formula*. In turn, a sequence formula is formed by recursively composing *frame assertions* (Φ) holding in the individual frames of σ and relational assertions on temporal freeze variables, through the freeze operator ($t.[\theta]$), the Boolean connectives and the temporal *until* operator:

$$\theta = \Phi | t.[\theta] | \neg\theta | \theta_1 \wedge \theta_2 | \theta_1 unt_t \theta_2 | |t_a - t_b| = l$$

where:

- Φ is a frame assertion;
- t_a and t_b belong to a set T of temporal freeze variables;
- l is a *qualitative distance* between two time instants and belongs to an enumeration set which can be defined with any appropriate granularity so as to match the relevant phenomena of the specific application context

$$l = \text{SOON} | \neg\text{SOON} | \ldots | \text{LATE} | \neg\text{LATE}.$$

Given a sequence σ and an interpretation Γ for the set T of temporal freeze variables[2], a sequence assertion $(j) \models_t \theta$ is interpreted over σ and Γ according to the following semantic clauses:

- if Φ is a frame assertion, the basic sequence assertion

$$(j) \models_t \Phi$$

means that Φ holds in the jth frame of σ;
- the freeze operator assigns the index of the *current frame* to a freeze variable; thus

$$(j) \models_t t.[\theta]$$

means that the assertion $(j) \models_t \theta$ holds if the frame index j is assigned to the freeze variable t;
- Boolean connectives $\wedge$ and $\neg$ have their usual meaning:

$$(j) \models_t \neg\theta$$

means that $(j) \models_t \theta$ does not hold;

$$(j) \models_t \theta_1 \wedge \theta_2$$

means that both $(j) \models_t \theta_1$ and $(j) \models_t \theta_2$ hold;
- the temporal operator *until* permits the statement of *frame assertions* over multiple frames of the sequence

$$(j) \models_t \theta_1 \; unt_t \; \theta_2$$

means that there exists an index $k \geq j$ such that θ_2 holds in the kth frame and θ_1 holds at least from the jth to the kth frame of the sequence
- finally, relational assertions on temporal freeze variables express conditions on the distance between freezed time instants:

$$(j) \models_t |t_a - t_b| = l$$

means that the interpretation Γ associates the variables t_a and t_b with two instants of time whose distance is in the range defined by the time distance quantifier l.

---

[2] An interpretation for Γ is a relation which associates each temporal freeze variable with a value in the set of frame indexes.

3.1.1. Shorthand operators

Further operators can be derived as shorthands. As usual, the Boolean *disjunction* and *implication* connectives ($\lor$, $\rightarrow$) are obtained by composing *negation* and *conjunction* connectives:

$$\theta_1 \lor \theta_2 = \neg(\neg\theta_1 \land \neg\theta_2)$$

$$\theta_1 \rightarrow \theta_2 = \neg(\theta_1 \land \neg\theta_2)$$

In addition, temporal *eventually* ($\Diamond_t$) and *always* ($\Box_t$) operators are derived from the temporal *until* operator. Specifically,

$$(j) \models_t \Diamond_t\theta = (j) \models_t \neg(\neg\theta \; unt_t \; \text{FALSE})$$

means that there exists an index $k \geq j$ such that θ holds in the kth frame of the sequence, while

$$(j) \models_t \Box_t\theta = (j) \models_t \neg(\Diamond_t\neg\theta)$$

means that θ holds in any frame subsequent to j.

3.2. Frame assertions

A *frame assertion* Φ on a generic frame of a sequence σ is expressed in the form:

$$\Phi = (r) \models_s \phi$$

where r is a point in the scene represented by the frame and ϕ is a spatial formula. In turn, a spatial formula ϕ is formed by inductively composing object identifiers and relational assertions on the values taken over time by a set V of *spatial freeze variables* through the *freezing operator* $(v.[\phi])$, the Boolean connectives, and the *spatial until* operators:

$$\phi = p|v.[\phi]|\neg\phi|\phi_1 \land \phi_2|\phi_1 \; |unt_{e\pm}\phi_2|$$

$$\|v_1(t_a) - v_2(t_b)\| = D|\|v_1(t_a) - v_2(t_a)\| \leq \|v_1(t_b) - v_2(t_b)\|$$

where:

- p is the identifier of an object;
- v is a spatial freeze variable belonging to a set V;
- $unt_{e\pm}$ is a positive (unt_{e+}) or negative (unt_{e-}) until operator referring to the positive or negative direction of an axis e of the reference system assumed for the description;

- $v_1(t_a)$, $v_1(t_b)$, $v_2(t_a)$ and $v_2(t_b)$ are the values taken by the freeze variables v_1 and v_2 in the sequence frames with indexes equal to the values of the temporal freeze variables t_a and t_b, respectively;
- D is a distance-quantifier belonging to an enumeration set which can be defined with any granularity so as to match the actual characteristics of spatial phenomena in the environment under consideration:

$$D = \text{NEAR} \mid \neg \text{NEAR} \mid \ldots \mid \text{FAR} \mid \neg \text{FAR}.$$

Given a frame S in a sequence σ, and given an interpretation Υ for the set V of spatial freeze variables freezed along the frames of σ and an interpretation Γ for the set T of temporal freeze variables of σ itself, the spatial assertion $(r) \models_s \phi$ is interpreted according to the following semantic clauses:

- if p is the identifier of an object in the sequence, the basic frame assertion

$$(r) \models_s p$$

means that the the object p stands on the point r;
- the freeze operator assigns the *current position* to a freeze variable:

$$(r) \models_s v.[\phi]$$

it means that the assertion $(r) \models_s \phi$ holds if the position of the point r is assigned to the freeze variable v; after this freezing, the variable v has a *global scope* along the frames of the sequence: for any frame index $k \geq j$, the variable $v(k)$ contains the position to which the point r has moved.
- Boolean connectives $\wedge$ and $\neg$ have their usual meanings; thus,

$$(r) \models_s \neg \phi$$

means that $(r) \models_s \phi$ does not hold, while

$$(r) \models_s \phi_1 \wedge \phi_2$$

means that both $(r) \models_s \phi_1$ and $(r) \models_s \phi_2$ hold.
- the *until* operators state a formula over multiple points of the scene; specifically,

$$(r) \models_s \phi_1 unt_{e+} \phi_2$$

means that there exists a point r' which is reached moving from r in the positive direction of the axis e such that ϕ_2 holds in r' and ϕ_1 holds in all the points along the line from r to r'. Besides,

$$(r) \models_s \phi_1 \, unt_{e-} \phi_2$$

means that there exists a point r' which is reached moving from r in the *negative* direction of axis e such that ϕ_2 holds in r' and ϕ_1 holds in all the points along the line from r to r';

- finally, relational assertions on freeze variables express conditions on the distances between positions freezed by the variables themselves:

$$(r) \models_s \|v_1(t_a) - v_2(t_b)\| = D$$

means that D is equal to the distance between the positions returned by the spatial variables v_1 and v_2 in the frames with indexes freezed in t_a and t_b, respectively. Besides,

$$(r) \models_s \|v_1(t_a) - v_2(t_a)\| \le \|v_1(t_b) - v_2(t_b)\|$$

means that the distance between the positions returned by the spatial variables v_1 and v_2 in the frame with index freezed in t_a is not greater than the distance in the frame with index freezed in t_b.

3.2.1. *Shorthand operators*

Further operators can be derived as shorthands. In particular, spatial *eventually* ($\Diamond_{e\pm}$) and *always* ($\Box_{e\pm}$) operators are derived from the spatial *until* operators:

$$\Diamond_{e\pm} \phi = \neg(\neg\phi \, unt_{e\pm} \, \text{FALSE})$$

$$\Box_{e\pm} \phi = \neg(\Diamond_{e\pm} \neg\phi)$$

According to the semantics of the *until* operators, the assertion $(r) \models_s \Diamond_{e\pm} \phi$ means that moving from point r in the direction of the axis e (in either the positive or the negative direction depending on the sign $\pm$), a point r' is reached where assertion ϕ holds. Besides, $(r) \models_s \Box_{e+} \phi$ means that, in the jth frame of the sequence, moving from point r along the direction of the axis e, the assertion ϕ holds in all the visited points.

Further shorthand operators can be defined so as to match relationships that are of relevant interest in the specific application context in which XSTL is employed.

3.3. *Context declarators*

The spatial relationship of an object p with respect to the point r may be represented by the set of the possible walkthroughs from r to any of the points in p. By extending this paradigm, the spatial relationship of an object p with respect to a second object q can be represented by the set of the walkthroughs from the points in q to the points in p. To this end, *context declarators* are introduced so as to refer frame assertions to the overall set of the points in an object: if q is an object identifier, the assertion $(q) \models_s \phi$ (read "ϕ holds in q") expresses that, for each point r in q, there exists a walkthrough originating in r which satisfies ϕ. For instance, the assertion $(q) \models_s \Diamond_{e_1^+} \Diamond_{e_2^+} p$ means that, for any point r in q, there exists a walkthrough along the positive directions of the axes e_1 and e_2 which leads into a point r' belonging to p (see Fig. 2).

It should be noted that, in XSTL, negation does not distribute with respect to context declaration. In fact, in general

$$\neg(q) \models_s \phi \neq (q) \models_s \neg\phi$$

the right-hand side being stronger than the left. This fact permits the expression of *weak context* assertions, i.e. assertions referring to *some* rather than *all* the points in a context object q. For instance, to state that in the jth frame,

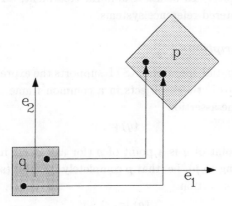

Fig. 2. Walkthroughs expressed by the assertion $(q) \models_s \Diamond_{e_1^+} \Diamond_{e_2^+} p$.

two objects are *near*, we need to express that in that frame, "there *exist* two points, one in p and the other in q, whose distance is lower than some threshold", and this can be done by stating that "it is not the case that, for any point in q, there is no point in p whose distance is lower than some threshold":

$$(j) \models_t ((q) \models_s \Diamond_{e_1^+} \Diamond_{2+} p \quad \wedge \quad \neg(q) \models_s v_q.[\Diamond_{e_1^+} \Diamond_{e_2^+} v_p.[p]]$$

$$\rightarrow \neg(\|v_p(j) - v_q(j)\| = \text{NEAR})) \, .$$

Context declarations have a critical impact on the feasibility of a decision algorithm checking frame assertions for satisfaction. In fact, in order to check for satisfaction a frame assertion of the form $(q) \models_s \phi$, the formula ϕ must be verified for *all* the points of the object q, which may be not feasible if q stands over a dense set of points. To overcome this problem, each object q may be associated with a finite set of representative points, and the assertion $(q) \models_s \phi$ may be read as "for any representative point r in q, the assertion $(r) \models_s \phi$ holds". The selection of these representative points determines the model of objects assumed for the descriptions. Note that different selections may be considered so as to accomplish different levels of detail and accuracy in the representation of the contents of a scene.

4. Representing Significant Conditions Through XSTL

In this section, the use of XSTL for the expression of some spatial and temporal conditions are discussed. For the sake of simplicity, we will refer to bi-dimensional scenes. To attain a uniform treatment, all the examples will refer to object-centered reference systems.

4.1. *Static descriptions*

Through the use spatial operators, XSTL supports the expression of qualitative spatial relationships between objects in a common frame. Given a couple of objects p and q, the assertion

$$(q) \models_s p$$

means that any point of q is a point of p (for any point in q, there is a null walkthrough leading to p), i.e. that p completely covers q (see Fig. 3(a)). As a different case, the assertion

$$(q) \models_s \Diamond_{e_1^+} p$$

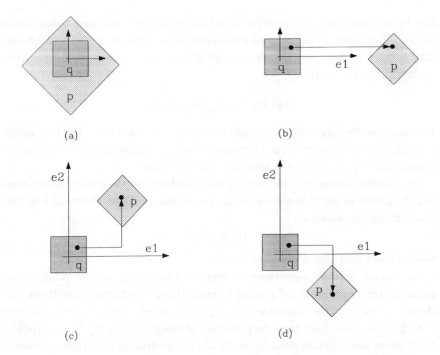

Fig. 3. Some possible spatial relationships between a couple of objects q and p.

means that, starting from any point in q, there exists a walkthrough which leads to a point in p by moving along the positive direction of the first coordinate axis of the reference system E (see Fig. 3(b)). In the same way, the assertion

$$(q) \models_s \Diamond_{e_1^+} \Diamond_{e_2^+} p$$

means that, starting from any point in q, there exists a walkthrough which leads to a point in q by moving along the positive direction of the first and of the second coordinate axis of the reference system E (see Fig. 3(c)).

The insertion of *eventually* operators stepping along opposite directions of the same axis permits to disregard the alignment condition orthogonal to that axis. For instance, the assertion

$$(q) \models_s \Diamond_{e_1^+} \Diamond_{e_2^+} \Diamond_{e_2^-} p$$

which is satisfied by both the conditions of Figs. 3(c) and 3(d), means that, starting from any point in q, there exists a walkthrough which leads to a point in p by moving along the positive direction of the first axis and along one of the two directions of the second coordinate axis, thus modeling a *don't care* condition for e_2 direction. *Don't care* conditions can be used for multiple axes; for instance, the assertion

$$(q) \models_s \Diamond_{e_1^+} \Diamond_{e_1^-} \Diamond_{e_2^+} \Diamond_{e_2^-} p$$

does not specify any ordering condition along any reference axis, but rather starting from any point in q, there exists some walkthrough which leads to some point of p, i.e. that p is *somewhere* in the scene.

It is worth noting that the correspondence between the above descriptions and the scenes of Fig. 3 is not univocal. For instance, the condition of Fig. 3(c) also satisfies the assertion

$$(q) \models_s \neg p$$

which means that q and p do not overlap.

In general, different assertions can be stated for a single scene. While giving means to the description refinement in manual construction of assertions, this absence of univocality clashes with the possible need of automatic generation of XSTL assertions from the interpretation of sample scenes [9]. To resolve this clash, some assumptions must be made about the kind of assertions generated by the system so as to obtain only one description for each scene. These assumptions involve the structure of Boolean composition of the different spatial operators as well as the number of objects considered in each assertion, and define the *fragment* of XSTL that will be actually exploited by the automatic generator of assertions.

As an example, a possible fragment is made up of the assertions which are formed through the use of *eventually* operators to relate a couple of objects. Using this structure of assertions, the spatial position of p with respect to q in Fig. 4 can be expressed by two possible walkthroughs:

$$(q) \models_s \Diamond_{e_1^+} \Diamond_{e_2^+} p$$

which is possible for all the points in q, and

$$(q) \models_s \Diamond_{e_2^+} p$$

which is possible only for the points of q in the dark-gray area of the figure.

Note that, saying that the spatial position of p is expressed by two walk-throughs means that for each point in q, at least one of the two walkthroughs is

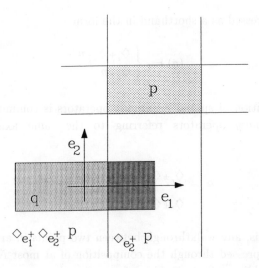

Fig. 4. Walkthroughs $(q) \models_s \Diamond_{e_1^+} \Diamond_{e_2^+} p$ and $(q) \models_s \Diamond_{e_2^+} p$ holding in different regions of q.

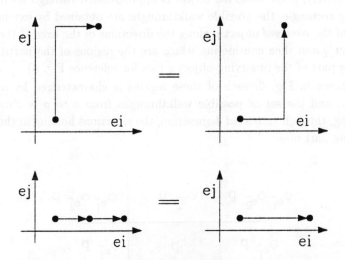

Fig. 5. Visual meaning of commutation and absorption properties of *eventually* operators.

possible and that each of the two walkthroughs is possible at least in one point of q. For the sake of notation, this condition which we refer to as *restricted disjunction*, is formally defined as

$$(q) \models_s \Diamond_{e_1^+} \Diamond_{e_2^+} p \vee \Diamond_{e_2^+} p \quad \wedge \quad \neg(q) \models_s \neg \Diamond_{e_1^+} \Diamond_{e_2^+} p \quad \wedge \quad \neg(q) \models_s \neg \Diamond_{e_2^+} p,$$

and will be expressed as a shorthand in the form

$$(q) \models_s \begin{cases} \Diamond_{e_1^+} \Diamond_{e_2^+} p \\ \Diamond_{e_2^+} p \end{cases}$$

The composition of spatial *eventually* operators is commutative and that multiple *eventually* operators referring to the same axis are *absorbed* (see Fig. 5):

$$\Diamond_{e_i^{\pm}} \Diamond_{e_j^{\pm}} = \Diamond_{e_j^{\pm}} \Diamond_{e_i^{\pm}}$$

$$\Diamond_{e^{\pm}} \Diamond_{e^{\pm}} = \Diamond_{e^{\pm}}$$

According to this, any walkthrough between two points in an N-dimensional scene can be expressed through the composition of at most N *eventually* operators, thus yielding a finite number of assertions.

Operatively, if the observed object is approximated through its minimum bounding rectangle, the possible walkthroughs are obtained by extending the bounds of the *observed* object p along the directions of the axes of the *observing* object q and then considering which are the regions of the partitionment including part of the observing object q (see for reference Fig. 4).

As shown in Fig. 6, each of these regions is characterized by a specific assertion, and the set of possible walkthroughs from q to p is obtained by combining, through *restricted disjunction*, the assertions holding in the regions containing part of q.

$\Diamond_{e_1^+} \Diamond_{e_2^-} p$	$\Diamond_{e_2^-} p$	$\Diamond_{e_1^-} \Diamond_{e_2^-} p$
$\Diamond_{e_1^+} p$	p	$\Diamond_{e_1^-} p$
$\Diamond_{e_1^+} \Diamond_{e_2^+} p$	$\Diamond_{e_2^+} p$	$\Diamond_{e_1^-} \Diamond_{e_2^+} p$

Fig. 6. Partitionment of the space defined by the bounds of the *observed* object and corresponding assertions.

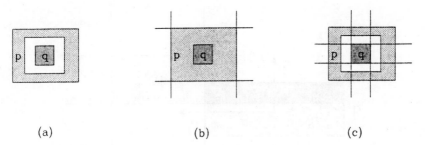

(a)   (b)   (c)

Fig. 7. An object q surrounded by a second object p (a), and the partitionments of the space defined by the bounds of p (b) and q (c).

As an example, consider the case of Fig. 7(a) where an object q is completely surrounded by a second object p.

In the representation of the position of p with respect to q, p is the *observed* object, thus p is approximated by its minimum enclosing rectangle and its bounds are extended along the directions of the *observing* object q (see Fig. 7(b)); in this condition, since the minimum enclosing rectangle of p completely covers q, the only path from q to p is the null walkthrough and the position of p with respect to q is defined by the assertion

$$(q) \models_s \{\, p$$

Conversely, in the representation of the position of q with respect to p (see Fig. 7(c)), all the walkthroughs except the null one are possible paths from p to q:

$$(p) \models_s \begin{cases} \Diamond_{e_1^+} \Diamond_{e_2^+} q \\ \Diamond_{e_2^+} q \\ \Diamond_{e_1^-} \Diamond_{e_2^+} q \\ \Diamond_{e_1^-} q \\ \Diamond_{e_1^-} \Diamond_{e_2^-} q \\ \Diamond_{e_2^-} q \\ \Diamond_{e_1^+} \Diamond_{e_2^-} q \\ \Diamond_{e_1^+} q \end{cases}$$

Please note that, if object p was a filled rectangle covering object q, this latter assertion would change as also the null walkthrough would be a possible path from p to q.

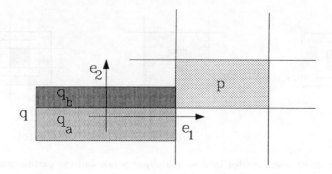

Fig. 8. An alignment condition between two objects q and p.

A different fragment providing a finer description can be defined by using walkthroughs which refer to more than two objects and include the spatial *until* operator. In this latter case, alignment conditions between the extreme bounds of the objects can be expressed.

For instance, the condition in Fig. 8 can be represented as

$$(q) \models_s \begin{cases} (q \ \wedge \ \neg p) \ unt_{e_1^+}(\neg q \ \wedge \ p) \\ (q \ \wedge \ \neg\Diamond_{e_2^+}p) \ unt_{e_1^+}(\neg q \ \wedge \ \Diamond_{e_2^+}p) \end{cases}$$

where:

- the walkthrough $(q \ \wedge \ \neg p) \ unt_{e_1^+} (\neg q \ \wedge \ p)$ holds for the points standing in the region q_A and expresses that moving along the positive direction of axis e_1, the points encountered belong to q and not to p, until points belonging to p and not to q are reached;
- the walkthrough $(q \wedge \neg\Diamond_{e_2^+}p) \ unt_{e_1^+} (\neg q \wedge \Diamond_{e_2^+}p)$ holds for points standing in the regions q_A and q_B and expresses that moving along the positive direction of axis e_1, each point encountered belongs to q with no point of p along e_2, until points are reached which do not belong to q but such that moving along e_2 direction points of p are reached.

All the assertions in both the fragments considered capture pure qualitative relationships in that they define the existence of walkthroughs without constraining the distance between their intermediate or extreme points. The use of freeze variables permits to refine the descriptions with metric information about the walkthroughs. For instance, referring again to the case of Fig. 3(c), the assertion

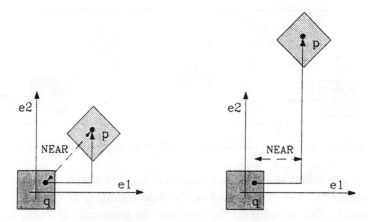

Fig. 9. Metric constraints on walkthrough elongation expressed through spatial freeze variables.

$$(j) \models_t ((q) \models_s v_1.[\Diamond_{e_1^+} \Diamond_{e_2^+} v_2.[p]] \wedge \|v_1(j) - v_2(j)\| = \text{NEAR})$$

means that, in the jth frame, starting from any point in q, there exists a *short* walkthrough leading to q along the positive directions of the first and second axes (see Fig. 9(a)) whose extreme points are at a distance which can be characterized as NEAR. Note that, if the freeze operator is introduced between the *eventually* operators, metric constraints between intermediate points of the walkthrough can be expressed. For instance, the assertion

$$(j) \models_t ((q) \models_s v_1.[\Diamond_{e_1^+} v_2.[\Diamond_{e_2^+} p]] \wedge \|v_1(j) - v_2(j)\| = \text{NEAR})$$

states that in the walkthrough $\Diamond_{e_1^+} \Diamond_{e_2^+}$ the step along the first axis is short while the second is not constrained. This condition, which is illustrated in Fig. 9(b), corresponds to the condition of *almost aligned* along the orthogonal direction to the first axis.

4.2. *Dynamic descriptions*

Temporal operators permit the description of time ordering relationships between frames in which different spatial conditions hold. For instance, the sequence assertion

$$(t_a) \models_t ((q) \models_s \Diamond_{e_1^+} \Diamond_{e_2^+} p) \wedge \Diamond_t((q) \models_s \Diamond_{e_1^-} \Diamond_{e_2^+} p)$$

means that, object p is initially right of object q and that, eventually, it will be left of it (see Fig. 10).

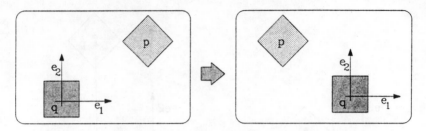

Fig. 10. An object q moving from the left to the right side of an object p.

It is worth noting that the above assertion permits any change of the spatial relationships between q and p before the final condition in which p is left of q is reached. This depends on the fact that the temporal *eventually* operator does not state a condition in the *next* state but rather in *some state in the future*. In general, the temporal *eventually* operator can be used to attain *partial* descriptions of a sequence in which only some relevant conditions are encountered. On the contrary, the temporal *until* operator permits the description of sequences in which *all* the subsequent conditions are defined.

Metric relationships between time instants in which different spatial relationships hold can be expressed by the use of temporal freeze variables. For instance, the assertion

$$(t_a) \models_t (q) \models_s \Diamond_{e_1^+} p) \wedge \Diamond_t t_b.[((q) \models_s \Diamond_{e_1^-} p)] \wedge |t_b - t_a| = \text{SOON}$$

means that object p is initially right of object q and that it will be left of it within a time which can be characterized as SOON.

The joint use of spatial and temporal freeze variables permits the representation of relationships and conditions where space and time are inherently tangled, such as, for instance, advancement and approaching of objects.

The approaching of an object q towards an object p (see Fig. 11) can be expressed through the following assertion:

$$(t_a) \models_t ((q) \models_s v_q.[q] \wedge (p) \models_s v_p.[p]) \wedge \Diamond_t t_b.[\|v_q(t_a)$$
$$- v_p(t_a)\| \leq \|v_q(t_b) - v_p(t_b)\|]$$

which states that, freezed in v_q and v_p any two points belonging to p and q, there will eventually be a frame t_b in which the distance between v_q and v_p is lower than in the first frame t_a. Note that this basically states that there will be a frame in which *any* couple of points in p and q will be nearer than they

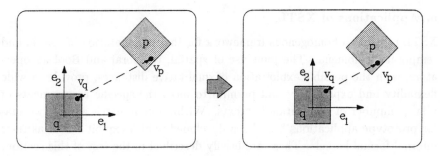

Fig. 11. An object q approaching an object p.

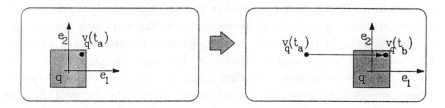

Fig. 12. An object q advancing along the direction of the axis e_1.

are in the first frame. The context declaration can be weakened through the use of negation connectives so as to state that the approaching condition holds not for all the couples of points but only for some of them.

The expression of the advancement of an individual object requires the comparison of the positions of the same object in different frames (see Fig. 12). This is accomplished by the following assertion:

$$(t_a) \models_t ((q) \models_s v_q.[q]) \wedge \Diamond_t t_b.[(v_q(t_a)) \models_s \Diamond_{e_1^+} q]$$

which asserts that, for any point v_q belonging to q, there will be a time t_b in which the point v_q is right of the position of v_q in the initial frame.

Reasoning about the *speed* of changes in the spatial relationships between the objects is supported by the joint use of spatial and temporal quantifiers. For instance, a distance which changes of a quantity FAR in a time interval SOON certainly corresponds to a FAST motion. The appropriate combination of temporal and spatial relationships also permits the description of composite spatio temporal relationships such as *zigzag, backward and forward* or *revolution* motions.

5. Applications of XSTL

XSTL provides a homogenous framework for the representation of spatial and temporal phenomena. The joint use of spatial, temporal and Boolean operators, with the possible exploitation of qualitative distances, provides a wide flexibility and expressivity and permits to meet the specific requirements of a large number of application contexts. Within our research group, two major prototype applications have been developed, which exploit XSTL as their internal formal kernel[3]. These are briefly described in the rest of this section.

5.1. *Retrieval by contents of image sequences*

A subset of XSTL has been exploited in the development of a system which supports retrieval by contents of image sequences through iconic querying by example [9, 11]. In the system, image sequences are stored in a database along with a spatio-temporal description of their contents. Queries are specified through a dynamic iconic interface which permits the creation of sample dynamic scenes reproducing the contents of sequences to be retrieved. Sample scenes are then automatically parsed and translated into a spatio-temporal assertion, and retrieval is accomplished by checking the specification of sample scenes against the descriptions of the sequences in the database.

A block diagram of the system is sketched in Fig. 13. Raw digital image sequences are stored in the *Database* along with sequence assertions describing their salient contents. For each sequence stored, the description is created with the assistance of the *Sequence Recorder* module which provides the means to reproduce the contents of the sequence through a visual iconic interface. The iconic sequences that are produced through the Sequence Recorded are then interpreted by the *Spatio-Temporal Parser* which automatically generates a sequence assertion capturing the contents of the reproduced scene. Queries are expressed visually through the use of the *Visual Scene Editor*. Following a multitrack recorder metaphor, this allows the user to arrange and move icons within a virtual space so as to reproduce the contents of the sequences to be retrieved. Sample scenes are then interpreted by the *Spatio-Temporal Parser* and translated into sequence assertions. In this translation, different target fragments can be selected by the user to obtain more or less precise queries so as to match the user's prior knowledge about the actual contents of sequences

---

[3] Both the systems presently run under AIX 3.1 operating system on an IBM RISC 6000 equipped with a 7235 Power GTO accelerator for 3D graphics support.

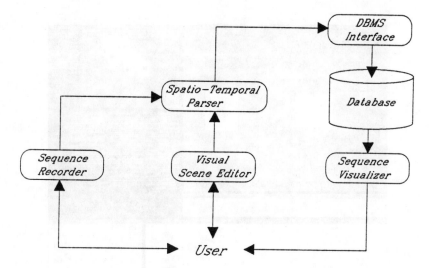

Fig. 13. A block diagram of the retrieval system.

to be retrieved. When the translation has been completed, retrieval is accomplished by the *DBMS Interface* by checking the querying assertions against the descriptions associated with the sequences in the database. Matched sequences are visualized on the screen by the *Sequence Visualizer*.

An example of use of Visual Scene Editor is described in Fig. 14. Here, the user is retrieving sequences in which a car has not given the right of way to another car coming from its right side at a crossroad. After the icons representing the objects have been selected and placed in the appropriate positions, the trajectory of one car (the white car) is recorded first. Hence, it is rewound and played-back during the specification of the trajectory of the second car (the gray car). In the resulting scene, the two cars are made to come to a crossroad, at approximately the same time, and the gray car is made to pass before the white one without giving it the right of way (see Figs. 14(a) and 14(b)). The result of the retrieval is shown in Fig. 15, where a single matching sequence is visualized.

5.2. *Virtual agents visual programming*

XSTL was employed in the development of a prototype tool supporting an evolutionary approach to the visual specification of the behavior of actors running within virtual reality environments [12]. This tool enforces the concept

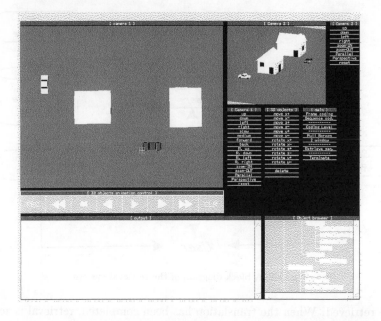

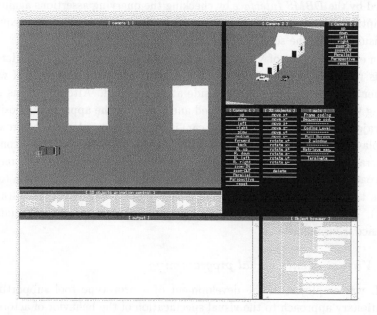

Fig. 14. Use of the Visual Scene Editor in the construction of a sample querying scene.

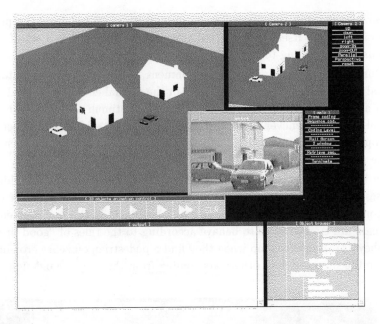

Fig. 15. Result of retrieval for the query of Fig. 14.

of *behavioral training*, i.e. a specification-by-example process in which the behavior of each agent is defined by visually replicating its reaction pattern to specific perceived stimuli coming from its embedding virtual environment. Afterwards, during the operation of the virtual environment, the system operates these models so as to make agents run in the virtual environment in accordance with the behavioral patterns emerging from the specification examples.

In the creation of specification examples, the designer interacts with a 3D iconic environment so as to visually compose dynamic training scenes populated by a number of standing or moving *background* agents which reproduces the spatio-temporal conditions to which the agent is to react. The spatio-temporal contents of the training scenes created by the designer are automatically interpreted by a *spatio-temporal parser* and described in terms of XSTL assertions.

Once a training scene has been created, the designer specifies through an example how the agent will respond to the spatio-temporal stimuli occurring within that scene. In order to support this specification with immersive engagement of the designer, icons representing agents are provided with an *internal appearance* showing the environment contents as perceived from the point of view of the agent itself; this internal appearance also features a set of *control buttons* corresponding to the control actions of the agent.

During the operation of the environment, a *Global Parser* monitors the spatial relationships among the objects in the virtual environment and checks them against the XSTL description of perceived stimuli associated with each virtual agent. Whenever the occurrence of a relevant stimulus is detected, an appropriate signal is posted to the interested agents so as to make them react in the proper way.

In Fig. 16, an example of operation of the system is described which addresses the behavioral training of a car-like agent to be run within a virtual environment for giving driving lessons to a beginner. In this environment, virtual cars are trained so as to behave according to the rules of "good driving", i.e. they are trained to stop when they find a pedestrian on zebra crossing and to give the precedence to other cars coming from their right hand side.

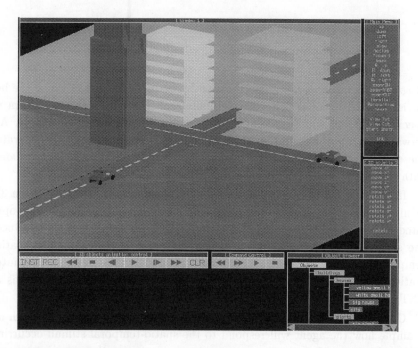

Fig. 16. An example scene to train a car-agent to stop at a crossroad when a car approaches from the right side.

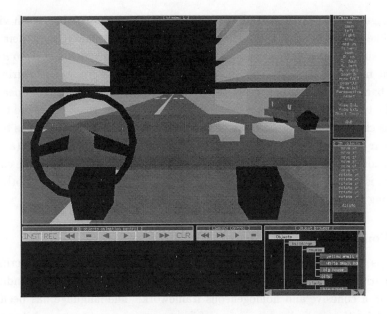

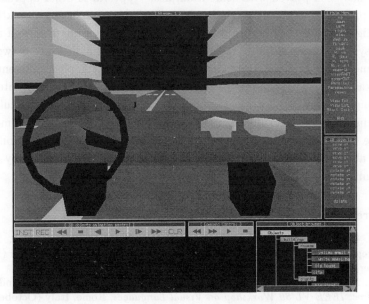

Fig. 17. The drive of a virtual car through the training scene of Fig. 16.

Figure 16 depicts the training scene that has been created to teach virtual car-like agents to give the precedence to other cars coming from their right hand side. To this end, a training scene is composed in which a *background* car agent moves along a straight line and goes through a crossroad. During the playback of this training scene, the designer assumes the internal appearance of the trainee virtual car and drives it towards the crossroad; when the trainee car is close to the crossroad, the designer pushes the brake button so as to stop the car and give the precedence to the *background* agent. (see Figs. 17(a)–(b)). As a consequence of this training example, the behavioral model of the car-like agent is modified so as impose the car to stop whenever it detects another car coming from its right-hand side at a near distance.

6. Conclusions

In this chapter we have presented a new language encompassing descriptions of spatial and temporal relationships between entities with metric conditions, within a cohesive and homogeneous framework. The language has been proposed for the symbolic description of image sequence contents and its expressivity has been proved with some examples. Opposite to other approaches in the representation of spatial relationships, the language relies on a walkthrough paradigm, rather than on projections of objects on coordinate axes of a reference system, thus naturally encompassing the concept of distance between the extreme points of a walkthrough. Description can accomplish different levels of detail and can be tailored to the needs of specific application contexts by defining appropriate shorthand operators and relationships. In particular, not only distances but also angular metric conditions can be easily accommodated in the model by natural extension of its syntax and semantics. Considerations about relative speeds between the objects can be supported by a joint reasoning on spatial and temporal descriptions.

References

1. R. Alur and T. Henzinger, "A really temporal logic", Tech. Rep. 92-1310 Department of Computer Science, Cornell University, Ithaca, New York (November 1992).
2. T. Arndt, and S. K. Chang, "Image sequence compression by iconic indexing", *Proc. IEEE VL'89 Workshop on Visual Languages*, Rome, Italy (October 1989) 177–182.

3. S. K. Chang, and S. H. Liu, "Picture indexing and abstraction techniques for pictorial databases", *IEEE Transactions on Pattern Analysis and Machine Intelligence*, **6**, 4 (July 1984) 475–484.

4. S. K. Chang, Q. Y. Shi, and C. W. Yan, "Iconic indexing by 2-D strings", *IEEE Transactions on Pattern Analysis and Machine Intelligence* **9**, 3 (July 1987) 413–428.

5. S. K. Chang, C. W. Yan, D. C. Dimitroff, and T. Arndt, "An intelligent image database system", *IEEE Transactions on Software Engineering* **14**, 5 (May 1988) 681–688.

6. S. K. Chang, and E. Jungert, "Pictorial data management based upon the theory of symbolic projections", *Journal of Visual Languages and Computing* **2** (June 1991) 195–215.

7. G. Costagliola, G. Tortora, and T. Arndt, "A unifying approach to iconic indexing for 2D and 3D scenes", *IEEE Transactions on Knowledge and Data Engineering*, **4** 3 (June 1992) 205–219.

8. A. Del Bimbo, M. Campanai, and P. Nesi, "A three-dimensional iconic environment for image database querying", *IEEE Transactions on Software Engineering*, **19** 10 (October 1993) 997–1010.

9. A. Del Bimbo, E. Vicario, and D. Zingoni, "Sequence retrieval by contents through spatio temporal indexing", *Proc. IEEE VL'93 Workshop on Visual Languages*, Bergen, Norway (August 24–27, 1993), pp. 88–92.

10. A. Del Bimbo, E. Vicario, and D. Zingoni, "A spatial logic for symbolic description of image contents", *Journal on Visual Languages and Computing* **5** (October 1994) 267–286.

11. A. Del Bimbo, E. Vicario, and D. Zingoni, "Symbolic indexing of image sequences with spatio temporal logic", *IEEE Transactions on Knowledge and Data Engineering* **7**, 4 (August 1995) 609–622.

12. A. Del Bimbo, E. Vicario, and D. Zingoni, "An interactive environment for the visual programming of virtual agents", *Proc. IEEE VL'94, Int. Symp. on Visual Languages*, St.Louis, MI (October 1994).

13. A. Frank, "Qualitative spatial reasoning about distances and directions in geographic space", *Journal of Visual Languages and Computing* **3** (September 1992) 343–371.

14. C. Freksa, "Using orientation information for qualitative spatial reasoning", *Proc. Int. Conf. Theories and Methods of Spatio-Temporal Reasoning in Geographic Space*, Pisa, Italy (September 21–23, 1992), *Lecture Notes in Computer Science*, (Springer Verlag, 1992) pp. 162–178.

15. E. Jungert, "The observer's point of view, an extension of symbolic projections", *Proc. Int. Conf. Theories and Methods of Spatio-Temporal Reasoning in Geographic Space*, Pisa, Italy (September 21–23) 1992, *Lecture Notes in Computer Science*, (Springer Verlag, 1992) pp. 179–195.

16. P. Holmes, and E. Jungert, "Symbolic and geometric connectivity graph methods for route planning in digitized maps", *IEEE Transactions on Pattern Analysis and Machine Intelligence* **14**, 5 (May 1992) 549–565.

17. S. Y. Lee, and F. J. Hsu, "2D C-string: A new spatial knowledge representation for image database systems", *Pattern Recognition* **23**, 10 (October 1990) 1077–1087.

18. S. Y. Lee, and F. J. Hsu, "Spatial reasoning and similarity retrieval of images using 2D-C-string knowledge representation", *Pattern Recognition* **25**, 3 (March 1992) 305–317.

19. S. Y. Lee, M. Shan, and W. Pang, "Similarity retrieval of iconic image database", *Pattern Recognition* **22**, 6 (June 1989) 675–682.

20. Z. Manna, and A. Pnueli, "The temporal logic of reactive and concurrent systems", (Springer Verlag, New York, 1992).

21. G. Petraglia, M. Sebillo, M. Tucci, and G. Tortora, "Similarity retrieval of images by indexed 2D C-string", Techn. Report Univ. of Salerno, 1992.

22. G. Petraglia, M. Sebillo, M. Tucci, and G. Tortora, "A normalized index for image databases", *Proc. Workshop on Spatial Reasoning*, Bergen, Norway (August 1993).

23. E. Petrakis, and S. Orphanoudakis, "Methodology for the representation, indexing and retrieval of images by content", *Image and Vision Computing* **11**, 8 (October 1993) 504–521.

24. C. Schlieder, "Representing visible locations for qualitative navigation", in: *Qualitative Reasoning and Decision Technologies*, eds., N. Piera Carrete and M. Singh (CIMNE, Barcelona, 1993) pp. 523–532.

A GENERALIZED APPROACH TO IMAGE INDEXING AND RETRIEVAL BASED ON 2D STRINGS

EURIPIDES G. M. PETRAKIS

Department of Computer Science, University of Crete

STELIOS C. ORPHANOUDAKIS

*Institute of Computer Science, Foundation for Research and Technology-Hellas
Heraklion, Crete, Greece*

2D strings are one of a few representation structures originally designed for use in an IDB environment. In this chapter, a generalized approach for 2D string based indexing, which avoids an exhaustive search through the entire database of previous 2D string based techniques, is proposed. The classical framework of representation of 2D strings is also specialized to the cases of scaled and unscaled images. Index structures for supporting retrieval by content, utilizing the 2D string representation framework, are also discussed. The performance of the proposed method is evaluated using a database of simulated images and compared with the performance of existing techniques of 2D string indexing and retrieval. The results demonstrate a very significant improvement in retrieval performance.

1. Introduction

Much attention has been given during the past few years to the design and development of Image DataBase (IDB) systems which support the archiving and retrieval of images by content [1, 2, 3]. In such systems, images are analyzed so that descriptions of their content can be extracted and stored in the IDB together with the original images. These descriptions are then used to search the IDB and to determine which images satisfy the query selection criteria. However, the problem of retrieving images by content is difficult for reasons related to the complexity and uncertainty inherent in image analysis and interpretation tasks, the large amounts of data involved in derived image descriptions, as well as the dependence of such descriptions on the content of images relating to a specific application. Furthermore, the time efficiency of the processing and database search techniques which are applied may not satisfy the speed requirements of many IDB applications.

Prior to storage, derived image descriptions need to be appropriately represented (mapped) in database storage structures and models (e.g. relational tables). The amount of data stored, data processing and communication overhead can be reduced by using compact image representations. Furthermore, retrieval responses can be speeded up by incorporating into the IDB storage and search mechanisms efficient techniques which support the indexing of images by content.

Once image representations are stored in database storage structures, they can be indexed using the indexing mechanisms provided by the particular DBMS [4, 5]. Queries specifying constraints on object properties are then easy to answer. Queries specifying object properties and relationships between objects (e.g. queries by example image) have to be translated into conditional statements involving constraints on object properties and relationships. However, such queries are difficult to process and image comparisons involve time-intensive operations such as graph matching [6, 7]. The time complexity of matching increases with the number of objects in the images which are compared.

2D strings by S.K. Chang *et al.* [8] is one of a few representation structures originally designed for use in an IDB environment. The technique provides a simple and compact representation of spatial image properties in the form of two one-dimensional strings. 2D strings can be used to resolve queries based on image content. A query is specified by providing an example image or icon. After computing its 2D string representation, the problem of image retrieval is transformed into one of two-dimensional string matching. However, the search based on 2D strings is exhaustive: in order to determine which images must be retrieved, 2D string representations corresponding to all stored images are compared with a similar representation extracted from the query image.

A technique for indexing 2D strings stored in an IDB has been proposed by C.C. Chang and S.Y. Lee in [9]. Specifically, 2D strings are indexed based on representations corresponding to all pairs of objects. Each pair of objects is assigned an address (index) and entered into a hash table. Similarly, the objects contained in a given query image are taken in pairs. Each pair of query objects acts as a separate query and is used to retrieve a set of images. The intersection of the retrieved sets contains images which are then compared to the original query.

In this chapter, a generalized scheme for 2D string indexing and retrieval is proposed. Indexing is based not only on pairs of objects, but also on groups consisting of more than 2 objects. These groups are first represented by 2D strings. An address is then computed for each one of the above 2D strings. The representation of 2D strings is specialized to the cases of scaled and unscaled images.

The addressing scheme proposed in [9] requires that the images to be stored in the IDB are given in advance. A preprocessing step is needed to derive a hash function which is perfect (i.e. guarantees that no two pairs of objects are mapped to the same address unless they have the same properties) for this particular set of images. However, if new images are entered into the IDB, the hash function ceases to be perfect. The addressing scheme used in this work requires no preprocessing, the images need not be given in advance, and it is not affected (i.e. remains perfect) by the number of images which are entered in the IDB.

The performance (given in terms of the average size of the space searched and of the average retrieval response time) of the proposed methodology is compared against the performance of the 2D string matching algorithms of [8] and of the indexing mechanism of [9]. To our knowledge, the performance of the techniques under consideration has not been studied elsewhere in the literature. Indexing based on pairs of objects incurs a significant overhead due to excessive processing of intermediate query results. Retrieval responses are speeded up significantly when indexing is based on groups consisting of more than 2 objects. However, retrieval response times and storage space are traded off. An IDB of 1000 simulated images has been used as a testbed for all comparisons.

This work completes and extends previous work by the authors: a similar addressing scheme and a general approach to represpresenting spatial image properties has been presented in [10]. String representations taking into account any number of object properties and the inclusion relationships between objects have been proposed. The effectiveness of such representations in retrieving images by content has been investigated. However, certain retrievals incur a significant processing overhead and are relatively slow. In this chapter, string image presentations and similar indexing structures are combined with known 2D string matching algorithms to provide a more time efficient but less space demanding approach of image indexing and retrieval.

The rest of this chapter is organized as follows: an overview of 2D strings is presented in Sec. 2. A specialization of 2D strings in the cases of scaled and unscaled images is presented in Sec. 3. Our approach to indexing 2D strings is presented in Sec. 4. The proposed search strategy and evaluations of the performance of retrievals based on exhaustive search, the indexing scheme of [9], and our approach are discussed in Sec 5, followed by conclusions in Sec. 6.

2. Overview of 2-D Strings

To produce the 2D string representation of a given image, the image is segmented and the positions of all objects (i.e. their centers of mass) are projected along the x and y directions. By taking the objects from left to right and from below to above, two one-dimensional strings are obtained forming the 2D string representation of the image. The objects themselves are represented by values corresponding to classes or names. For example, the objects contained in the image of Fig. 1 can be of one of 4 classes, namely a, b, c and d, and are numbered from 0 to 6. Their indices are shown on the left of their classes. Object indices (numbers) and object classes will be used alternatively in this chapter to denote objects.

The 2D string representation of a given image may take various forms, namely "reduced", "augmented" etc. Details about these forms and the transformations between them can be found in [8]. The reduced 2D string representation of the image of Fig. 1 is

$$(u,v) = (a\,d\,c < b < c\,a < d,\ a\,b < c < d\,c\,d < a) \qquad \text{(reduced 2D string)}.$$

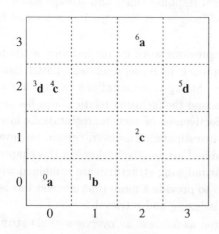

Augmented 2D string:
$$(u,v) = (adc < b < ca < d,$$
$$03 < 4 < 126 < 5)$$

Fig. 1. A symbolic image (left) and its corresponding augmented 2D string (right).

The symbol "<" denotes the "left/right" relationships in string u and the "below/above" relationships in string v. Notice that objects having the same x or y projection can be written in any order. For example, objects 0, 3 and 4 have the same x projection and can be written as acd or cad or dca etc. To obtain the augmented 2D string, we substitute each object in string v by its position in string u. For example, object a is first in u and it is substituted by 0 in v, object b is fourth in string u and it is substituted by 3 in v etc. The augmented 2D string representation of the image of Fig. 1 is

$$(u, v) = (a\, d\, c < b < c\, a < d,\ 0\, 3 < 4 < 1\, 2\, 6 < 5) \qquad \text{(augmented 2D string)}.$$

In this chapter, we make use of a form, which will henceforth be called "expanded 2D string": the augmented 2D string representation (u, v) of a given image is expanded into a form (z, r, s) of three one-dimensional strings, where z contains the names or the classes of all objects in the same order as they appear in u, while strings r and s contain the projections of all objects along the horizontal and vertical directions respectively. The values in strings r and s will henceforth be called "ranks". In this example, r and s take values in the range $[0, 3]$. However, the range for r and s need not be always equal. For example, object b in the image of Fig. 1 has rank 1 along the x axis and rank 0 along the y axis. Objects c and d in the cell with coordinates $(0, 2)$, share the same position and have the same ranks. The expanded 2D string representation of the image of Fig. 1 is

$$(z, r, s) = (a\, d\, c\, b\, c\, a\, d,\ 0\, 0\, 0\, 1\, 2\, 2\, 3,\ 0\, 2\, 2\, 0\, 1\, 3\, 2) \qquad \text{(expanded 2D string)}.$$

2D strings are an adequate representation of spatial image properties in the case of images consisting of nonoverlapping objects (i.e. their minimum enclosing rectangles do not intersect) having simple shapes. Various extensions of 2D strings, such as 2D G strings and 2D C strings have been proposed in [11] and [12] respectively, and deal with situations of overlapping objects with complex shapes. However, such representations are not as simple and compact as the original 2D string representation, nor can they be produced very efficiently. Extensions of 2D strings for representation of three-dimensional scenes can be found in [13].

2.1. *Image similarity based on 2D strings*

The similarity between two images (e.g. a query and a retrieved image), whose contents are represented by two-dimensional strings, can be determined based either on exact or approximate matching techniques. In the first case, every object in the query image has to be associated to at least one similar object (i.e. an object having the same name or class) in the retrieved image and the matched objects in these two images must have exactly the same relationships. In the case of a successful match, there is at least one 2D subsequence within the second 2D string matching the query. An algorithm must determine the existence of a match and, in the case of a successful match, it must find all the matching subsequences. Three algorithms for 2D string matching and three types of similarity criteria, namely type-0,1,2, have been defined in [8]. The first algorithm, referred to as $2DmatchA$, is a more general one and may be used with all types of similarity criteria. The other two, referred to as $2Dquery1$ and $2Dquery2$, may be used only with the type-1 and type-2 similarity criteria, respectively.

The effectiveness of 2D string based representations in retrieving images by content has been investigated in [10]. It has been shown that, in certain cases, such representations are not tolerant to small variations of property values and become unstable (i.e. change drastically). Due to unstable representations, retrievals may be proven to be inaccurate, yielding images that a user would not consider similar to the query. In addition, not all images which a user would consider similar to a query are retrieved.

In 2D string matching, a query and its retrieved subsequence must have exactly the same representation (exact match retrievals). However, image retrieval is not an exact process. Images are rarely identical. To be effective, database search must seek for images having approximately similar representations with the query. Then, appropriate distance (or similarity) measures must be adopted. An approach to dealing with such issues by making use of alternative representations of image content (e.g. attributed graphs) is discussed in [14].

The definition of similarity is less strict in the case of approximate matching techniques, since the two-dimensional string of the query need not be an exact subsequence of the second string. The approximate similarity between two 2D strings can be determined based on either a maximum likelihood or a minimum distance criterion. In the first case, the similarity is determined based on the longest 2D string subsequence that the two 2D strings under consideration have in common. Regarding image retrieval, the problem is then to retrieve the most similar image from a set of stored images. This is the one having the longest common subsequence with the query among the images stored in the IDB. The problem of finding the longest common subsequence between two 2D strings is transformed into a problem of finding the maximal complete subgraphs (cliques) of a given graph. Therefore, the 2D string longest common subsequence problem has nonpolynomial time complexity. The problem of finding the longest common subsequence between 2D strings is treated in [15]. The problem of finding the longest common subsequence between 2D C strings is treated in [16].

The similarity between two 2D strings can also be determined based upon a minimum distance criterion. For example, the minimum distance between two 2D or 2D C strings can be defined as the cost of the minimum-cost transformations required in order to transform the first string to the second. Algorithms for determining the minimum distance between 1D strings do exist [17, 18] and have to be generalized to the case of two dimensional strings.

In this chapter, we focus our attention on 2D strings and on exact-match retrievals. We make use of the original algorithms for 2D string matching of [8] and propose a generalized approach for indexing and retrieval based on 2D string subsequences extracted from all stored images. However, to increase the accuracy of retrievals, techniques of indexing 2D G strings or 2D C strings need to be developed. To our knowledge, no such techniques have been proposed so far. The proposed approach may be regarded as a first step in this direction.

2.2. *Correctness of 2D string matching*

The algorithm $2DmatchA$ allows "false drops" in certain cases [19] (i.e. there may exist instances in the answer set which do not actually match the query). The conditions of occurrence of false drops are discussed in [19] and an algorithm which avoids false drops has been proposed. False drops may occur with type-0 and type-1 matchings, while false drops cannot occur with type-2 matching. Moreover, the original algorithms for 2D string matching are, in certain cases, inexact (i.e. mismatched subsequences). These algorithms have been corrected in [20] to list all matched subsequences and have been extended to take into account any number of object properties and the inclusion relationships between objects.

3. Extensions to 2D Strings

So far, we have assumed that objects which are close enough to each other may be assigned the same position and the same rank. This is possible in cases where images are at a fixed scale. However, when images are scaled with respect to each other, there is no reference distance for comparing the relative distances between objects. Therefore, objects which are close enough to each other may not be assigned the same position or have the same rank. Therefore, there is a need to specialize the representation of 2D strings to the cases of scaled and unscaled images separately.

Without loss of generality, we require that objects are ordered. Ordering is mainly required for indexing, but it also helps us to derive representations which are easier to understand and use. In the following, two criteria for ordering image objects are presented and discussed. The first ordering criterion can be used even in cases where images are scaled with respect to each other, while the second ordering criterion can be used only in cases where images are found at a fixed scale.

3.1. First ordering criterion

Let $(a[0], a[1], \ldots, a[n-1])$ be the set of image objects. For any two objects $a[i]$, $a[j]$, $i, j \in [0, n-1]$ with centers of mass $(cg_x[i], cg_y[i])$ and $(cg_x[j], cg_y[j])$ respectively, either $a[i]$ is a "predecessor" of $a[j]$, which is written as $a[i] \prec a[j]$, or $a[i]$ is a "successor" of $a[j]$, which is written as $a[i] \succ a[j]$. Specifically, the first ordering criterion is written as follows:

$$\forall i, j \in [0, n-1] \begin{cases} a[i] \prec a[j], & \text{if } cg_x[i] < cg_x[j] \text{ OR} \\ cg_y[i] < cg_y[j] & \text{if } cg_x[i] = cg_x[j]; \\ a[i] \succ a[j], & \text{otherwise}. \end{cases} \tag{1}$$

We assume that no two objects have the same center of mass. However, cases where objects have the same center of mass are very rare and may occur only when objects contain other objects. By applying this ordering criterion to the objects contained in an image, a permutation string p is obtained which is the ordered sequence of indices corresponding to the above objects. In particular, string p corresponds to the sequence of objects produced by projecting their positions along the x axis, taking them from left to right. Henceforth, p will be used to characterize the image itself. The ordered sequence of objects corresponding to the example image of Fig. 1 is $p = (0\ 3\ 4\ 1\ 2\ 6\ 5)$. By substituting each object in p by its name or class, we obtain the string z of the expanded 2D string representation. Specifically, $z = (a\ d\ c\ b\ c\ a\ d)$.

The expanded 2D string representation makes use of strings r and s representing the ranks of objects along the x and y directions respectively. The first ordering criterion guarantees that objects are ordered from left to right, while no two objects may be assigned the same position and have the same rank. Therefore, string r takes the form $r = (0, 1, 2, \ldots, n - 1)$. A string s corresponding to the ranks of objects along the y direction is obtained by computing, for each object in p, the number of objects which are below it. To compute s we proceed as follows: first, a second permutation string p' is produced by projecting the positions of objects along the y axis and by taking them from below to above. In particular, string p' is produced by ordering objects according to the following rule:

$$\forall\, i, j \,\in\, [0, n - 1] \begin{cases} a_i \prec a_j, & \text{if } cg_y[i] < cg_y[j] \text{ OR} \\ cg_x[i] < cg_x[j] & \text{if } cg_y[i] = cg_y[j]; \\ a_i \succ a_j, & \text{otherwise}. \end{cases} \tag{2}$$

For example, the permutation string p' corresponding to the image of Fig. 1 is $p' = (0\ 1\ 2\ 3\ 4\ 5\ 6)$. The rank $s[i]$ of the ith object in p equals its position in string p'. Specifically, $s[i]$ is computed as follows:

$$s[i] = j \quad \Longleftrightarrow \quad p[i] = p'[j], \quad 0 \le i, j < n. \tag{3}$$

The string corresponding to the ordered sequence $p = (0\ 3\ 4\ 1\ 2\ 6\ 5)$ is $s = (0\ 3\ 4\ 1\ 2\ 6\ 5)$. Finally, the expanded 2D string representation corresponding to the example image of Fig. 1 and the first ordering criterion is

$$(z, r, s) = (a\,d\,c\,b\,c\,a\,d,\ 0\,1\,2\,3\,4\,5\,6,\ 0\,3\,4\,1\,2\,6\,5).$$

Representations derived by the application of the first ordering criterion are both translation and scale invariant (i.e. images translated or scaled with respect to each other result in the same representation). Translation invariance is assured, since only relative positions are taken into account in determining the order of objects. Similarly, scale invariance is assured, since no distance criterion is used.

3.2. Second ordering criterion

The image area is partitioned by an $M \times N$ rectangular grid. The position of an object with index i, where $i \in [0, n - 1]$, is defined by the pair of ranks $(r[i], s[i])$, where $r[i] \in [0, M - 1]$ and $s[i] \in [0, N - 1]$, corresponding to the coordinates of the grid cell containing its center of mass. Equivalently, the position of an object is represented by a single value $R[i]$ which is computed as a function of $r[i]$ and $s[i]$ as $R[i] = r[i] \cdot N + s[i]$. For any two objects $a[i]$, $a[j]$, $i, j \in [0, n-1]$, with values $R[i]$, $R[j]$ respectively, the second ordering criterion is written as

$$\forall \, i, j \, \in \, [0, n-1] \begin{cases} a[i] \prec a[j], & \text{if } R[i] < R[j] \text{ OR} \\ z[i] < z[j] & \text{if } R[i] = R[j]; \\ a[i] \succ a[j], & \text{otherwise}. \end{cases} \quad (4)$$

Objects sharing the same grid position are ordered based on their class values. We assume that an order can be defined over the set of names or classes (e.g. $a < b < c \cdots$). Objects sharing the same grid position and having the same name or class cannot be ordered. However, this situation is rather rare, especially when the grids are dense (e.g. $M, N > 3$); when the objects have various sizes (i.e. a large object is less likely to have the same position as other objects); when they are outside one another; and when the number of different classes is large (e.g. greater than 3).

The ordered sequence of objects corresponding to the example image of Fig. 1 is $p = (0\ 4\ 3\ 1\ 2\ 6\ 5)$. In this case $M = N = 4$. Object 4 is before object 3 in p, since $c < d$. The string R corresponding to p is $(0\ 2\ 2\ 4\ 9\ 11\ 14)$. By substituting each object in p by its name or class, we obtain the string z of the expanded 2D string representation. Specifically, $z = (a\ c\ d\ b\ c\ a\ d)$. Finally, the expanded 2D string representation corresponding to the image of Fig. 1 and the second ordering criterion is

$$(z, r, s) = (a\ c\ d\ b\ c\ a\ d,\ 0\ 0\ 0\ 1\ 2\ 2\ 3,\ 0\ 2\ 2\ 0\ 1\ 3\ 2).$$

Translation invariance of the derived representation is achieved by a simple coordinate transformation: let α and β be the minimum $r[i]$ and $s[i]$ values respectively. The ranks of each object i along x and y directions become $r[i] - \alpha$ and $s[i] - \beta$ respectively.

4. Indexing on 2D Strings

An image is decomposed into groups of objects called "image subsets". All image subsets from 2 up to a prespecified size K_{max} are produced; these are $\sum_{k=2}^{\min(n, K_{max})} \binom{n}{k}$. For example, when $K_{max} = 6$, 57 subsets are produced from the image of Fig. 1. The number of image subsets which are produced becomes very large especially when $K_{max} > 5$ and $n > 10$. Therefore, to reduce space demands, K_{max} must take low values. Methods for specifying K_{max} are discussed in Sec. 5.

An image is indexed based on the set of image subsets derived from it. First, the expanded 2D string representation corresponding to all image subsets is computed. Once the expanded 2D string representation of an image subset of size k has been derived, we compute two addresses, namely $I_k^{r,s}$ and I_k^z corresponding to spatial relationships and object classes respectively.

When the first ordering criterion is used, $I_k^{r,s}$ is computed based on string s. A string s completely characterizes the spatial relationships between the objects contained in an image subset. String s defines a permutation over the set $\{0, 1, \ldots, k-1\}$, since no two objects have equal ranks. Thus, string s may take $k!$ different values. An ordered image subset p is mapped to a unique address $I_k^{r,s}$ in an address space of size $D_k^{r,s} = k!$ by computing the rank (order) of r in a listing of permutations. The ranking algorithm we used is that by Johnson and Trotter [21]. For example, the ordered image subset $p = (0\ 1\ 2\ 5)$ derived from the image of Fig. 1 has $s = (0\ 1\ 2\ 3)$ and $I_k^{r,s} = 0$, while $D_4^{r,s} = 24$.

When the second ordering criterion is used, the spatial relationships between the objects contained in an ordered image subset are completely characterized by string R. The number of different ways for placing k objects on an $M \times N$ rectangular grid is equal to the number of the "l-part compositions of k elements", where $l = M \cdot N$. Therefore, the number of different values a string R may take is equal to $\binom{k+l-1}{k}$. An ordered image subset p is mapped to a unique address $I_k^{r,s}$ in an address space of size $D_k^{r,s} = \binom{k+l-1}{k}$ by computing the rank of string R in a listing of compositions [22]. For example, the ordered image subset $p = (0\ 1\ 2\ 5)$ derived from the image of Fig. 1 has $R = (0\ 4\ 9\ 14)$ and $I_k^{r,s} = 2555$, while $D_4^{r,s} = 3060$.

Finally, an address I_k^z corresponding to object classes is computed based on string z. A string z consists of k elements and each one may take q different values, where q is the number of object classes. A string z may be regarded as one of the "q-base representations of k elements"; these are $D_k^z = q^k$. An ordered image subset p is mapped to a unique address I_k^z in an address space of size D_k^z by computing the rank of string z in a listing of the q-base representations of k elements. For example, assuming 4 classes ($q = 4$), namely a, b, c and d, the ordered image subset $p = (0\ 1\ 2\ 5)$ has $z = (a\ b\ c\ d)$ and $I_4^z = 228$, while $D_4^z = 256$.

Once the indices $I_k^{r,s}$ and I_k^z have been computed, a 2D string corresponding to an image subset of size k is mapped to a unique address I_k in an address space of size $D_k = D_k^{r,s} \cdot D_k^z$ as follows:

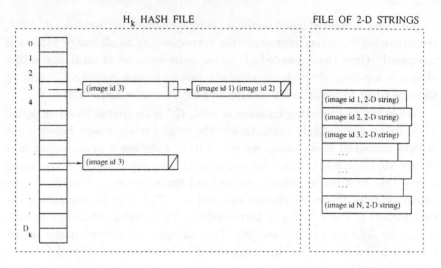

Fig. 2. Proposed file structure. Only one of the $(H_2, H_3, \ldots H_{K_{max}})$ hash files is shown.

$$I_k = I_k^{r,s} + D_k^{r,s} \cdot I_k^z, \quad 2 \le k \le K_{max}. \tag{5}$$

The pair $(I_k^{r,s}, I_k^z)$ is considered to be the representation of I_k in the "mixed radix system" $(D_k^{r,s}, D_k^z)$. I_k is unique in the sense that only image subsets having exactly the same 2D string, and therefore the same indices $I_k^{r,s}$ and I_k^z are mapped to the same address I_k.

The proposed addressing scheme guarantees that only image subsets having the same 2D string representation are mapped to the same index. Therefore, hashing is perfect and remains perfect regardless of the number of images which are entered in the IDB. The addressing scheme discussed in this section can be extended to take into account any number of properties representing global object characteristics (i.e. area, roundness, orientation etc.), as well as the inclusion ("inside/outside") relationships between the objects contained in a given image or image subject. For further details, the reader is referred to [10].

An index (e.g. an image identifier) to the image from which the image subset has been derived is then entered into a hash table of size D_k. The storage space consists of data pages of fixed capacity. Overflows are handled by creating linked lists of data pages. The IDB consists of a set $(H_2, H_3, \ldots, H_{K_{max}})$

of such index structures corresponding to subsets consisting of $2, 3, \ldots, K_{max}$ objects respectively.

The 2D string representations of the original images are stored in a separate indexed file using the image identifiers as keys. A pointer is kept from each image in H_k to its 2D string. Figure 2 shows the file structure of the data on the disk. Only one hash file ($H_k, 2 \leq k \leq K_{max}$) with address space D_k holding indices to three images is shown.

5. Image Retrieval

We distinguish between "direct access" queries corresponding to $2 \leq m \leq K_{max}$ and "indirect access" queries corresponding to $m > K_{max}$, where m is the number of query objects and K_{max} is the maximum size of image subsets used for indexing.

Direct access queries: The 2D string representation and the index I_m corresponding to the query are computed first. The query addresses the H_m hash file. The 2D strings corresponding to all images having indices stored in the list of data pages pointed by I_m are retrieved from the file of 2D strings. These are images matching the query (i.e. each image contains at least one 2D subsequence matching the query). To produce all 2D subsequences matching the query, all retrieved 2D strings are compared with the 2D string of the query using a 2D string matching algorithm.

Indirect access queries: The query is decomposed into $\rho = \binom{m}{K_{max}}$ subsets, thus creating ρ new queries. Each of these queries performs as a direct access query on the $H_{K_{max}}$ file. Their answer sets, namely $S_0, S_1, \ldots, S_{\rho-1}$, are derived and their intersection $S = S_0 \cap S_1 \cdots \cap S_{\rho-1}$ is obtained. S consists of indices corresponding to candidate images matching the original query (i.e. there may exist images in S not matching the query). To determine which images match the original query and to produce all 2D matching subsequencies, the 2D strings corresponding to all images in S are retrieved from the file of 2D strings and compared with the 2D string of the query using a 2D string matching algorithm.

5.1. *Performance evaluation*

Before producing the 2D string representation of a given image, the image must first be segmented into disjoint regions corresponding to image objects.

It is assumed that objects are not hidden or overlapped with others so that their positions can be computed correctly and their classes can be identified (by a human expert or by applying a computer algorithm). Producing such segmentations from images of a real application is a very hard task and is beyond the scope of this chapter.

To evaluate the performance of the alternative indexing and retrieval techniques under consideration we make use of an IDB consisting of 1000 simulated images: a random number generator has been used to produce 1000 2D strings corresponding to images containing between 4 and 10 objects. The positions of objects in a 3×3 rectangular grid have been generated at random. Objects are distinguished in 3 categories ($q = 3$). Each object is assigned a class at random. All images are considered to be at a fixed scale and the second ordering criterion has been used. The IDB has been implemented on a magnetic disc connected to a SUN SPARCstation ELC.

The access methods which are compared are the following: (a) The original method proposed by S. K. Chang *et al.* [8]. An exhaustive search through the entire database of 2D strings is performed using one of the 2D string matching algorithms mentioned in Sec. 2. All these algorithms, namely *2DmatchA*, *2Dquery*1 and *2Dquery*2, have been implemented as in [20] and support either type-0, type-1 or type-2 matching; (b) Indexed search based on the technique proposed by C. C. Chang and S. Y. Lee [9] in combination with the above algorithms. Indexing is based on pairs of objects ($K_{max} = 2$); (c) Indexed search using our method in combination with 2D string matching. Indexing is based on groups of objects having size greater than 2 ($3 \leq K_{max} \leq 6$).

The performance of each of the above access methods is given in terms of (a) the retrieval response time and, (b) the size of the space searched. The size of the searched space is given as a percentage of images which are retrieved and compared with the query. To obtain average performance measures, for each value of m ranging from 2 to 6, 20 image queries have been applied and the average performance of queries specifying an equal number of objects has been computed.

The average size of the answer set as a function of the number of query objects and of K_{max} is shown in Fig. 3. The shape of the curves can be justified as follows.

The size of the answer set returned decreases with m. Queries address hash tables holding subsets of equal size, or at most of size K_{max}. However, the

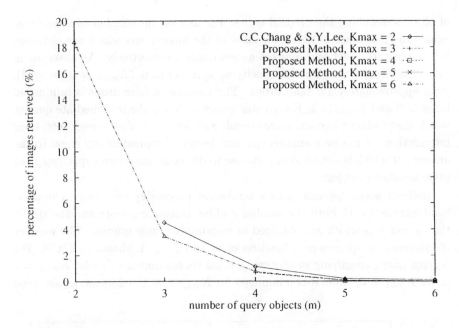

Fig. 3. Average size of space searched as a percentage of images retrieved, plotted against the number of query objects for (a) $K_{max} = 2$ following C.C. Chang and Y.S. Lee and (b) for $K_{max} \in [3,6]$ according to the proposed method.

size of the hash table addressed increases with the size of stored image subsets. Similarly, the size of the hash table holding subsets of size K_{max} increases with K_{max}. The size of an address space increases also with q (the number of object classes).

As the size of the address space increases, the subsets are distributed over larger address spaces and less image subsets are stored per index. Therefore, queries specifying more objects result in smaller searched spaces. For example, the address space has size 405 for $m = 2$, 4455 for $m = 3$ and 40095 for $m = 4$ (we assumed $M = N = 3$ and $q = 3$). Queries specifying two objects ($m = 2$) retrieve approximately 18.5% of the images stored in the IDB. The size of the searched space drops to less than 5% for queries specifying more than 2 objects ($m > 2$). For $m > 5$, most queries return empty answer sets.

Indirect access queries ($m > K_{max}$) return answer sets which may contain images not matching the query (false drops). A 2D string matching algorithm must then be applied to eliminate the false drops and to produce all sequences of objects matching the original query. For any m, the number of false drops equals the difference between the sizes of the answer sets which are obtained in response to direct and indirect access queries respectively. As observed in Fig. 3, indirect access queries specifying three objects ($K_{max} = 2$, $m = 3$), yield approximately 1% false drops. The number of false drops is minimized for $m > 3$ and $K_{max} > 2$. For greater values of K_{max} the intermediate queries which are produced become more specific and return smaller answer sets; their intersection set has even smaller size and becomes approximately equal to the answer set which is obtained in response to direct access queries specifying the same number of objects.

Indirect access queries incur a significant processing overhead. The overhead increases with both the number ρ of intermediate queries and the size of the answer sets which are obtained in response to these queries. The number of intermediate queries as a function of m and K_{max} is shown in Fig. 4. For a given query specifying m objects, ρ takes its maximum value for $K_{max} = 2$ or for $K_{max} = 3$, while it is minimized for $K_{max} > 3$. In addition, as observed

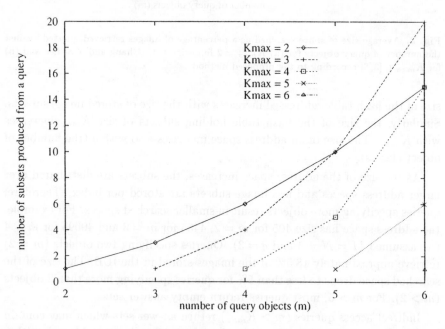

Fig. 4. Number ρ of intermediate queries produced from a query specifying m objects, as a function of m and of the maximum size of image subsets K_{max}.

in Fig. 3, the size of an answer set decreases with K_{max}. For example, if $K_{max} = 2$, queries specifying 5 objects ($m = 5$) have to retrieve and process $\rho = 10$ answer sets each consisting of 18.5% of the total number of images stored in the IDB. If $K_{max} = 4$, 5 answer sets are produced each holding less than 1% of the total number of images stored in the IDB. Therefore, to minimize the overhead and to speed-up retrievals, a value of K_{max} greater than 2 must be selected (e.g. $K_{max} = 4$).

The average retrieval response time corresponding to indexed and exhaustive search utilizing $2DmatchA$ is shown in Fig. 5. Indexed search always results in faster retrieval response times. Retrievals become faster with K_{max}. However, as observed in Fig. 4, as m increases, the number ρ of intermediate queries specifying K_{max} objects increases too, the processing overhead increases and retrievals are slowed down.

The average retrieval response times corresponding to indexed and exhaustive search utilizing $2Dquery1$ or $2Dquery2$ algorithm are shown in Fig. 6.

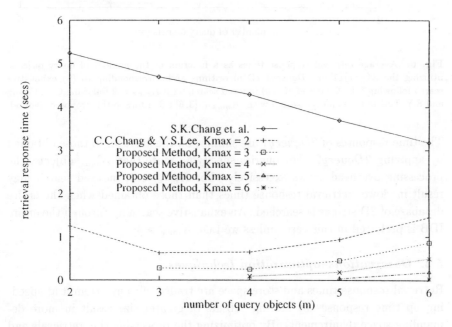

Fig. 5. Average retrieval response time as a function of the number of query objects, utilizing $2Dmatch\,A$ algorithm and corresponding to (a) exhaustive search following S.K. Chang *et al.*, (b) indexed search with $K_{max} = 2$ following C.C. Chang and S.Y. Lee and (c) indexed search with $K_{max} \in [3, 6]$ according to the proposed method.

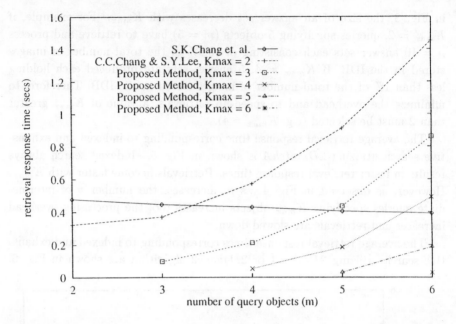

Fig. 6. Average retrieval response times as a function of the number of query objects, utilizing the *2Dquery1* or *2Dquery2* 2D algorithms and corresponding to (a) exhaustive search following S.K. Chang *et al.*, (b) indexed search with $K_{max} = 2$ following C.C. Chang and S.Y. Lee and (c) indexed search with $K_{max} \in [3, 6]$ according to the proposed method.

The time responses of *2Dquery1* are similar, on the average, to those obtained by applying *2Dquery2*. For queries specifying more than K_{max} objects, the processing overhead grows excessively. For $K_{max} < 5$, indexed search may result in slower retrieval response times than those obtained when the entire database of 2D strings is searched. An exhaustive searching through the entire IDB is preferred in this case, unless we take $K_{max} > 4$.

5.2. *Observations–optimization techniques*

Retrieval response times and store space are traded off: any attempt at speeding up time responses by storing subsets of greater size result in more demanding space requirements. By optimizing the processing (i.e. retrievals and set intersections) of indirect access queries, retrieval responses can be further speeded up and K_{max} may take lower values. So far, retrievals and intersections have not been optimized.

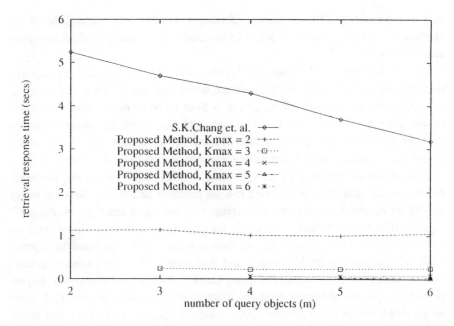

Fig. 7. Average retrieval response time as a function of the number of query objects, utilizing $2DmatchA$ algorithm and corresponding to (a) exhaustive search following S.K. Chang *et al.*, (b) indexed search with $K_{max} \in [2,6]$ utilizing one query subset.

We attempted to minimize the processing overhead by applying, instead of ρ, only one intermediate query. The time responses obtained utilizing the $2DmatchA$ algorithm are shown in Fig. 7. Similar results are obtained when $2Dquery1$ or $2Dquery2$ is applied. Although the size of the answer sets returned in response to this query is, on the average, greater than that obtained when all ρ queries are applied, retrieval responses are speeded up significantly, since no intersections are necessary. The time responses do not decrease with m since the size of the answer set obtained for all $m > K_{max}$ is the same. A value of 3 or 4 for K_{max} can be used in this case.

Whether retrievals are always speeded up by applying all or just one intermediate query is an open question. There may exist cases (e.g. specific kinds of images) where the maximum speedup is encountered for some particular number ρ' of intermediate queries between 1 and ρ.

Two important parameters must be specified: the maximum size of images subsets K_{max} and the number p' of intermediate queries. To specify K_{max}

and ρ' a prototype IDB consisting of images which are characteristic of the application under consideration has to be used and an analysis of performance has to be performed.

In the experiments discussed in this chapter, retrievals are faster compared to retrievals in [10]. Specifically, indirect access queries in [10] incur a significant processing overhead: all images in S have to be retrieved, their representations have to be computed and matched with the query. By maintaining the indexed file of 2D strings, the above processing overhead is eliminated. As a consequence, K_{max} takes lower values and space demands are lower.

The shape of the curves corresponding to database search using the original 2D string matching algorithms can be justified as follows: Given a query specifying m objects, matching with images consisting of less than m objects is rejected immediately (early rejection). As m increases, the number of early rejections increases too. Notice that all images contain between 4 and 10 objects, while all queries specify between 2 and 6 objects. Therefore, time responses become faster with the number of query objects. $2DmatchA$ algorithm, in particular, makes use of termination conditions (see [8]) which are satisfied faster as queries become more specific. Algorithms $2Dquery1$ and $2Dquery2$ result in faster time responses than $2DmatchA$ due to their lower time complexity.

6. Conclusions

In this chapter, a new method which supports efficient indexing of 2D strings stored in an IDB has been proposed and its performance compared with the performance of three 2D string matching algorithms proposed in [8] and with the performance of the indexing method proposed in [9].

Our approach to indexing 2D strings is based on the idea of computing addresses to equal size 2D strings corresponding to image subsets derived from all stored images. All subsets up to a prespecified size K_{max} are considered. Searching through the entire IDB is avoided and retrievals are speeded up significantly when $K_{max} > 2$. The time responses become faster for greater values of K_{max}. Methods for the specification of K_{max} have also been discussed. However, any attempt at speeding up time responses by storing subsets of greater size would result in more demanding average space requirements. This is a trade off which must be carefully considered in the context of specific applications.

The addressing scheme used is perfect (i.e. no two subsets are mapped to the same address unless they have the same properties) and, in contrast to the addressing scheme of [9], remains perfect regardless of the number of images which are entered in the IDB. We have shown extensive experimental results analyzing the performance of the indexing technique presented in comparison with the performance of the previous approaches.

This work completes and extends the work of others. In particular, the technique of [9] may be regarded as a special case of the proposed indexing scheme when the maximum size of image subsets is 2 ($K_{max} = 2$). In addition, the work of [10] has been extended to take advantage of the effectiveness of known 2D string matching algorithms and a more general, more time efficient but less space demanding approach to image indexing and retrieval has been proposed.

Indexing techniques with lower space demands have to be developed. Furthermore, attempts must be made to extend this method to include indexing of 2D C string representations which has been shown to be better suited for applications where objects are overlapping and have complex shapes. Retrievals based on 2D C strings are less efficient compared with retrievals based on 2D strings, and indexing could speed up time responses significantly.

Acknowledgements

We would like to thank Prof. Stavros Christodoulakis for valuable contributions in this work.

References

1. Hideyuki Tamura and Naokazu Yokoya, "Image database systems: A survey", *Pattern Recognition* **17**, 1, pp. 29–49 (1984).
2. Petros Kofakis and Stelios C. Orphanoudakis, "Image indexing by content", in M. Osteaux et al., eds., *A Second Generation PACS Concept*, chap. 7, (Springer-Verlag, 1992) pp. 250–293.
3. Shi-Kuo Chang and Arding Hsu, "Image information systems: Where do we go from where?", *IEEE Trans. on Knowledge and Data Engineering* **4**, 5, (1992) 431–442.
4. Shi-Kuo Chang and King-Sun Fu, "A relational database system for images", in Shi-Kuo Chang and King-Sun Fu, eds., *Pictorial Information Systems*, (Springer-Verlag, 1980) pp. 288–321.
5. Stelios C. Orphanoudakis, Euripides G. Petrakis, and Petros Kofakis, "A medical image database system for tomographic images", In *Proc. of Comput. Assisted Radiology, CAR89*, (Berlin, June 1989) pp. 618–622.
6. Martin A. Fischler and Robert A. Elschlager, "The representation and matching of pictorial structures", *IEEE Trans. on Comput.* **C-22**, 1 (1973) 67–92.

7. Linda G. Shapiro and Robert M. Haralick, "Structural descriptions and inexact matching", *IEEE Trans. on Pattern Analysis and Machine Intelligence* **3**, 5 (1981) 504–519.

8. Shi-Kuo Chang, Qing-Yun Shi, and Cheng-Wen Yan, "Iconic indexing by 2D strings", *IEEE Trans. on Pattern Analysis and Machine Intelligence* **9**, 3 (May 1987) 413–428.

9. Chin-Chen Chang and Suh-Yin Lee, "Retrieval of similar pictures on pictorial databases", *Pattern Recognition* **24**, 7 (1991) 675–680.

10. Euripides G. M. Petrakis and Stelios C. Orphanoudakis, "Methodology for the representation, indexing and retrieval of images by content", *Image and Vision Computing* **11**, 8 (October 1993) 504–521.

11. Shi-Kuo Chang, Erland Jungert, and Y. Li, "Representation and retrieval of symbolic pictures using generalized 2D strings", In *SPIE Proc. Visual Comm. and Image Processing*, (Philadelphia, November 1989) 1360–1372.

12. Suh-Yin Lee and Fang-Jung Hsu, "2D C-string: A new spatial knowledge representation for image database systems", *Pattern Recognition* **23**, 10 (1990) 1077–1087.

13. Gennaro Costagliola, Genoveffa Tortora, and Timothy Arndt, "A unifying approach to iconic indexing for 2D and 3D scenes", *IEEE Trans. on Knowledge and Data Eng.* **4**, 3 (June 1992) 205–222.

14. Euripides G. M. Petrakis and Christos Faloutsos, "Similarity searching in large image databases", Technical Report MUSIC/TR-94-01, MUltimedia Sys. Inst. of Crete (Chania, Crete, July 1994).

15. Suh-Yin Lee, Man-Kwan Shan, and Wei-Pang Yang, "Similarity retrieval of iconic image databases", *Pattern Recognition* **22**, 6 (1989) 675–682.

16. Suh-Yin Lee and Fang-Jung Hsu, "Spatial reasoning and similarity retrieval of images using 2D C-string knowledge representation", *Pattern Recognition* **25**, 3 (1992) 305–318.

17. Robert A. Wagner and Michael J. Fischer, "The string-to-string correction problem", *J. of the Assoc. for Computing Machinery* **21**, 1 (January 1974) 168–173.

18. Patrick A. V. Hall and Geoff R. Dowling, "Approximate string matching", *ACM Computing Surveys* **12**, 4 (December 1980) 381–402.

19. John Drakopoulos and Panos Constantopoulos, "An exact algorithm for 2D string matching", Technical Report 021, Inst. of Comp. Sci., Foundation for Research and Technology - Hellas (Heraklion, Greece, November 1989).

20. Euripides G. M. Petrakis, *Image Representation, Indexing and Retrieval Based on Spatial Relationships and Properties of Objects*, PhD thesis, Univ. of Crete, Dep. of Comp. Sci. (March 1993). Available as Technical Report FORTH-ICS/TR-075.

21. Dennis Stanton and Dennis White, *Constructive Combinatorics*, chap. 1 (Springer-Verlag, 1986).

22. Edward M. Reingold, Jurg Nievergelt, and Narsingh Deo, *Combinatorial Algorithms*, chap. 5 (Prentice Hall, 1977).

USING 2D-STRING DECISION TREES
FOR SYMBOLIC PICTURE RETRIEVAL

DANIEL J. BUEHRER, C. C. CHANG, and S. M. LING

Institute of Computer Science and Information Engineering,
National Chung Cheng University Chia Yi, Taiwan, 62107 Republic of China

We now consider the problem of how to efficiently retrieve pictures from a large database. A query should retrieve all input pictures which satisfy a given pattern expression, where this pattern expression may involve Boolean operators applied to a given set of permissible subpatterns. The number of permissible subpatterns determine whether a simple linear search, hashing, or a decision tree would give the best performance. For on the order of 1,000,000 patterns or more, the decision tree algorithm which we present here has the advantage of being able to rule out most nonmatching patterns without performing any disk accesses. Similar to the trie-hashing algorithm [8], this decision tree indexing method stores only those subpatterns which are needed to distinguish a set of input pictures, and the decision tree does not need to store the whole patterns. The whole indexing structure can thus be usually stored in the main memory, making it possible to access the needed data with a single disk access. We describe in detail how the decision tree algorithm works on 2D strings [6], which are short representations of the spatial relationships between the elements of a given symbolic picture is corresponding to a real image.

1. Introduction

There is a plethora of image data (e.g. from satellites) which is not of much use unless it can be indexed and stored in a way which permits quick retrieval. Sometimes the pictures need to be retrieved based on the spatial relationships (e.g. left, right, above, below) between the objects or feature points in the image. For such applications, symbolic pictures [6] are generally used to perform the indexing. The symbolic picture consists of icons which represent feature points in the original picture, such as the center of objects, the endpoints of lines, etc. These icons all have integer (X,Y) coordinates. As in previous spatial pattern matching algorithms, we will assume that two icons can have only one of nine spatial relationships, depending on whether their (X,Y) coordinates are <, =, or >. These nine spatial relationships are shown in Fig. 1.

Northwest 3	North 2	Northeast 9
West 4	Same 1	East 8
Southwest 5	South 6	Southeast 7

Fig. 1. Nine spatial directions.

There have been many papers describing the problem of querying a large spatial database to find all the pictures which have certain objects in certain relative locations with respect to each other (e.g. [1, 5, 7]). Usually symbolic pictures are first defined for each real image, where a symbolic picture contains an icon at each position which corresponds to a feature point of a real object in the real image. These symbolic pictures may then be matched using various techniques for checking the spatial relationships between the icons. In an exact match, the number of icons in the subject, and pattern must be the same, and these icons must all have the same relative spatial directions. We are concerned mainly with what are known as "type 1" matches [3], where the icons of a pattern correspond to a subset of the icons of the subject, and the icons in the pattern all have the same spatial relationships as the corresponding subject icons.

2. 2D Strings

One often-used representation of symbolic pictures is the 2D string. We briefly review the 2D string by looking at an example. Suppose that we have the following symbolic picture composed of icon types "a" through "g", and where icons "e" and "g" are at the same location:

Column	1	2	3	4
Row 1	f			b
Row 2	b	a	d	
Row 3	e,g	c		

This picture may be stored as the following 2D string:
  "e:g =b =f <c =a <d <b. e:g =c <b=a =d <f =b."

This string represents the reduced symbolic picture, where empty rows and columns have been deleted. The first half of the string gives the spatial relationships between the x coordinates, subsorted by the y coordinates and by the icon type. The second half of the string gives the relationships between the y coordinates, subsorted by the x coordinates and icon type. Rather than using icon types, the second half of the "augmented 2D string" uses indices on the icons in the first half of the string:

"e:g =b =f <c =a <d <b. 1:2 =5 <3 =6 =7 <4 =8."

This augmented 2D string is sometimes used in order to disambiguate the icons in case there are multiple occurrences of the same icon type. There is a 1-1 correspondence between the augmented 2D string and the symbolic picture.

Since we are only using the 2D string as a filter to rule out impossible matches, it is more efficient to use the simple 2D string. The 2D string of a pattern picture must be a subsequence of a subject picture if it is to be contained in the subject. (The converse is only true for augmented 2D strings.) If the 2D string of a pattern P is not contained in a subject, then neither will other patterns containing P be contained in the subject. This property is used to construct a decision tree for indexing and efficiently searching the patterns.

The problem which we consider here is how to construct an indexing scheme which can allow us to find all subject (i.e. input) pictures which satisfy Boolean expressions involving certain pattern pictures. For instance, the expression

(pat6 or pat14) and pat 7 and not pat4

should return a vector of pointers to all subject images whose symbolic pictures contain (either pattern 6 or pattern 14) and pattern 7, minus those subject pictures which contain pattern 4. We will assume that, for convenience, the subject images are assigned successive numbers as they are streamed onto disk or tape. At that time, their feature points are extracted, and their symbolic pictures are stored onto the disk or tape along with the subject image.

We assume that the user may wish to ask queries involving a very large number of patterns. This chapter is concerned with devising an indexing scheme which can fit into the main memory (e.g. 64 megabytes), and which can quickly add a pointer to all patterns which are contained in a given subject picture. Then, for any pattern, the set of pointers to all subject pictures containing that pattern can be quickly retrieved. Thus, union, intersection, and difference operations involving these sets of pointers can quickly retrieve the indices of all subject pictures which satisfy a given Boolean expression involving certain subpatterns. From the pointers, the corresponding real images can also be quickly retrieved.

Although a million pattern pictures sounds like a lot, there are many cases for which this will prove to be insufficient. For instance, suppose that a pattern contains 20 icons, and we want to match any subject picture which contains up to 15 corresponding icons with the correct spatial relationships. This is already $20!/(15! \cdot 5!) = 15,504$ patterns.

It may be worthwhile in such cases to use a special indexing technique. The subpatterns can be represented by bit strings. In this example, the bit strings have size 20 and have 15 bits which are 1. But even using such compression techniques, the 2D strings for the patterns will often not fit into the main memory.

For small numbers of patterns, simple linear search of an array or hashing suffices. However, for very large numbers of patterns, the decision tree structure below often performs better. We shall show how such an indexing scheme can make use of a decision tree structure, and how databases containing millions of pictures can be indexed while performing few disk accesses for each subject picture. The decision tree structure which is in memory is used to look up all buckets on the disk. Each bucket contains some 2D string patterns, and for each pattern, the corresponding vector of pointers point to the subject images which contain this pattern.

The advantage of using the decision tree algorithm to look up matching pattern 2D strings is that usually only a small subsequence of the keys needs to be stored in the main memory in order for the correct disk bucket to be located. That is, even for very large pictorial databases, the symbolic indices can be stored in the main memory, making it possible to retrieve a pattern in one disk access or to rule out impossible matches with no disk accesses.

3. Constructing the Decision Tree

We consider only what are known as type-1 matches [3], where rows, columns, and individual icons can be removed from the subject picture to make it the same as the pattern picture. A pattern picture type-1 matches a subject picture if and only if its 2D string is in a way a "2D subsequence" of the 2D string for the subject picture. The 2D subsequence problem is much more difficult than for standard 1D strings, since it can be proven to be NP-complete. However, since we are only using the 2D strings to rule out impossible matches (so that not all patterns have to be checked), the algorithm below is able to use a standard 1D $O(n \cdot m)$ longest common subsequence algorithm to rule out most of the impossible matches.

We will assume for simplicity that there are at most 16,384 icon types, so that each icon in the 2D string takes at most 14 bits. 2 bits will be used to store the spatial relation symbols $<$, $:$, $=$, and period. Therefore, each icon and its following operator symbol will be assumed to take 2 bytes. That is, a 2D string for n icons would take $4n$ bytes.

Our problem is to find an indexing scheme that will fit into the memory (e.g. 64 megabytes) and which can locate the numbers of all pictures containing a given pattern picture. In order to do this, for every new subject picture, we insert that picture's number into the list for each pattern which is contained in the picture. The number of subpictures of a picture with n icons is 2^n. For example, a picture with 200 icons has 2^{200} subpictures, which is many trillions of trillions of times larger than the number of atomic particles in the visible universe. Therefore, we limit the queries to a fairly small number of possible patterns, say about 1,000,000. In the worst case, all patterns will be contained in the given subject picture, which means that all buckets on the disk will have to be updated. But usually, most patterns will not be contained in the subject. We will now show how to quickly skip through the set of patterns in order to efficiently find all of the patterns that type-1 match a given subject picture.

A decision tree is used to group the patterns which contain similar subpatterns. Only patterns which contain a given subpattern are stored below that subpattern in the decision tree. Therefore, when looking for all the patterns which are contained within a given subject picture, this tree can be searched efficiently. If the pattern associated with a node is not contained in the subject picture, then the patterns which are below it in the decision tree also could not possibly be contained in the subject picture. The leaf nodes of the decision tree point to buckets on the disk where the full 2D strings associated with the patterns are stored. However, usually only a small substring of the patterns is stored in the decision tree, and that is sufficient to rule out most impossible pattern matches.

The root node contains a subpattern of size 0, so that it matches every subject image. The first pattern will be inserted immediately beneath the root. When the second pattern arrives, the longest common subsequence (lcs) with the first pattern is found, this lcs replaces the first subpattern, and the first and second subpatterns are moved below the lcs. If the lcs is empty, then the new pattern is simply added on as a brother of the original node.

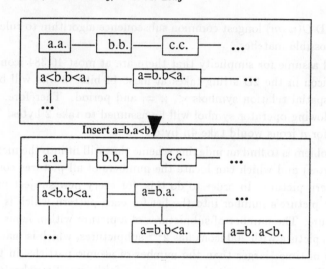

Fig. 2. Inserting the string "a =b.a <b." into the decision tree.

The decision tree has "yes" edges going downward and "no" edges going to the right. To insert a new pattern into the decision tree, each row is searched, and the node which has the longest (one-dimensional) common subsequence (lcs) with the given pattern is chosen. The node with the lcs is replaced by the lcs, and the original node is moved down as a son of the lcs node. The node to be inserted is then recursively inserted into the level below the lcs node. See Fig. 2 for an example of how the 2D string "a=b.a <b." is inserted into the decision tree.

The one-dimensional lcs problem must be modified somewhat to perform matching of the 2D strings. For instance, the 2D string "a=b" should not be considered to be a substring of "a<c=b" because the intervening "<" operator overrides the meaning of the "=" operator (since the "=" no longer indicates that "a" and "b" are in the same row or column). That is, for the simple 2D lcs, intermediate operators of lower precedence are not permitted, where the operators in order of increasing precedence are ".", "<", "=", and ".".

Since most 2D strings are fairly short, we can modify the simple $O(nm)$ lcs algorithm rather than the more complex $O(m \log(n))$ algorithm. We recursively use the 1D lcs on substrings involving only operators higher than a certain precedence level.

For matrix M, one of the traditional 1D lcs algorithms uses the following formula to fill in a matrix:

$$M[i,j] = \max(M[i-1,j], M[i,j-1], M[i-1,j-1])$$
$$+ \text{match}(\text{first}[i], \text{second}[j])$$

where match(first[i], second[j]) is either 0 or 1 depending on whether the letter at position i of the first string is the same as the letter at position j of the second string. Now, rather than matching letters, we are recursively matching substrings, so the value of match may be more than 1. At each level of recursion, however, the algorithm basically works the same as for the one dimensional case, except that we are matching substrings rather than letters, so the lengths of the subsequences in the matrix may grow by more than one.

For example, in Fig. 3, the "2" in the lower right-hand corner indicates that the longest common subsequence of "a < c = b =a:d" and "a:d=c<b" has length 2. This "2" at M[2,2] can be derived either by adding M[1,1] to match ("c= b= a:d", "b") = 1, or by using the "match" substring "a:d" from M[2,1], as calculated in Fig. 4.

To work most efficiently, the algorithm requires that the icons at each position (connected by ":" operators) must be in sorted order. In that case a simple left-right scan can determine the number of common icons in two strings containing only ":" operators. Therefore, each half of the 2D string takes only two levels of recursion to eliminate the < and = operators.

We did not worry about correspondences between the first half of the 2D string and the second half of the 2D string. The icons in the two halves may turn out to be completely different.

	a:d=c	b
a	1	1
c=b=a:d	2	2

Fig. 3. Modified lcs algorithm.

	a:d	c
c	0	0
b	0	1
a:d	2	2

Fig. 4. Recursively finding "match" for entry in row 2, column 1 of Fig. 3.

Assuming that each bucket contains an average of 25 patterns, then 10,000,000 patterns would have about 400,000 bucket pointers pointing to them. There would then also be about 400,000 internal nodes. Assuming that each node takes about 8 bytes, then approximately 6.4 megabytes of memory would be needed. Therefore, any one of the 10,000,000 patterns could be located in 1 disk access. It may require another disk access to find the beginning of the vector of subject images which contain this pattern.

4. Results of Simulation

For this simulation we used a 486-66 PC with 64 megabytes of real memory and 1 gigabyte of disk.

A linear search was compared to the decision tree search. As each subject picture of 5 icons was read in, all of the buckets were retrieved which potentially held pattern pictures that matched the subject picture. The simulation times do not include the time for adding pointers to the matching pattern pictures, since that time is relatively independent of the search time. The results of the experiment are shown in Table 1 below:

The results show that even a PC can efficiently index millions of subject pictures against millions of patterns, so that the indices of all subjects that match a given Boolean query involving the patterns may be retrieved in a few seconds. This means that the response time is fast enough to develop an interactive query environment.

Of course, searching the decision tree for a given Boolean expression of subpatterns is much faster than finding feature points, creating the symbolic images, and creating the decision tree. In order to get a reasonable processing time (e.g. one 24-hour day), all of the feature points in an image would have to be extracted in less than a tenth of a second, which may require the use of a supercomputer. The construction of the decision tree for the 800k random

Table 1. Experimental run times (seconds) for 2 icons in each pattern, 5 icons in each subject, 8192 icon types.

Number of pattern pictures	20k	100k	200k	400k	800k
Exhaustive search of 2D strings on disk	22	77	225	445	1192
Decision tree	0.02	0.16	0.32	0.65	1.30

symbolic pictures in Table 1 took around 20 hours on our PC. This is less than a tenth of a second per picture, so the speed is still acceptable for an interactive environment.

We also performed some experiments to test the effects of the total number of icon types and the number of icons per pattern. The results are shown below in Table 2. The total number of icon types seem to have very little effect on search times.

One interesting effect that can be observed from Table 2 is that the search times actually decrease as the pattern lengths increase. This is due to the fact that the decision trees in Table 2 all have 80,000 nodes, and the longer patterns cause each node to have a longer common subsequence. The longer lcs's in turn permit quicker elimination of impossible matches, so that fewer nodes have to be searched.

Table 2. Effect of # Icons/pattern and # Icon types/pattern for 40,000 patterns, 10 icons per subject. (Runtime is given in seconds.)

# icons/pattern	8 icon types	8,192 icon types
1	0.06	0.06
2	0.05	0.05
4	0.05	0.05
8	0.05	0.05

5. Conclusions

Suppose that we are receiving images in real time. These images are analyzed and appropriate feature points are extracted. Suppose that we want to index these images by whether or not they contain certain spatial arrangements of such feature points. We have shown how to get an efficient indexing scheme for answering queries which are Boolean combinations of these patterns. Although, as mentioned previously, there are an extremely large number of subpictures in the subject pictures, the decision tree method will quickly skip over large groups of impossible patterns, permitting quick retrieval of matching patterns and their vector of subject image pointers. As for trie-hashing, the decision tree method only stores substrings of the patterns, so that the whole decision tree can be kept in memory even for millions of patterns. This permits speedups of between 500 to 1000 over disk-based indexing methods.

References

1. C. C. Chang and D. J. Buehrer, "A survey of some spatial match query algorithms", *Database Systems for Advanced Applications '91*, **2**, *Advanced Database Research and Development Series* (World Scientific Publishing Co., 1992) pp. 218–223.
2. C. C. Chang and S. Y. Lin, "Retrieval of similar pictures on pictorial databases", *Pattern Recognition* **24**, 7 (1991) 675–680.
3. S. K. Chang, *Principles of Pictorial Information Systems Design* (Prentice Hall, 1989).
4. S. K. Chang and K. S. Fu, "Query-by-pictorial-example", *IEEE Trans. Softw. Eng.* **SE-6**, 6 (1980) 519–524.
5. S. K. Chang, C. W. Yan, C. C. Dimitroff, and T. Arndt, "An intelligent picture database system", *IEEE Trans. Softw. Eng.* **14**, 5 (1988) 681–688.
6. S. K. Chang, Q. Y. Shi, and C. W. Yan, "Iconic indexing by 2D strings", *IEEE Trans. Pattern Anal. Mach. Intell.* **PAMI- 9**, 3 (1987) 413–428.
7. S.-Y. Lee, M.-K. Shan, and W. P. Yang, "Similarity retrieval of iconic picture databases", *Pattern Recognition* **22**, 6 (1989) 675–682.
8. W. Litwin, "Trie hashing", Research Report, MAP-I-014, I.R.I.A., Le Chesnay, France (1981).

EFFICIENT IMAGE RETRIEVAL ALGORITHMS
FOR LARGE SPATIAL DATABASES*

JUDY C. R. TSENG

Department of Computer Science, Chung-Hua Polytechnic Institute,
30 Tung Shiang, Hsinchu, Taiwan, Republic of China
Email:judycrt@cc.nctu.edu.tw

TSONG-FENG HWANG and WEI-PANG YANG

Department of Computer and Information Science,
National Chiao Tung University, Hsinchu, 300, Taiwan, Republic of China,
Email:wpyang@cis.nctu.edu.tw

The 2D string, proposed by Chang *et al.* is a spatial index structure which preserves the information of spatial relationships in a spatial database. In this paper, two new image retrieval algorithms for 2D string are proposed. The first one improves the retrieval efficiency, while the second reduces the space requirement. The performance analysis shows that the two methods perform much better than previous works especially when the spatial database is large.

Keywords: Spatial database, image retrieval, 2D string, signature file.

1. Introduction

With the growth of applications which heavily rely on spatial data, *spatial database* (also named *image database*) has become an important issue. To avoid on-line image processing and to speed up the spatial searching while answering user queries, various spatial indexing techniques have been proposed [2, 8, 11, 14]. Among them, the *2D string* [2-4] proposed by Chang *et al.* is ideal for retrieving images by the spatial relationships between objects, while others generally focus on the range queries and the point search.

The 2D string indexing method works as follows. For a gray scale image, the techniques of image processing and pattern recognition are applied first

---

*This study was supported, in part, by the National Science Council, Republic of China, under the contract no.: NSC82-0408-E009-044.

Fig. 1. A symbolic picture f.

to recognize the *pictorial objects* contained in the image. The image is then represented by a *symbolic picture*, in which each symbol represents a pictorial object in the raw image. The 2D string of the symbolic picture is a pair of 1D strings, say (u, v). The first 1D string u represents the spatial relationships between the pictorial objects along the x axis, and the second, v, represents those along the y axis. In u and v, "$<$" denotes is-west-of and is-south-of relationships, respectively.

For example, consider the symbolic picture f shown in Fig. 1. The symbols a, b, c and d represent pictorial objects. The 2D string representing f is $s = (ad < b < c, ac < b < d)$. Associated with each 2D string is a pointer to the image it represents.

The collection of the 2D strings and the pointers constitutes the index structure of the spatial database. Interested readers may refer to [2] for the generation of the symbolic picture and the detailed descriptions of the 2D string. In this paper, we assume that the 2D string index structure has been generated and stored in the spatial database.

A query that retrieves images by pairwise spatial relationships can also be represented by a 2D string. Therefore, the problem of image retrieval becomes that of *2D subsequence matching*. There are three types of 2D *subsequences*, namely type-0, type-1, and type-2. They describe the degrees of similarity between two 2D strings. The three types of 2D subsequences are defined as follows [2]:

A string u is contained in a string v, if u is a subsequence of a permutation string of v. A string u is a type-i 1D subsequence of string v, if

1. u is contained in v, and
2. $a_1 w_1 b_1$ is a substring of u, a_1 matches a_2 in v and b_1 matches b_2 in v, then

$$
\begin{aligned}
&\text{(type-0)} \quad && r(b_2) - r(a_2) \geq r(b_1) - r(a_1) && \text{or} \\
& && r(b_1) - r(a_1) = 0 \\
&\text{(type-1)} \quad && r(b_2) - r(a_2) \geq r(b_1) - r(a_1) > 0 && \text{or} \\
& && r(b_2) - r(a_2) = r(b_1) - r(a_1) = 0 \\
&\text{(type-2)} \quad && r(b_2) - r(a_2) = r(b_1) - r(a_1)
\end{aligned}
$$

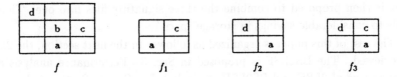

Fig. 2. Picture matching example.

where $r(x)$, the rank of symbol x, is defined to be one plus the number of "$<$" preceding x.

Let (u, v) and (u', v') be the respective 2D string representation of f and f'. (u', v') is a type-i 2D subsequence of (u, v), if u' is type-i 1D subsequence of u, and v' is type-i 1D subsequence of v. f' is then said to be a type-i subpicture of f.

For example, suppose there are four images f, f_1, f_2 and f_3 as shown in Fig. 2. The 2D string representations of $f, f_1, f_2,$ and f_3 are

$$f : (d < ab < c, a < bc < d),$$
$$f_1 : (a < c, a < c),$$
$$f_2 : (d < a, a < d), \text{ and}$$
$$f_3 : (d < ac, a < dc).$$

Then type-0 subpictures of f are f_1, f_2, f_3, type-1 subpictures of f are f_1, f_2, and type-2 subpicture of f is f_1.

To efficiently solve the 2D subsequence matching problem, Lee *et al.* proposed a 2D Longest Common Subsequence method [9]. However, a spatial database may contain hundreds of thousands of images and sequential 2D subsequence matching is still costly. In [10], Lee and Shan proposed a fast preselection algorithm, we call it a *two-level spatial filter* (2LSF), to speed up the retrieval of images indexed by the 2D string. The algorithm uses a *two-level signature file* [12] to represent the 2D strings in the spatial database, and acts as a *search filter* [1, 15, 16] to quickly filter out impossible images.

In this paper, a new image retrieval algorithm for 2D string, called a *bit-sliced two-level spatial filter* (BS2LSF), is proposed to further improve the performance of image retrieval. The new proposed spatial filter applies the concept of *bit-transposed file* [17] to speed up the filtering process. The 2LSF and the BS2LSF both employ one signature file for each type of 2D subsequences. Therefore, three signature files in total are required. A refined method, called

1SF, is then proposed to combine the three signature files into one. Thus it leads to considerable savings in storage space.

The rest of this paper is organized as follows. In the next section, the 2LSF is reviewed. The BS2LSF is proposed in Sec. 3. Performance analysis and comparisons of 2LSF and BS2LSF are included in Sec. 4. Section 5 describes the refined method, 1SF. Conclusions are given in Sec. 6.

2. Review of the Two-Level Spatial Filter (2LSF)

The 2LSF [10] is based on the *signature file* technique [6] to speed up the retrieval of images indexed by 2D strings. The signature file method has been widely employed in information retrieval systems to speed up the retrieval of both formatted and unformatted data.

In 2LSF, each pairwise spatial relationship contained in a 2D string (u, v), is represented by a spatial string as described below. Suppose the two objects that participated in the pairwise spatial relationship are A and B, where A is less than B in alphabetical order. The spatial relationships between A and B can be denoted by spatial characters, which are determined by the ranks of A and B. Let $r(X)$ be the rank of object X in a 1D string. The type-i spatial character, $V^i(A, B)$, denoting the type-i spatial relationship between A and B is defined as follows:

$$
\begin{array}{lll}
\text{(type-0)} & V^0(A, B) = \text{``0''} & \text{if } r(A) = r(B) \\
& V^0(A, B) = \text{``1'' or } V^0(A, B) = \text{``0''} & \text{if } r(A) < r(B) \\
& V^0(A, B) = \text{``2'' or } V^0(A, B) = \text{``0''} & \text{if } r(A) > r(B) \\
\text{(type-1)} & V^1(A, B) = \text{``0''} & \text{if } r(A) = r(B) \\
& V^1(A, B) = \text{``1''} & \text{if } r(A) < r(B) \\
& V^1(A, B) = \text{``2''} & \text{if } r(A) > r(B) \\
\text{(type-2)} & V^2(A, B) = \text{``00''} & \text{if } r(A) = r(B) \\
& V^2(A, B) = \text{``1''} + str(r(B) - r(A)) & \text{if } r(A) < r(B) \\
& V^2(A, B) = \text{``2''} + str(r(A) - r(B)) & \text{if } r(A) > r(B)
\end{array}
$$

where "+" denotes string concatenation, and $str(X)$ is a transformation function from integer X to string "X".

The type-i spatial string, $S^i(A, B)$, is the concatenation of the two symbols A, B and the two type-i spatial characters $V_u^i(A, B)$ and $V_v^i(A, B)$, where $V_u^i(A, B)$ and $V_v^i(A, B)$ are the type-i spatial characters of A, B in 1D strings u and v, respectively. For example, in $s = (u, v) = (ad < b < c, ac < b < d), r_u(a) = 1 < r_u(c) = 3$ and $r_v(a) = 1 = r_v(c) = 1$. The type-i

spatial strings, $S^i(a, c)$, representing the type-i spatial relationships between a and c for $i = 0$ to 2 are:

$$S^0(a, c) = \text{``ac10''} \text{ or } \text{``ac00''} ,$$
$$S^1(a, c) = \text{``ac10''} , \text{ and}$$
$$S^2(a, c) = \text{``ac1200''} .$$

In 2LSF, several 2D strings are grouped as a *block*. Each 2D string is associated with a *record signature* of b_r bits, and each block of 2D strings is associated with a *block signature* of b_b bits. The record signature of a 2D string for type-i subpicture matching is generated as follows:

Step 1. Extract the type-i spatial strings from the 2D string.

Step 2. Generate a *record term signature* of b_r bits for each of the type-i spatial strings by hash functions. Each record term signature contains exactly k_r 1 bits. (In general, k_r hash functions are used to decide the positions of 1-bits. The k_r positions hashed are all distinct.)

Step 3. OR all the record term signatures together to result in a record signature.

For example, suppose $b_r = 8, k_r = 2$, and the record term signatures of the type-1 spatial strings extracted from $s = (ad < b < c, ac < b < d)$ are shown in Table 1. The record signature of s for type-1 subpicture matching is 01111001.

The block signature of a block of 2D strings for type-i subpicture matching is generated in the similar way. A *block term signature* of b_b bits is generated for each type-i spatial string extracted from the 2D strings of the block. Each block term signature contains exactly k_b 1 bits. ORing all the block term

Table 1. The record term signatures for some spatial strings.

Spatial String	Record term signature
ab11	01000001
ac10	00100001
ad01	01010000
bc12	00101000
bd21	01001000
cd21	00110000

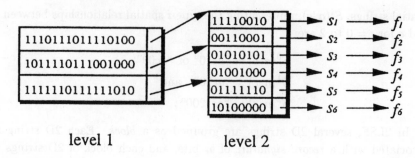

level 1   **level 2**

Fig. 3. A two-level signature file.

signatures together results in the block signature. In general, b_b is larger than b_r, since much more information is to be represented in a block signature.

Associated with each block signature is a pointer pointing to the record signatures of the 2D strings contained in the block. A pointer is also associated with each record signature to point to the corresponding 2D string. The block signatures (together with the pointers) are stored sequentially to constitute the first level of the two-level signature file, and the record signatures of a block are also stored sequentially to constitute the second level. For example, consider a spatial database with six images, $f_1, f_2, \ldots, f_6$. Let the 2D strings of the six images be $s_1, s_2, \ldots, s_6$. A two-level signature file for the spatial database is shown in Fig. 3.

Note that one two-level signature file is needed for each type of subpicture matching. Therefore, three two-level signature files are employed in 2LSF.

While processing a query represented by a 2D string, the block signature and the record signature of the query are generated. The *query block signature* (the block signature of the query) is ANDed to each block signature. If the result is equal to the query block signature (i.e. all the 1's in the query block signature are also contained in the block signature examined), the corresponding block may contain a 2D string that qualifies the query; otherwise, it can be certain that no qualified 2D string is contained in the block. Because of the information loss in representing a block of 2D strings by a block signature, the block that matches the query may not contain any answer. We call the case a *false block match*. The probability that a flase record match occurs is known as the *false* record match probability. To exclude a flase block match occurs is the *false block match probability*. Each record signature of the matched block is then ANDed to the *query record signature* (the record signature of the query).

If the result is equal to the query record signature, the 2D string s pointed by the record signature is a possible answer. Similarly, s may not be a true answer, because of the information loss in representing a 2D string by a record signature. The case is called a *false record match*. While examining a block of record signatures, the probability that a false record match occurs is known as the *false record match probability*. To exclude a false record match, the 2D subsequence matching is performed. If the query is a 2D subsequence of s, then the image pointed by s qualifies the query.

The two-level spatial filter provides an efficient way to retrieve images from spatial database. However, all the bits of the block signatures should be examined, as well as all the bits of the record signatures contained in a matched block. It is time consuming when the signature file is large. In the next section, a new spatial filter is proposed to improve the performance of the image retrieval.

3. The Bit-Sliced Two-Level Spatial Filter (BS2LSF)

3.1. *The algorithm*

The new proposed method, $BS2LSF$, uses the *bit-slice* storage technique [17] to reduce the amount of signature data examined. In BS2LSF, the record signatures and the block signatures are generated in a similar way as in 2LSF. However, the block signatures and the record signatures are not stored sequentially. They are stored by *bit-slices*.

Suppose there are N_b block signatures, each of which is b_b bits long. The collection of the block signatures can be viewed as a $N_b \times b_b$ two-dimensional bit array. A row of the two-dimensional bit array is a block signature, and a column is a *block bit-slice*. The two-level spatial signature file suggests that the two-dimensional bit array is to be stored row by row. On the contrary, the bit-sliced two-level spatial filter suggests storing the two-dimensional bit array column by column. Suppose a query is issued and the query block signature contains Q_b 1's. In the bit-sliced two-level spatial filter, only the relevant Q_b block bit-slices, rather than all the block signatures, have to be examined. That is, only $Q_b N_b$ bits rather than $b_b N_b$ bits have to be examined. Since in general $Q_b \ll b_b$, it is clear that considerable costs for retrieval are saved.

The same storage technique is also applied to store each block of record signatures. In the two-dimensional bit array constituted by a block of record signatures, a column is a *record bit-slice*. The two-dimensional bit array is then stored by record bit-slices. In our scheme, we will choose appropriate design parameters in order that the record signatures of a block can fit entirely within a disk page, ensuring that retrieving the record signatures of a block costs only one disk access.

The pointers associated with the block signatures are stored sequentially in another file, and so are the pointers associated with the record signatures. The block bit-slices and the pointers associated with the block signatures constitute the first level of the bit-sliced two-level signature file; the record bit-slices and the pointers associated with the record signatures constitute the second. When a query is issued, the process of image retrieval via the bit-sliced two-level spatial filter follows.

Step 1. The block signature and the record signature of the query (represented by a 2D string q) is generated.

Step 2. For each 1's in the query block signature, corresponding block bit-slices are retrieved and successively ANDed. Let the result be BBS. The block that corresponds to a 1 bit in BBS is a match.

A block whose signature contains all the 1's of the query block signature is a match. Since the relevant bit-slices is successively ANDed to be BBS, the block that corresponds to a 1-bit in BBS contains all the 1's of the query block signature and is a match. However, the matched block may not contain any 2D string that qualifies the query since a false block match may occur.

Step 3. For each matched block, the record bit-slices corresponding to the 1's in the query record signature are retrieved and successively ANDed. Let the result be RBS. The record signature that corresponds to a 1-bit in RBS is a match. Let the 2D string pointed by the matched record signature be s.

Likewise, s may not qualify the query since a false record match may occur. Therefore the following step is required.

Step 4. The 2D subsequence matching is performed. If the query, q, is a 2D subsequence of s, then the image pointed by s is retrieved as an answer to the query.

The complete algorithm follows.

Algorithm: Retrieval-of-images-via-bit-sliced-two-level-spatial-filter

INPUT: the 2D string, q, that represents the query.

OUTPUT: the images which qualify the query.

BEGIN

generate the query block signature QBS and the query record signature QRS initialize all bits in a block bit-slice, BBS, for the result of successively AND to be 1

FOR each bit B_i in QBS **DO**

 IF B_i is a 1-bit **THEN**

  retrieve the ith block bit-slice BS^i

  $BBS = BBS \cap BS^i$

 END-IF

END-FOR

FOR each bit C_i in BBS **DO**

 IF C_i is a 1-bit **THEN**

  initialize all bits in a record bit-slice, RBS_i, for the result of successively AND to be 1

  FOR each bit D_j in QRS **DO**

   IF D_j is a 1-bit **THEN**

    retrieve the jth record bit-slice RS_i^j of block i

    $RBS_i = RBS_i \cap RS_i^j$

   END-IF

  END-FOR

  FOR each bit E_j in RBS_i **DO**

   IF E_j is a 1-bit **THEN**

    let the 2D string pointed by the jth record signature of block i be s

    IF q is a 2D subsequence of s **THEN**

     output the image pointed by s

    END-IF

   END-FOR

 END-IF

END-FOR

END-OF-ALGORITHM

3.2. *An example*

Suppose there are six images $f_1, f_2, \ldots, f_6$ in the spatial database. The symbolic pictures of the six images are:

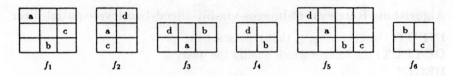

The 2D string representations of $f_1, f_2, \ldots, f_6$ are:

$$s_1 = (a < b < c,\, b < c < a),$$
$$s_2 = (ca < d,\, c < a < d),$$
$$s_3 = (d < a < b,\, a < db),$$
$$s_4 = (d < b,\, b < d),$$
$$s_5 = (d < a < b < c,\, bc < a < d),\text{ and}$$
$$s_6 = (b < c,\, c < b)\text{ respectively}.$$

Suppose there are three blocks: block 1 contains f_1, f_2, block 2 contains f_3, f_4, and block 3 contains f_5, f_6. Let the lengths of each block and each record signature be 16 and 8, respectively. For each 2D spatial strings, two bits are set to 1 in the record signature while three bits are set to 1 in the block signature. The record and block term signatures for the 2D spatial strings are shown in Table 2.

Table 2. Block term signatures and record term signatures generated for the 2D spatial strings in the illustrating example.

Spatial string	Record term signature	Block term signature
ab11	01000001	1000100001000000
ab12	01000010	1000010000100000
ac02	00100001	1000010000010000
ac12	00100010	0100100010000000
ad11	00010001	0100100000100000
ad21	00010100	0010010001000000
bc10	00100100	0100100001000000
bc11	10010000	0010001000100000
bc12	10100000	0001000100010000
bd20	01010000	0001000100001000
bd21	01001000	0000100010001000
cd11	00110000	0000100001000100
cd21	00010010	0010010000000010

The construction of the bit-sliced two-level signature file is shown below.

Step 1. The sets S_j^1 of type-1 spatial strings of f_j for $j = 1$ to 6 are generated as

$$S_1^1 = \{\text{``ab12''}, \text{``ac12''}, \text{``bc11''}\}$$
$$S_2^1 = \{\text{``ac02''}, \text{``ad11''}, \text{``cd11''}\}$$
$$S_3^1 = \{\text{``ab11''}, \text{``ad21''}, \text{``bd20''}\}$$
$$S_4^1 = \{\text{``bd21''}\}$$
$$S_5^1 = \{\text{``ab12''}, \text{``ac12''}, \text{``ad21''}, \text{``bc10''}, \text{``bd21''}, \text{``cd21''}\}$$
$$S_6^1 = \{\text{``bc12''}\}$$

Step 2. The sets, B_j^1, $j = 1$ to 3, of type-1 spatial strings for the three blocks are

$$B_1^1 = \{\text{``ab12''}, \text{``ac12''}, \text{``bc11''}, \text{``ac02''}, \text{``ad11''}, \text{``cd11''}\}$$
$$B_2^1 = \{\text{``ab11''}, \text{``ad21''}, \text{``bd20''}, \text{``bd21''}\}$$
$$B_3^1 = \{\text{``ab12''}, \text{``ac12''}, \text{``ad21''}, \text{``bc10''}, \text{``bd21''}, \text{``cd21''}, \text{``bc12''}\}$$

Step 3. The record term signatures of S_j^1 and the block term signatures of B_j^1 are generated according to Table 2. ORing the record term signatures of R_j^1 results in the record signature, RS_j, of f_j, where

$$RS_1 = 11110010, \quad RS_2 = 00110001,$$
$$RS_3 = 01010101, \quad RS_4 = 01001000,$$
$$RS_5 = 01111110, \quad RS_6 = 10100000.$$

ORing the block term signatures of B_j results in the block signature, BS_j, of block j, where

$$BS_1 = 1110111011110100,$$
$$BS_2 = 1011110111001000,$$
$$BS_3 = 1111110111111010.$$

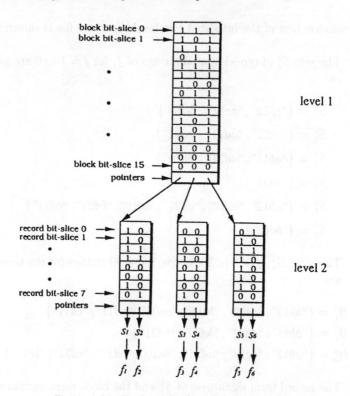

Fig. 4. A bit-sliced two-level spatial signature file.

Fig. 5. The symbolic picture of the query.

Step 4. Storing the block signatures by block bit-slice and the record signatures of a block by record bit-slice, the type-1 bit-sliced two level signature file is constructed as shown in Fig. 4. (Note: Fig. 3 is its two-level counterpart.)

Suppose the query is: "Find all the images in which a is northwest of c, d is northwest of a, and c is southeast of d." The 2D string representing the query is $(d < a < c, c < a < d)$, and the symbolic picture of the query is shown in Fig. 5. The process of type-1 image retrieval via BS2LSF follows:

Step 1. The type-1 spatial strings of the query are generated as $Q_1 = \{$ "ac12", "ad21", "cd21" $\}$.

Step 2. The query block signature QBS and the query record signature QRS are generated according to Table 2 as $QBS = 0110110011000010$, $QRS = 00110110$.

Step 3. According to the positions of 1's in QBS, block bit-slices 1,2,4,5,8,9 and 14 are retrieved and ANDed. The result is 001. Therefore, only the third block is matched.

Step 4. According to the position of 1's in RBS, record bit-slices 2, 3, 5 and 6 of the third block record signatures are retrieved and ANDed. The result is 10. It indicates that f_5 is a possible solution.

Step 5. Because the 2D string representing the query $(d < a < c, c < a < d)$, is a type-1 2D subsequence of $s_5 = (d < a < b < c, bc < a < d)$, f_5 is retrieved as the answer to the query.

In this example, the amount of signature data retrieved is 29 bits. However, if the two-level spatial filter is used, 64 bits have to be retrieved. Above half of the retrieval time is saved in this example.

4. Performance Analysis and Comparisons

In this section, the costs of the two spatial filters (2LSF and BS2LSF) for image retrieval are analyzed. Comparisons of the two filters are also given.

Notations used in this section are described as follows.

k_r: number of bits set to 1 in a record term signature.
k_b: number of bits set to 1 in a block term signature.
K_r: expected weight (number of 1's) of a record signature.
K_b: expected weight of a block signature.
Q_r: expected weight of the query record signature.
Q_b: expected weight of the query block signature.
b_r: length of a record signature.
b_b: length of a block signature.
N_r: number of 2D strings in a block.
N_b: number of blocks.
N : number of 2D strings in the spatial database. (equals to $N_b \cdot N_r$.)
n_r: average number of spatial terms contained in a 2D string.

n_b: average number of spatial terms contained in a block of
       2D strings.
n_q: number of spatial terms contained in the query.
P_r: false record match probability.
P_b: false block match probability.
P :   page size in bit.
T_s: average seek time.
T_d: time required to transfer a bit from disk.
T_a: time required to perform an AND on two bits.
T_o: time required to locate the position of 1 within a word.
T_c: time required to compare two bits.
T_r: time required to retrieve a 2D string and perform the 2D
       subsequence matching.
T_h: time required to calculate a hash function.

We assume that k_r (k_b) hash functions are used to decide the k_r (k_b) distinct positions to be set to 1 in the record (block) term signature for each spatial term. Moreover, the spatial terms appearing in each image are of uniform distribution.

Since the number of blocks of record signatures to be examined depends on the false block match probability, and the number of 2D strings to be examined depends on the false record match probability, P_b and P_r are derived first. The signatures of the two spatial filter are generated by the same method, therefore the false block match probability of the two spatial filters is the same, and so is the false record match probability. The derivations follow.

The expected proportion of 1's in a block signature is

$$1 - \left(1 - \frac{k_b}{b_b}\right)^{n_b}.$$

A false block match is detected if in a block signature the bits positioned by the 1's in the query block signature are all 1's. Therefore the false block match probability is

$$\left[1 - \left(1 - \frac{k_b}{b_b}\right)^{n_b}\right]^{Q_b}.$$

Since there is $1 - (1 - \frac{k_b}{b_b})^{n_q}$ of 1's in the query block signature, the expected weight of the query block signature is

$$Q_b = \left[1 - \left(1 - \frac{k_b}{b_b}\right)^{n_q}\right] \cdot b_b.$$

The false block match probability is then

$$P_b = \left[1 - \left(1 - \frac{k_b}{b_b}\right)^{n_b}\right]^{[1-(1-\frac{k_b}{b_b})^{n_q}]\cdot b_b}.$$

The false record match probability can be derived in the same manner. It is

$$Pr = \left[1 - \left(1 - \frac{k_r}{b_r}\right)^{n_r}\right]^{[1-(1-\frac{k_r}{b_r})^{n_q}]\cdot b_r}.$$

4.1. Cost formulas for the two spatial filters

In the following, the image retrieval cost of the two-level spatial filter is analyzed step by step.

First the cost for generating the query block signature and the query record signature is

$$\begin{aligned} C_1 &= n_q \cdot k_b \cdot T_h + n_q \cdot k_r \cdot T_h \\ &= n_q \cdot T_h \cdot (k_b + k_r). \end{aligned}$$

The cost for retrieving all the block signatures is

$$C_2 = \left\lceil \frac{b_b \cdot N_b}{P} \right\rceil \cdot (T_s + P \cdot T_d).$$

To decide which block is matched, the query block signature is ANDed to each block signature. If the result is equal to the query block signature, the block is matched. Therefore the cost for deciding the matched block is

$$C_3 = N_b \cdot (b_b \cdot T_a + b_b \cdot T_c) = N_b \cdot b_b \cdot (T_a + T_c).$$

For each matched block, the cost for retrieving all the record signatures in this block is

$$C_{41} = \left\lceil \frac{b_r \cdot N_r}{P} \right\rceil \cdot (T_s + P \cdot T_d),$$

and the cost for deciding matched records of this block is

$$C_{42} = N_r \cdot b_r \cdot (T_a + T_c).$$

Since the expected number of matched blocks is $N_b \cdot P_b$, total cost of this step is

$$C_4 = N_b \cdot P_b \cdot \left[\left\lceil \frac{b_r \cdot N_r}{P} \right\rceil \cdot (T_s + P \cdot T_d) + N_r \cdot b_r \cdot (T_a + T_c) \right].$$

The expected number of matched 2D strings can be evaluated by $N \cdot P_b \cdot P_r$, therefore the cost for retrieving the matched 2D strings and performing 2D subsequence matching is

$$C_5 = N \cdot P_b \cdot P_r \cdot T_r.$$

The total cost of image retrieval via the two-level spatial filter is then

$$C = C_1 + C_2 + C_3 + C_4 + C_5$$
$$= n_q \cdot T_h \cdot (k_b + k_r) + \left(\left\lceil \frac{b_b \cdot N_b}{P} \right\rceil + N_b \cdot P_b \cdot \left\lceil \frac{b_r \cdot N_r}{P} \right\rceil \right) \cdot (T_s + P \cdot T_d)$$
$$+ (N_b \cdot b_b + N \cdot P_b \cdot b_r) \cdot (T_a + T_c) + N \cdot P_b \cdot P_r \cdot T_r.$$

The image retrieval cost of the bit-sliced two-level spatial filter is analyzed in a similar mannar as follows.

The cost for generating the query block signature and the query record signature is

$$D_1 = n_q \cdot k_b \cdot T_h + n_q \cdot k_r \cdot T_h$$
$$= n_q \cdot T_h \cdot (k_b + k_r).$$

The cost for retrieving the block bit-slices according to the positions of l's in the query block signature is

$$D_2 = Q_b \cdot T_o + Q_b \cdot \left\lceil \frac{N_b}{P} \right\rceil \cdot (T_s + P \cdot T_d).$$

After retrieving all the block bit-slices, the cost for successively ANDing the block bit-slices is

$$D_3 = (Q_b - 1) \cdot N_b \cdot T_a.$$

Let the result of successive AND be BBS. For each block which corresponds to a 1-bit in BBS, three steps are performed:

Step 1.   Retrieve the record bit-slices of the block according to the positions of 1's in the query record signature.

Since all the record bit-slices of a block are stored in a disk page in our design, one disk access is required in this step. Hence this step costs

$$D_{41} = Q_r \cdot T_o + T_s + P \cdot T^d.$$

Step 2. Successively AND the record bit-slices retrieved. Let the result be *RBS*. It costs

$$D_{42} = (Q_r - 1) \cdot N_r \cdot T_a.$$

Step 3. Retrieve each 2D string that corresponds to a 1-bit in *RBS* and perform 2D subsequence matching.

Since the number of 1's in the result of the last step is the number of matched record signatures in the block, and can be estimated by $N_r \cdot P_r$, this step costs

$$D_{43} = N_r \cdot P_r \cdot (T_o + T_r).$$

The number of 1's in *BBS* is the number of matched blocks, and can be estimated by $N_b \cdot P_b$. Therefore

$$
\begin{aligned}
D_4 &= N_b \cdot P_b \cdot T_o + N_b \cdot P_b \cdot (D_{41} + D_{42} + D_{43}) \\
&= N_b \cdot P_b \cdot [T_o + Q_r \cdot T_o + T_s + P \cdot T_d \\
&\quad + (Q_r - 1) \cdot N_r \cdot T_a + N_r \cdot P_r \cdot (T_o + T_r)].
\end{aligned}
$$

The total retrieval cost of the bit-sliced two-level signature file is then

$$
\begin{aligned}
D &= D_1 + D_2 + D_3 + D_4 \\
&= n_q \cdot T_h \cdot (k_b + k_r) + \left(Q_b \cdot \left\lceil \frac{N_b}{P} \right\rceil + N_b \cdot P_b \right) \cdot (T_s + P \cdot T_d) \\
&\quad + [(Q_b - 1) \cdot N_b + (Q_r - 1) \cdot N \cdot P_b] \cdot T_a \\
&\quad + (Q_b + N_b \cdot P_b + N_b \cdot P_b \cdot Q_r + N \cdot P_b \cdot P_r) \cdot T_o + N \cdot P_b \cdot P_r \cdot T_r.
\end{aligned}
$$

4.2. *Comparisons*

Subtracting D from C and simplifying the result by assuming that $T_o = T_c$, we have

$$C - D = \left(\left\lceil \frac{b_b \cdot N_b}{P} \right\rceil - Q_b \cdot \left\lceil \frac{N_b}{P} \right\rceil \right) (T_s + P \cdot T_d) \qquad (1)$$

$$+N_b \cdot P_b \cdot \left(\left\lceil \frac{b_r \cdot N_r}{P} \right\rceil - 1 \right) \cdot (T_s + P \cdot T_d) \tag{2}$$

$$+N_b \cdot (b_b - Q_b + 1) \cdot T_a \tag{3}$$

$$+N \cdot P_b \cdot (b_r - Q_r + 1) \cdot T_a \tag{4}$$

$$+N_b \cdot \left(b_b - \frac{Q_b}{N_b} - P_b - P_b \cdot Q_r \right) \cdot T_c \tag{5}$$

$$+N \cdot P_b \cdot (b_r - P_r) \cdot T_c . \tag{6}$$

Since typically $Q_b \ll b_b, Q_r \ll b_r$ and $b_r < b_b$, the terms from (2) to (6) of the above equation are all ≥ 0. In the following, the condition that $(1) \geq 0$ is derived. By using the inequation $x \leq \lceil x \rceil < x + 1$,

$$(1) > \frac{N_b \cdot b_b}{P} - Q_b \cdot \left(\frac{N_b}{P} + 1 \right) = N_b \cdot \frac{b_b - Q_b}{P} - Q_b .$$

Since $N_b \cdot \frac{b_b - Q_b}{P} - Q_b > 0$ when $N_b > P \cdot \frac{Q_b}{b_b - Q_b}$, we have

$$(1) > 0, \text{ if } N_b > P \cdot \frac{Q_b}{b_b - Q_b} .$$

It is then concluded that $C > D$ when $N_b > P \cdot \frac{Q_b}{b_b - Q_b}$. That is, the bit-sliced two-level spatial filter has a lower cost for image retrieval if the number of blocks, N_b, is large.

$$k_r = 2,$$
$$k_b = 2,$$
$$P = 8192.$$
$$b_r = \text{varying from 40 to 120},$$
$$b_b = b_r \cdot 30,$$
$$N_r = P/b_r,$$
$$N_b = N/N_r,$$
$$n_r = 20,$$
$$n_b = N_r \cdot n_r,$$
$$n_q = 2,$$
$$T_s = 35 \text{ milliseconds},$$
$$T_d = T_a = T_o = T_c = 0.2 \text{ microseconds},$$
$$T_r = 40 \text{ milliseconds},$$
$$T_h = 9 \text{ microseconds} .$$

Fig. 6. The design parameters used in analytical comparisons.

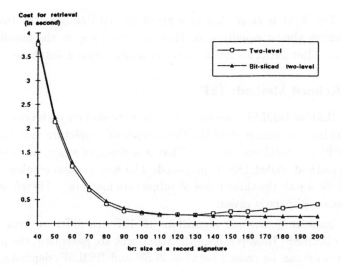

Fig. 7. Comparison of the two schemes when the number of 2D strings $N = 1024$.

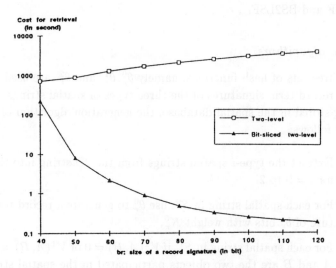

Fig. 8. Comparison of the two schemes when the number of 2D strings $N = 1048576$.

Figures 7 and 8 show the retrieval costs of the two spatial filters. In Fig. 7, the number of 2D strings, N is 1024, and in Fig. 8, $N = 1048576$. Both figures are draw under the operating environments depicted in Fig. 6. Some of the parameters are adopted from [13, 15, 16].

From Fig. 7, it is clear that in a small spatial database the two spatial filters perform almost equally well. However, from Fig. 8, the bit-sliced two-level spatial filter performs much better in a large spatial database.

5. The Refined Method: 1SF

In either 2LSF or BS2LSF, one signature file is needed for each type of subpicture matching. To accomodate the three types of subpicture matching, three signature files in total are created. That is a waste of space. In this section, a refined method, called 1SF, is proposed. The new method employs only one signature file for all the three types of subpicture matching. Therefore, a great deal of memory space is saved.

The signature generation algorithms in 1SF are different from those in 2LSF and BS2LSF. However, once the signatures are generated, the process of image retrieval can be chosen between 2LSF and BS2LSF, depending on the organization of the signature file. That is, the idea of 1SF can be applied to both 2LSF and BS2LSF.

5.1. *The algorithms*

In 1SF, three sets of hash functions, namely θ_r^0, θ_r^1, and θ_r^2, are used to determine the record term signatures of the three types of spatial strings. For each 2D string stored in the spatial database, the generation algorithm of a record signature follows:

Step 1. Extract the type-i spatial strings from the 2D string into the set S^i, for $i = 0$ to 2.

Step 2. For each spatial string in S^0, use θ_r^0 to generate a record term signature of b_r bits with weight K_r^0.

Step 3. For each spatial string in S^1, if $V_u^1(A, B) = 0$ or $V_v^1(A, B) = 0$ (where A and B are the two objects participated in the spatial string), use θ_r^1 to generate a record term signature of b_r bits with weight k_r^1.

Step 4. For each spatial string in S^2, use θ_r^2 to generate a record term signature of b_r bits with weight k_r^2.

Step 5. OR all the record term signatures generated in Steps 2, 3, and 4 together to result in a record signature.

The block signature of a block of 2D strings is generated in a similar way. Three sets of hash functions, namely θ_b^0, θ_b^1, and θ_b^2, are used to determine the block term signatures of the three types of spatial strings. The generation algorithm of a block signature follows:

Step 1. Extract the type-i spatial strings from the 2D strings contained in the block into the set B^i, for $i = 0$ to 2.

Step 2. For each spatial string in B^0, use θ_b^0 to generate a block term signature of b_b bits with weight k_b^0.

Step 3. For each spatial string in B^1, if $V_u^1(A, B) = 0$ or $V_v^1(A, B) = 0$ (where A and B are the two objects participating in the spatial string), use θ_b^1 to generate a block term signature of b_b bits with weight k_b^1.

Step 4. For each spatial string in B^2, use θ_b^2 to generate a block term signature of b_b bits with weight k_b^2.

Step 5. OR all the block term signatures together to result in a block signature.

Once all the record signatures and the block signatures are generated, the signatures can be stored as a two-level signature file or a bit-sliced two-level signature file as described in the previous sections.

For a query expressed as a 2D string, the generation algorithms of a record signature and a block signature are different from those for the 2D strings stored in the spatial database. The generation algorithm of a query record signature follows:

Step 1. Extract the type-i spatial strings from the 2D string that represents the query into the set Q^i, for $i = 0$ to 2.

Step 2. For each spatial string in Q^0, use θ_r^0 to generate a record term signature of b_r bits with weight k_r^0.

Step 3. If the query is of type-1 or type-2, then for each spatial string in Q^1, if $V_u^1(A, B) = 0$ or $V_v^1(A, B) = 0$ (where A and B are the two objects participating in the spatial string), use θ_r^1 or generate a record term signature of b_r bits with weight k_r^1.

Step 4. If the query is of type-2, then for each spatial string in Q^2, use θ_r^2 to generate a record term signature of b_r bits with weight k_r^2.

Step 5. OR all the record term signatures generated in Steps 2, 3, and 4 together to result in a query record signature.

The generation algorithm of a query block signature is similar:

Step 1. Extract the type-i spatial strings from the 2D string that represents the query into the set Q^i, for $i = 0$ to 2.

Step 2. For each spatial string in Q^0, use θ_b^0 to generate a block term signature of b_b bits with weight k_b^0.

Step 3. If the query is of type-1 or type-2, then for each spatial string in Q^1, if $V_u^1(A, B) = 0$ or $V_v^1(A, B) = 0$ (where $A\ B$ are the two objects participating in the spatial string), use θ_b^1 to generate a block term signature of b_b bits with weight k_b^1.

Step 4. If the query is of type-2, then for each spatial string in Q^2, use θ_b^2 to generate a block term signature of b_b bits with weight k_b^2.

Step 5. OR all the record term signatures generated in Steps 2, 3, and 4 together to result in a query block signature.

When a query is issued, the query record signature and the query block signature are generated by using the above algorithms. To find out the 2D strings that match the query, the retrieval algorithm of either 2LSF or BS2LSF is used according to the organization of the signature file. As we have seen in the previous section, the image retrieval is more efficient if BS2LSF is used.

5.2. *An example*

Suppose the spatial database contains the four images f_1, f_2, f_3, and f_4 shown in Fig. 9.

The 2D string representations of f_1, f_2, f_3, and f_4, are

$$f_1 : (a < c, c < a)$$
$$f_2 : (a < b < c, b < ac)$$
$$f_3 : (ac, c < a)$$
$$f_4 : (a < c, ac)$$

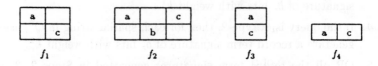

Fig. 9. The symbolic pictures of the four images.

Table 3. The record and block term signatures generated by θ_r^0 and θ_b^0.

Spatial string	Record term signature	Block term signature
ab12	0010001000	000010001000000000
ab10	1001000000	010000000100000000
ab02	0000010001	000001000000001000
ab00	0100001000	100000000001000000
ac12	0001010000	001000000000000010
ac10	0100000100	000010000100000000
ac02	0010000010	010000010000000000
ac00	1000010000	000001000000001000
bc11	0010100000	001000000100000000
bc10	0010000001	000000100000000100
bc01	0100000100	000100000000000001
bc00	0010001000	000000010000000010

Table 4. The record and block term signatures generated by θ_r^1 and θ_b^1.

Spatial string	Record term signature	Block term signature
ab12	0000001000	001000000000000000
ac12	0001000000	000000000100000000
ac10	0000000001	000001000000000000
ac02	0100000000	000000000001000000
bc11	0000010000	000000000000000010

Table 5. The record and block term signatures generated by θ_r^0 and θ_b^0.

Spatial string	Record term signature	Block term signature
ab1121	0000001000	001000000000000000
ac1200	0001000000	000000000000100000
ac1121	0000000100	000001000000000000
ac1100	0000000010	000000000000010000
ac0021	0000100000	000000000010000000
bc1111	0010000000	000000000100000000

The generation of record signatures for the four images is shown below.

Step 1. The sets S_j^i of type-i 2D spatial strings extracted from f_j for $i = 0$ to 2 and $j = 1$ to 4 are

$$S_1^0 = \{\text{``ac12''}, \text{``ac10''}, \text{``ac02''}, \text{``ac00''}\},$$

$$S_2^0 = \{\text{``ab12''}, \text{``ab10''}, \text{``ab02''}, \text{``ab00''}, \text{``ac10''}$$
$$\text{``ac00''}, \text{``bc11''}, \text{``bc10''}, \text{``bc01''}, \text{``bc00''}\},$$

$$S_3^0 = \{\text{``ac02''}, \text{``ac00''}\},$$

$$S_4^0 = \{\text{``ac10''}, \text{``ac00''}\},$$

$$S_1^1 = \{\text{``ac12''}\},$$

$$S_2^1 = \{\text{``ac12''}, \text{``ac10''}, \text{``bc11''}\},$$

$$S_3^1 = \{\text{``ac02''}\},$$

$$S_4^1 = \{\text{``ac10''}\},$$

$$S_1^2 = \{\text{``ac1121''}\},$$

$$S_2^2 = \{\text{``ab1121''}, \text{``ac1200''}, \text{``bc1111''}\},$$

$$S_3^2 = \{\text{``ac0021''}\}, \text{ and}$$

$$S_4^2 = \{\text{``ac1100''}\}.$$

Step 2. For the spatial strings in S_j^0, the record term signatures generated by using Table 3 for $j = 1$ to 4 are

$\theta_r^0(S_1^0) = \{0001010000, 0100000100, 0010000010, 1000010000\},$

$\theta_r^0(S_2^0) = \{0010001000, 1001000000, 0000010001, 0100001000, 0100000100,$
$\quad\quad 1000010000, 0010100000, 0010000001, 0100000100, 0010001000\},$

$\theta_r^0(S_3^0) = \{0010000010, 1000010000\},$ and

$\theta_r^0(S_4^0) = \{0100000100, 1000010000\}.$

Step 3. For the spatial strings in S_j^1 where $V_u^1(A, B) = 0$ or $V_v^1(A, B) = 0$(A and B are the two objects participating in the spatial string), the record term signatures generated by using Table 4 for $j = 1$ to 4 are

$$\theta_r^1(S_1^1) = \{\},$$

$$\theta_r^1(S_2^1) = \{0000000001\},$$

$$\theta_r^1(S_3^1) = \{0100000000\}, \text{ and}$$

$$\theta_r^1(S_4^1) = \{0000000001\}.$$

Step 4. For the spatial string in S_j^2, the record term signatures generated by using Table 5 for $j = 1$ to 4 are

$$\theta_r^2(S_1^2) = \{0000000100\},$$

$$\theta_r^2(S_2^2) = \{0000001000, 0001000000, 0010000000\},$$

$$\theta_r^2(S_3^2) = \{0000100000\}, \text{ and }$$

$$\theta_r^2(S_4^2) = \{0000000010\}.$$

Step 5. ORing the record term signatures in $\theta_r^0(S_j^0), \theta_r^1(S_j^1)$, and $\theta_r^2(S_j^2)$ results in the record signature RS_j of image f_j for $j = 1$ to 4, where

$$RS_1 = 1111010110,$$

$$RS_2 = 1111111101,$$

$$RS_3 = 1110110010, \text{ and }$$

$$RS_4 = 1100010111.$$

The generation of block signatures for the two blocks of images is shown below.

Step 1. The sets B_j^i of type-i 2D spatial strings extracted from block j for $i = 0$ to 2 and $j = 1$ to 2 are

$$B_1^0 = \{\text{``ac12''}, \text{``ac10''}, \text{``ac02''}, \text{``ac00'}, \text{''ab12''}, ab10\text{''},$$
$$\text{``ab02''}, \text{``ab00''}, \text{``bc11''}, \text{``bc10''}, \text{``bc01''}, \text{``bc00''}\},$$

$$B_2^0 = \{\text{``ac02''}, \text{``ac00''}, \text{``ac10''}\},$$

$$B_1^1 = \{\text{``ac12''}, \text{``ab12''}, \text{``ac10''}, \text{``bc11''}\},$$

$$B_2^1 = \{\text{``ac02''}, \text{``ac10''}\},$$

$$B_1^2 = \{\text{``ac1121''}, \text{``ab1121''}, \text{``ac1200''}, \text{``bc1111''}\}, \text{ and }$$

$$B_2^2 = \{\text{``ac0021''}, \text{``ac1100''}\}.$$

Step 2. For the spatial strings in B_j^0, the block term signatures generated by using Table 3 for $j = 1$ to 2 are

$\theta_b^0(B_1^0) = \{001000000000000010, 000010000100000000, 010000010000000000,$

$\qquad\qquad 000001000000001000, 000010001000000000, 010000000100000000,$

$\qquad\qquad 000001000000001000, 100000000001000000, 001000000100000000,$

$\qquad\qquad 000000100000000100, 000100000000000001,$

$\qquad\qquad 000000010000000010\}$, and

$\theta_b^0(B_2^0) = \{010000010000000000, 000001000000001000, 000010000100000000\}$.

Step 3. For the spatial strings in B_j^1 where $V_u^1(A, B) = 0$ or $V_v^1(A, B) = 0$ (A and B are the two objects participating in the spatial string), the block term signatures generated by using Table 4 for $j = 1$ to 2 are

$\theta_b^1(B_1^1) = \{000001000000000000\}$,

$\theta_b^1(B_2^1) = \{000000000001000000, 000001000000000000\}$,

Step 4. For the spatial strings in B_j^2, the block term signatures generated by using table 5 for $j = 1$ to 2 are

$\theta_b^2(B_1^2) = \{000001000000000000, 001000000000000000,$

$\qquad\qquad 000000000000100000, 000000000100000000\}$ and

$\theta_b^2(B_2^2) = \{000000000010000000, 000000000000010000\}$.

Step 5. ORing the block term signatures in $\theta_b^0(B_j^0), \theta_b^1(B_j^1)$, and $\theta_b^2(B_j^2)$ results in the block signature BS_j of block j for $j = 1$ to 2, where

$$BS_1 = 11111111101101111 \text{ and}$$
$$BS_2 = 010011010111011000.$$

Supposing we organize the record signatures and block signatures as a two-level signature file, we then have Fig. 10.

Suppose the user wants to retrieve images by the subpicture f_q shown in Fig. 11. The 2D string representing the query subpicture is $(a < c, ac)$.

Step 0.1. The sets Q^i of type-i 2D spatial strings extracted from the query 2D string for $i = 0$ to 2 are

$$Q^0 = \{\text{"ac10", "ac00"}\}$$
$$Q^1 = \{\text{"ac10"}\} \text{ and}$$
$$Q^2 = \{\text{"ac1100"}\}.$$

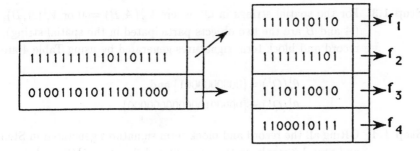

Fig. 10. The two-level signature file for three types of subpicture matching.

Fig. 11. The query subpicture f_q.

For type-0 subpicture matching, the query record signature and the query block signature are generated as follows.

Step 0.2. For the spatial strings in Q^0, the record and block term signatures generated by using Table 3 are

$$\theta_r^0(Q^0) = \{0100000100, 1000010000\} \text{ and}$$
$$\theta_b^0(Q^0) = \{000010000100000000, 000001000000001000\}.$$

Step 0.3. ORing all the record and block term signatures generated in Step 0.2 results in the query record signature QRS and the query block signature QBS, where

$$QRS = 1100010100 \text{ and}$$
$$QBS = 0000110001000010000.$$

Matching QBS and QRS through the two-level signature file shown in Fig. 10, we fine that f_1, f_2, and f_4 are possible answers.

For type-1 subpicture matching, the query record signature and the query block signature are generated as follows.

Step 1.1. The same as Step 0.1.

Step 1.2. The same as Step 0.2.

Step 1.3. For the spatial strings in Q^1 where $V_u^1(A, B) = 0$ or $V_v^1(A, B) = 0$ (A and B are the two objects participated in the spatial string), the record and block term signatures generated by using Table 4 are

$$\theta_r^1(Q^1) = \{0000000001\} \text{ and}$$
$$\theta_b^1(Q^1) = \{000001000000000000\}\,.$$

Step 1.4. ORing all the record and block term signatures generated in Step 1.2 and Step 1.3 results in the query record signature QRS and the query block signature QBS, where

$$QRS = 1100010101 \text{ and}$$
$$QBS = 000011000100001000\,.$$

Matching QBS and QRS through the two-level signature file shown in Fig. 10, we found that f_2 and f_4 are possible answers.

For type-2 subpicture matching, the query record signature and the query block signature are generated as follows.

Step 2.1. The same as Step 0.1.

Step 2.2. The same as Step 0.2.

Step 2.3. The same as Step 1.3.

Step 2.4. For the spatial strings in Q^2, the record and block term signatures generated by using Table 5 are

$$\theta_r^2(Q^2) = \{0000000010\} \text{ and}$$
$$\theta_b^2(Q^2) = \{000000000000010000\}.$$

Step 2.5. ORing all the record and block term signatures generated in Step 2.2, Step 2.3 and Step 2.4 results in the query record signature QRS and the query block signature QBS, where

$$QRS = 1100010111, \text{ and}$$
$$QBS = 000011000100011000.$$

Matching QBS and QRS through the two-level signature file shown in Fig. 10, we find that f_4 is a possible answer.

We can easily see from this example that only one signature file is constructed, and the three types of subpicture matching can all be accommodated. It is clear that 1SF requires far less disk space than the original 2LSF and BS2LSF.

6. Conclusions

A new image retrieval algorithm for 2D string, BS2LSF, is proposed. The cost formula of the proposed algorithm, as well as that of 2LSF, is derived. This is a difficult but important task for spatial query optimization. When comparing the costs of the two image retrieval algorithms, it is found that the proposed method is more suitable for large spatial database, which is generally the case.

As for all the algorithms that adopt the idea of the bit transposed file, BS2LSF suffers from the insertion difficulty. However, the batch processing proposed in [13] can control the cost of an insertion to within one disk access. We therefore conclude that if the retrieval frequency is much larger than the insertion frequency in a spatial database system and the spatial database is large, BS2LSF is advantageous in its low retrieval cost.

A refined image retrieval algorithm, 1SF, is also proposed in this paper. 1SF uses one signature file rather than three to accomodate three types of subpicture matching. The idea of 1SF can be applied to both 2LSF and BS2LSF to reduce the disk space needed for the filtering process. By applying 1SF to BS2LSF, both the time and space requirements of image retrieval are improved.

References

1. B. H. Bloom, "Space/time trade-offs in hash coding with allowable errors", *Commun. ACM* **13**, 7 (1970) 422–426.
2. S. K. Chang, Q. Y. Shi, and C. W. Yan, "Iconic indexing by 2D strings", *IEEE Trans. Pattern Anal. Mach. Intell.* **PAMI-9** (1987) 413–428.
3. S. K. Chang, C. W. Yan, D. Dimitrof, and T. Arndt, "An intelligent image database system", *IEEE Trans. Softw. Eng.* **14** (1988) 681–688.
4. S. K. Chang, *Principles of Pictorial information systems design* (Prentice-Hall, 1989).
5. D. J. Dewitt *et al.*, "Implementation techniques for main memory database systems", *Proc. ACM-SIGMOD Int. Conf. Management of Data*, (1984), pp. 1–8.
6. C. Faloutsos, "Access methods for text", *ACM Comput. Surv.* **17** (1985) 49–74.
7. O. Guenther and A. Buchmann, "Research issues in spatial databases", *SIGMOD Record* **19**, 4 (1990) 61–68.
8. A. Guttman, "R-trees: A dynamic index structure for spatial searching", *Proc. SIGMOD* (1984).

9. S. Y. Lee, M. K. Shan, and W. P. Yang, "Similarity retrieval of iconic image database", *Pattern Recogn.* **22** (1989) 675–682.

10. S. Y. Lee and M. K. Shan, "Access methods of image database", *Int. J. Pattern Recogn. Artif. Intell.* **4** (1990) 27–44.

11. J. T. Robinson, "The K-D-B-tree: A search structure for large multidimensional dynamic indexes", *Proc. SIGMOD* (1981) pp. 10–18.

12. R. Sacks-Davis and K. Ramamohanarao, "A two-level superimposed coding scheme for partial match retrieval", *Inform. Syst.* **8** (1983) 273–280.

13. R. Sacks-Davis and A. Kent, "Multikey access methods based on superimposed coding techniques", *ACM Trans. Database Syst.* **12** (1987) 655–696.

14. T. Sellis, N. Roussopoulos, and C. Faloutsos, "The R^+-tree: A dynamic index for multidimensional objects", *Proc. 13th Conf. on VLDB,* Brighton, England (1987).

15. J. C. R. Tseng and W. P. Yang, "2D random filter and analysis", *Int. J. Comput. Math.* **42** (1991) 33–45.

16. C. Y. Wong, W. P. Yang, J. C. R. Tseng, and M. Hsu, "Random filter and its analysis", *Int. J. Computer Math.* **33** (1990) 181–194.

17. H. K. T. Wong, H. Liu, F. Olken, D. Rotem, and L. Wong, "Bit transposed files", *Proc. 11th Conf. on Very Large Databases*, Stockholm, August 1985, pp. 448–457.

A PROTOTYPE MULTIMEDIA DATABASE SYSTEM
INCORPORATING ICONIC INDEXING

TIMOTHY ARNDT

Universita' di Salerno,
Facolta' di Ingegneria,
Sede di Benevento,
Plazzo Bosco,
82100 Benevento, Italy

and

RAVI KUPPANNA

Department of Computer Science,
Lamar University,
Beaumont, Texas 77710

A multimedia database is a database of multimedia documents and their constituent components (images, video, audio, and text). Efficient storage of the virious media aided by specialized indexing techniques and fast retrieval describes the essential functionality required of a multimedia database system. A prototype multimedia database system is described here. The prototype system incorporates iconic indexing for each of the major multimedia data types: image; audio; video; and document. The indexes provide a method for user-oriented, content-based retrieval of data. The indexes are based on spatial and/or temporal relationships between pairs of objects in the item being indexed.

1. Introduction

Multimedia computing has become possible largely because of the recent break-throughs in hardware technology as well as in software and algorithms. Com-mercial products are now available that are capable of making multimedia computing a reality. Low-cost, high speed input and output devices such as color scanners, digitizing cameras, sound boards, VCR controllers, and color laser printers are just a part of the enabling technology. Faster CPUs with vector processing capabilities and cheaper storage devices such as CD-ROMs, rewriteable optical disks, and digital audio tapes also contribute significantly to this next wave of computing. Research in areas of compression algorithms for multimedia data types is another reason why multimedia computing is becoming more widespread. Products incorporating this new type of computing are now widely available.

A multimedia database is a database of multimedia documents [5,17,18] that provides for storage and retrieval of these documents and their constituent components. Efficient storage of the various media comprising multimedia, aided by specialized indexing techniques and faster retrieval techniques, describes the essential functionality required of a multimedia database management system (MMDBMS).

A media-specific indexing and retrieval mechanism for multimedia databases has been provided in the prototype multimedia database management system described here. It is important to keep these media-specific mechanisms uniform. This means that the mechanisms are similar regardless of data type, but are specialized for the particular media/data type. It is also important that this mechanism be user-oriented and thus offer a way to address the contents of objects (this is known as content-addressability). The mechanism should allow queries based on specific properties of the contents such as the spatial arrangement of objects in an image.

Iconic indexing is a technique which assists in fast and easy retrieval of related images from a pictorial database by providing a mechanism for content-based queries. The image is first reduced to a symbolic picture. It is then converted to a 2D string [8] which is stored with appropriate pointers to the original image in the database. A 2D string is constructed from a user query and a 2D subsequence matching of this 2D query string with the 2D string of the images is performed to retrieve a group of images matching the query from the pictorial database. Iconic indexing, when extended to other data types, maintains uniformity. This technique holds much promise for future research.

One of the major requirements of a multimedia information processing system [21] is the development and maintenance of a multimedia document database. A multimedia document consists of multiple constituent objects of data types such as text, image, video, audio, and computer generated graphics, in a well-defined spatio-temporal arrangement. It should be possible to perform database operations on any one of the primitive objects individually or on a set of these objects grouped into a document. An example of a multimedia document is illustrated in Fig. 1.

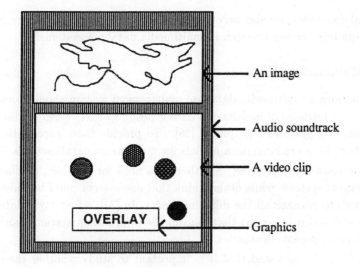

An image

Audio soundtrack

A video clip

OVERLAY

Graphics

Fig. 1. A multimedia document.

Operations such as add, delete and query are commonplace but important. It is necessary to provide these for a multimedia document database as well. It is also necessary to make these functions available for the individual objects so that alterations to a multimedia document are possible. This prototype multimedia database is part of an extended relational database and the tuples in the relational database help in relating objects to documents.

In the prototype system, a user can decide on the spatial arrangement of different objects that will eventually appear on the screen, in this way defining a multimedia document. The spatial arrangements of these objects can be decided dynamically or be statically bound during document creation.

The rest of this chapter is organized as follows. Section 2 surveys related research in the area of multimedia and pictorial database management systems. Section 3 describes the architecture of the prototype system. Section 4 shows how indexing is performed in the system. Section 5 describes the indexing methodology and the processing of queries. Section 6 contains a discussion of future research.

2. Related Research

In this section we survey related research in multimedia database systems. Since multimedia database research often builds on research in the area of pictorial databases, we also survey research in that area which is important for understanding further research in multimedia database systems.

2.1. *Multimedia databases*

The functions a multimedia database management system should provide are storage and retrieval of multimedia data types (e.g. text, video, audio, image, and computer generated graphics) [28]. To provide these capabilities, some researchers have explored data models for multimedia databases [16, 24, 29].

Some research groups feel that there is a need for multiple, media-specific management systems while others think that one system could be built powerful enough to manage all the different media. In [24], a four-layer data model is proposed and it is argued that multimedia information systems can best be queried using domain semantics.

In [28], it is suggested that it is important to study whether the existing services offered by textual DBMSs such as data independence, application neutrality, fault tolerance, access control, and multi-user operation are sufficient for a multimedia database management system. He argues that an MMDBMSs should concern itself only with storage and retrieval, nothing more and nothing less. Image processing, editing and other functions should not be part of the DBMS. However, such applications must be able to access the database for the objects and then should be able to store the results in the database. A file system, on the other hand, or a (relational) DBMs with just "binary large objects" (BLOBs) falls short of the quality of data management already available for formatted data, particularly with respect to data independence. Also, an "atomized" storage where words of a text or pixels of an image are stored as separate entities (e.g. in tuples of a relation), falls short of the needs of most applications that want to treat the data objects as a whole.

As regards which of the current DBMSs are best suited for multimedia, there are two schools of thought: one favors an extension of the relational model and the other favors object-oriented database systems. While the relationships among the data objects support navigational access, there is also a need to search in a descriptive way and DBMSs must address the problem of content addressability [29]. There are several major issues for research in this area:

– Performance of multimedia database systems is a very important issue since time-dependent media such as audio and video produce large amounts of data which affect, among other things, database buffer management.

Integration of continuous media is an important topic in the framework of database management systems, database integration, and database interoperability [29].

- Extensible DBMSs offer mechanisms to define abstract data types for multimedia objects. These mechanisms are widely used as a means to achieve data independence. Design of abstract data types for multimedia objects is a problem. There is a tradeoff between data independence and flexibility of use of data objects [28]. A proper embedding of these ADTs into a data model is required to allow for the representation of relationships among the objects and to get the power of a query language for accessing these objects.

- Research on standardizing formats of data objects is underway and this is an important part of any information system. This is especially important for multimedia information systems since the data objects consume much storage space. Compression mechanisms for efficient storage and various protocols for effective information exchange are to be standardized.

One of the most important parts of an MMDBMS is a support query language, and many researchers have proposed different ways of indexing to support query languages. One major concern is to support content-based queries. In one system, researchers have implemented a query language called EVA [13] which, in addition to the capabilities of an ordinary query language, deals with the spatial and temporal aspects of information retrieval and delivery. They accomplish this task with the help of query, update, computational, space management, and temporal operators. They provide DBMSs with some operators such as pan and zoom for images and clip and pace for video. Since multimedia data objects require huge amounts of storage space, replicating them is expensive. Therefore, sharing of data is required. If sharing is to be provided, then the problems of concurrency control and access control must be addressed.

Bertino, Rabitti, and Gibbs [5] describe a query language based on a conceptual document model that allows the users to formulate queries on both document content and structure. They outline a system in which multimedia data objects are stored on different storage media. They provide different strategies and algorithms for query processing for multimedia documents. Another group has provided a vector-based data model for content-based retrieval of multimedia objects from an MMDBMS [12]. They analyze an object and store its index in the database. Retrieval of objects is based on similarity estimation, a model that they propose, between query and, index vectors. They provide an example system with a polygon similarity estimation model implemented for geometrical objects, where each vector contains text and image objects. They consider images to be either geometrical or fractal objects in their analysis. Their main objective is to introduce the similarity estimation model for geometrical objects as a part of a query mechanism for a multimedia cognitive-based information retrieval.

Object-oriented database management systems are critically analyzed in [23]. The limitations of an object in modeling a time variant multimedia data type are noted. Objects are inherently discrete, conceptually containing the state of a system at a fixed point in space and time. Continuous media, such as voice and video, flow across time with no convenient boundaries for object representation. Objects can be used to represent discrete parts of this flow, but do not readily represent the entire flow. Object-based systems are being used for many tasks mainly because of their benefits of improved encapsulation. An object-oriented MMDBMS is implemented by breaking the continuous media into chunks and, instead of storing each chunk in an object, the objects are represented by points in space past which these chunks must flow over time.

Two temporal models are proposed in [16] for time-dependent data retrieval in a MMDBMS. These models are shown to be useful for facilitating storage and retrieval of time-dependent multimedia data. The models apply a temporal hierarchy supported by a relational model. They introduce temporal relations which permit forward, reverse and partial interval evaluation during multimedia object playout. An MMDBMS must have the capability for managing the aspects of time required for time-dependent media. Time-dependent multimedia objects require special considerations in presentations due to their real-time playout characteristics. Random system delays can cause short term jitter or long term skew on the synchronized streams of multimedia data when they are played out. These are real challenges to be addressed.

For efficient storage to help in playback [22] proposes a storage mechanism for audio and video data. A file system for storing "strands" of multimedia data on a disk is proposed. A strand is a sequence of continuously sampled video frames and/or audio samples. Techniques for merging the storage of multiple media strands, interleaved such that the continuity of retrieval of each media strand is preserved, are presented. Other issues such as database buffer management, read ahead requirements of merged strands, and media layout mechanisms are also discussed.

2.2. *Pictorial databases*

Most of the research reported above discusses multimedia database management systems when in fact their current implementation supports only text and images. In certain other cases, computer generated graphics are supported. The query processing and storage and indexing mechanisms discussed above are valid for pictorial databases as well, since pictorial databases form a subset of multimedia databases.

In [7], the various issues in managing pictorial databases are discussed. A unified approach to the retrieval and manipulation of pictorial information is provided. Data structures and improvement of algorithms to retrieve and manipulate either a database with a large number of pictures or a pictorial database with large pictures or pictures with great complexity are also discussed. It is shown that traditional algebras cannot analyze the spatial relationships among various picture objects. A set of picture operations are therefore provided for storage, retrieval, manipulation and transformation of spatial data.

In another approach to picture queries [6] describes a relational database system that is interfaced with an image understanding system. An algorithm to convert a relational graph into a relational database and the design of a flexible query language for the pictorial database based on Zloof's query-by-example approach [30] are described. The importance of spatial relationships as a means to retrieve images from a pictorial database is emphasized.

A survey of pictorial database systems is given in [25]. Various approaches and the elements of a pictorial database system design are also discussed. It is pointed out that man-machine communication with graphical aids greatly enhances queries facilities and therefore the QBE approach is highly commended. Any new pictorial database management system should always consider allowing for such query systems. The way in which the QBE approach helps query processing is not limited to Zloof's proposal. Many researchers have tried to use the concept of QBE adapted for their special needs. The origins of pictorial database are classified into the three categories shown below:

1. extensions of conventional databases by adding images as data types,

2. advanced image file systems in image processing systems, and

3. pictorial information systems which manage a large set of images in application areas.

Various data models which were available at the time, as well as querying methodologies, physical storage considerations, pictorial data structures and example image database systems are also considered.

Pictorial information systems are covered in a comprehensive way in [10], detailing all the previous work done and reporting various research results. The blending of image processing areas and image databases have led to a variety of pictorial information systems. Relational database extensions to pictorial databases and iconic indexing of images are some of the major issues discussed.

A method for iconic indexing of images based on the spatial relations of objects in the image is given in [8]. The methodology allows for the spatial information in an image to be stored as a textual string and for retrieval of images matching a query to be accomplished by subsequence matching of query string against the indexes stored in the database. A prototype system incorporating the iconic indexing methodology, as well as iconic index based spatial reasoning and visualization is given in [9]. Various proposals have been made to extend the iconic indexing of [8] (see, e.g. [11, 14, 26]).

2.3. *Discussion*

Although the above-mentioned authors provide much insight about iconic indexing techniques, they do not discuss ways of reducing an image to a sub-picture and labeling them so that they may be indexed using the given algorithms. In order for working systems to be produced, this step must be considered. In the prototype system described, the architecture of the system takes this problem into account.

The user of the system is responsible for classifying images that are to be added to the database. For each class of images, a plug-in module to do object recognition of the objects in that image may be provided. The module recognizes the objects, and this information is used to drive the indexing process. This mode of operation is known as automatic indexing. If no module is available for the given class of images, semi-automatic indexing is used. In this mode, the user may either point to an object or outline an object (using a mouse). If the user points to an object, the system employs a region-growing technique to discover the area covered by the object. In either case, the user inputs the name of the object, and indexing proceeds.

Note that in the case of images generated by computer graphics rendering systems, or video sequences generated by computer animation systems, the objects in the image (or image sequence) have been identified by the programmer.

In these cases, the prototype system will use the automatic indexing mode. Computer graphics are treated as a special case of the image data type, and computer animation as a special case of the video data type in the prototype system.

In the MMDBMSs surveyed above, indexing is supported only for the image data type. Video indexing has been discussed in other contexts ([2, 19]), while indexing of audio and document data types has not been discussed. In the prototype system, a uniform methodology is used to index images, video, audio, and document data types in an MMDBMS.

3. Architecture of Prototype System

The prototype multimedia database management system provides for the definition, storage and retrieval of multimedia documents. Another important feature is the incorporation of data specific indexes for the different multimedia data types. The indexes support content-based queries on the various data types. Examples of such queries include: "Retrieve all images having a tree to the left of a house"; "Retrieve all audio clips containing a gunshot during a presidential speech"; "Retrieve all video clips containing a car passing over a bridge". The high-level system architecture is sketched in Fig. 2.

The system is built on top of existing window and database management systems. The window system contains the facilities needed to display images and video as well as to play audio. In addition, it allows a graphical user interface to the MMDBMS to be constructed. The DBMS provides query

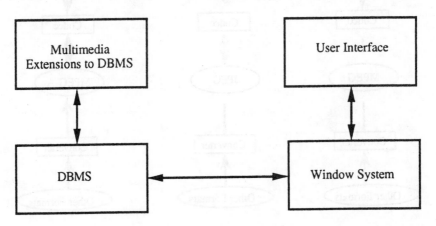

Fig. 2. High-level system architecture.

facilities, security, concurrency control, etc. for textual data. To allow for efficient treatment of multimedia data, an extension to the DBMS is defined. The extension provides for efficient storage of non-textual data, content-based queries, indexing, compression/decompression, and format conversion. The major multimedia data types — image, video, and audio — are stored in industry standard formats (JPEG [27], MPEG, and MPEG audio [15], respectively) to allow for ease of exchange with other applications, so compression/decompression modules for these formats are provided. Since not all of the data that the user wishes to store may be in this format, converters for a number of different formats are a part of the MMDBMS. Each of the data types also has an indexing module to build indexes which support

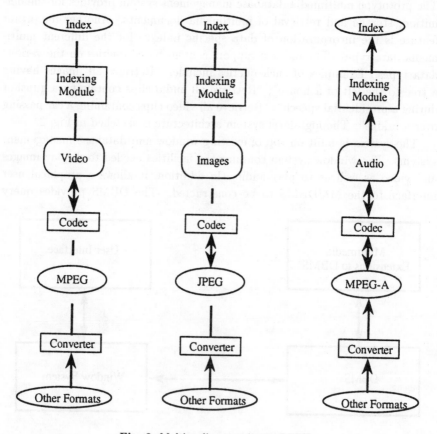

Fig. 3. Multimedia extension to DBMS.

content-based queries. These indexing modules operate in either automatic or semi-automatic mode. In automatic mode, the system uses object or speech recognition modules to autonomously generate an index. In semi-automatic mode, the system works interactively with the user to generate the index. The multimedia extension is sketched in Fig. 3.

3.1. *Prototype system*

The Multimedia Database System has been implemented on a DECsystem 5100 running Ultrix V4.2A using C and X11 Release 4 and OSF/Motif Version 1.1 [4, 20]. The user-interface part of the program is independent of the application program that creates and maintains the multimedia database. The multimedia database handles various data types such as images, video, audio, computer-generated graphics, and multimedia documents.

At present, indexing of images, documents, and audio is supported. Automatic indexing of images and documents is supported while only semi-automatic indexing of audio is supported. Automatic indexing is currently supported for images consisting of alpha-numeric characters.

Due to the use of X-windows in the implementation of the interface, the component objects of a multimedia document may be stored on a database server for viewing on a remote machine. The portability of the system is limited by the lack of a standard for audio corresponding to X-windows for images and video.

4. Index Construction

The MMDBMS uses the textual DBMS for efficient storage and retrieval of textual information such as indexes for the various data types and retrieval of multimedia objects by keyword.

A multimedia database management system requires careful attention to the attributes and properties of different data types, their storage requirements, their retrieval, manipulation and presentation methods. It has been suggested that an MMDBMS should only support storage and retrieval of multimedia objects, nothing more and nothing less [28]. We are interested in providing a better indexing techniques that will ease the retrieval process, and at the same time has nominal storage requirements.

The indexing techniques provided should not be limited to multimedia documents as a whole, but for individual data types as well. If it is possible to show that a uniform indexing mechanism works for individual data types, then this methodology may easily be extended to document indexing as a whole.

The storage and retrieval of text has been studied in detail, implemented in many information systems such as college and public libraries and the results reported. Most libraries use keyword search for retrieving textual records in a database, based on their "contents". For example, if a user looks for a keyword "motif", by doing a keyword search in a public library, the user would then get a listing of all books and papers that have the word "motif" in their "contents". This is because the database is capable of supporting queries based on a set of keywords that is present as one of the fields of the database.

For other data types such as images, for example, keywords that describe the objects/sub-pictures in the image can be stored and a keyword search supported. However, if user queries based on the spatial arrangement of these objects in an image are to be supported, keyword search is not a feasible idea. This is because the number of keywords required to describe all spatial relationships of objects in an image grows exponentially with the number of objects in an image. Moreover, while indexing image sequences such as a movie or a video clip, not only the spatial relationships of objects in a frame, but the temporal sequence of events are also important. This would require even more keywords, and thus not feasible. The notion of content addressability can be used here for storage and retrieval using iconic indexing.

The key concept of "content-addressability" is the following: The semantic information packed inside a data type is called the content, user queries that address the contents of a data type are supported. For example, in an image the sub-pictures of the image, the type of sub-pictures and/or the spatial arrangements of sub-pictures are the contents of that image. Similarly, in an audio sample, the acoustic events such as birds chirping or particular words spoken, are the contents of that sample. A given object is analyzed for its contents and the semantics of the object are stored in some suitable fashion. The information from this analysis or processing is used in indexing in such a way that the storage requirements of this indexing mechanism are minimized. The indexing is done so that it is easier to search through the indices than to retrieve the actual object from the database.

All the different multimedia objects have been stored in the multimedia database in compressed formats since the storage requirements of each of these objects are very high. The specific media that these data types are physically stored on are not considered in this research. There are numerous sources of multimedia objects and it is seldom the case that all the file formats for these objects from all these sources are uniform. Therefore, a way to convert an object from any given format to one of the known standard formats has been discussed. There are standard modules and sub-programs available to accomplish this task. They are made part of this system to accomplish the task. The standards used in the prototype system are JPEG for images, MPEG for video, and MPEG-A for audio.

Objects newly added to the database are first analyzed to form the indexes as described below, translated into the applicable standard, and stored along with the index in the database. If however, the objects are added in a known compressed format, it may have to be uncompressed so that indexing can be done.

The objects first undergo the process of recognition and analysis before indexing, since indexing is content-based. For example, for images, object recognition modules that have been implemented help to obtain a segmented picture which in turn is used to form the iconic index for the image. For audio, modules for speech recognition are available that can be made part of this system. These analysis and recognition modules are critical for indexing. This type of indexing, where plug-in modules do the analysis and recognition, followed by the processing provided by the indexing modules is known as automatic indexing. In automatic indexing, the system is capable of deciding on its own how to distinguish between objects and can form the index automatically without the intervention of the user. This is a very difficult task to accomplish due to the inherent difficulty of computer vision and speech recognition. In certain limited domains, however, it may be possible (e.g. for images containing only characters or audio containing only spoken words).

Semi-automatic indexing, on the other hand, is relatively easier, since the user participates in the process of object recognition. Once this is done, the system can easily form the objects. It is important to note here that for the analysis and object recognition to be completed automatically, it is imperative that suitable modules are available to complete this process. Alternatively, semi-automatic indexing is used when there are no object recognition modules available and when the user is willing to and capable of helping the system. In this case, there is one single module that provides the proper interface for the user to identify the objects. This module should also be capable of capturing the information that the user wishes to provide, in a suitable form, for indexing purposes.

When there are a large number of images with similar contents to be indexed, the effort in developing an automatic indexing module is justified. Such an example is the fax image. Fax is one of the fastest way of sending and receiving information between two points. People have felt the need to archive these facsimiles. The huge number of fax transactions everyday, and their consistent format is an example that is borrowed from the pictorial database field. An object recognition (specifically, character recognition) module has been provided to help in the automatic indexing of such images.

Similarly, there are many speech recognition systems available that can be used to process and analyze audio objects. Thus, it is possible to use automatic indexing in these cases. However, when the audio does not contain speech, but instead contain musical notes or natural sounds, it is very difficult to develop a recognition system. In such cases, semi-automatic indexing must be used to index the objects. From the image example, semi-automatic indexing is required when there is much detail in a given image or when a recognition technique for a particular class of images is not available. Automatic indexing of fax images has been implemented in the prototype system.

5. Indexing

In this section, the indexing methodology will be described. The basic idea is to use the relation between each pair of objects (or events for audio data) in each of one (for audio) two (for image) or three (for video or document) dimensions. In one dimension there are thirteen relations as shown in Fig. 4 (where the single dimension considered is the time dimension). In two dimensions there are 169 different relations between two objects, and in three dimensions, there are 2197 different relations between two objects.

5.1. *Image indexing*

The indexing of images may be performed either automatically or semi-automatically, as previously described. In the semi-automatic mode, the user marks the upper, lower, left, and right extents of the objects (using a mouse), and names each of the objects. In automatic mode, the system is responsible for recognizing the objects in the image. In either mode, the remainder of the indexing is done by the system. The projections of the objects onto the x- and y-axes are formed and the relation between each pair of objects in both the x- and y-directions is found. This pair of relations gives rise to the relations

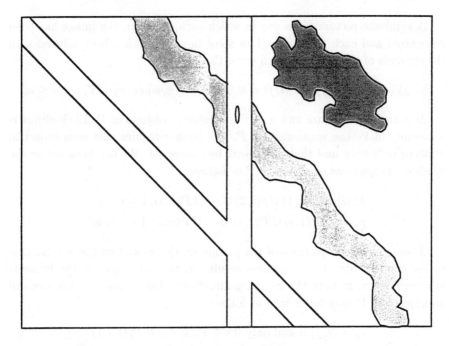

Fig. 4. A query-by-example.

between each pair of objects. The relation is denoted by a symbol, and the (object, relation, object) triple is stored in the relational database.

A query is given as an (object, relation, object) triple, or as a set of such triples, which is translated into a query in the language of the DBMS. The user may also form a query using a query-by-example approach as in [9]. A pallet of icons representing objects in the images is given, and the user is also given the opportunity to create new icons using an icon editor. The user then forms the icons into a spatial pattern on an area of the screen. This arrangement represents the arrangement of objects that images which match the user's query must have. An example of a query-by-example is shown in Fig. 4.

The system forms the query from the positions of pairs of objects in the drawing the user has created, and retrieves the matching images. The exact form of the indexes and the procedure for constructing them, as well as the methodology for constructing and performing queries is given in the rest of the section.

A symbolic picture [8] is one in which each object in the image has been recognized and each "slot" (pixel, or some larger area) has been labeled with the symbols of the objects which cover the slot:

$$P(i,j) = \{v_1, \ldots, v_p\} \text{ or } P(i,j) = \varnothing, 1 \leq i, j \leq n, \text{where } v_k \in V, 1 \leq k \leq m.$$

P is an $n \times n$ picture and m is the number of objects in P. Each object is a member of V, the vocabulary of P. We further require that each object in P occur only once and that all objects be connected. We can then define the symbolic projections of a picture P as follows:

$$P_x(i) = P(i,1) \cup p(i,2) \cup \cdots \cup P(i,n), 1 \leq i \leq n,$$
$$p_y(i) = P(1,i) \cup P(2,i) \cup \cdots \cup P(n,i), 1 \leq i \leq n.$$

These are the projections of the picture on the x- and on the y-axis. Due to the connectivity and uniqueness requirements, each object in the frame is now an interval in both the x- and y-directions. The x- and y-projections of an object $v \in V$ may be defined as follows:

$$v_x = (i,j) \text{ if and only if } v \in P_x(i) \wedge v \in P_x(i+1)$$
$$\wedge \cdots \wedge v \in P_x(j) \wedge v \notin P_x(k), k \leq i, k \geq j,$$
$$v_y = (i,j) \text{ if and only if } v \in P_y(i) \wedge v \in P_y(i+1)$$
$$\wedge \cdots \wedge v \in P_y(j) \wedge v \notin P_y(k), k \leq i, k \geq j.$$

In order to form the index of the frame, we sort both the x- and y-projections of all of the objects on (i,j). The result is two ordered sets:

$$P^*x = \{v_{x1}, v_{x2}, \ldots, v_{xm}\},$$
$$P^*y = \{v_{y1}, v_{y2}, \ldots, v_{ym}\}.$$

From these sets, form the following sets of pairs of projections:

$$SP_x = \{(v_{x1}, v_{x2}), (v_{x1}, v_{x3}), \ldots, (v_{x2}, v_{x3}), \ldots, (v_{x(m-1)}, v_{xm})\},$$
$$SP_y = \{(v_{y1}, v_{y2}), (v_{y1}, v_{y3}), \ldots, (v_{y2}, v_{y3}), \ldots, (v_{y(m-1)}, v_{ym})\}.$$

There are $(m^2 - m)/2$ pairs in each set. We now need to find the relationship existing between each pair of projections. Since we are working with intervals, we will use the result of [1] which shows that there are only 13 relations between two intervals P_a and P_b. These relations are shown in Fig. 5.

Due to symmetry it is only necessary to consider 7 of the 13 relations. If we choose to let P_a be the first interval in the sorted order, then the 7 necessary relations are the following:

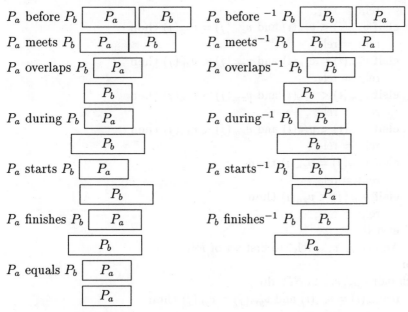

Fig. 5- The 13 relations between two objects in one dimension.

$$\text{rel}_1 \equiv P_a \text{ equals } P_b$$
$$\text{rel}_2 \equiv P_a \text{ finishes}^{-1} P_b$$
$$\text{rel}_3 \equiv P_a \text{ starts } P_b$$
$$\text{rel}_4 \equiv P_a \text{ during}^{-1} P_b$$
$$\text{rel}_5 \equiv P_a \text{ overlaps } P_b$$
$$\text{rel}_6 \equiv P_a \text{ meets } P_b$$
$$\text{rel}_7 \equiv P_a \text{ before } P_b .$$

Let R be the set $\{\text{rel}_i\}, 1 \leq i \leq 7$. Then a pictorial index PI of a symbolic picture P is composed of two sets of triples:

$$PI = \{(v_{x1}, v_{x2}, \text{rel}_{i1}), (v_{x1}, v_{x3}, \text{rel}_{i2}), \dots, (v_{x(m-1)}, v_{xm}, \text{rel}_{i[m(m-1)/2]})\},$$
$$\{(v_{y1}, v_{y2}, \text{rel}_{j1}), (v_{y1}, v_{y3}, \text{rel}_{j2}), \dots, (v_{y1}, v_{y2}, \text{rel}_{j[m(m-1)/2]})\} .$$

For a symbolic picture P we can construct the correct pictorial index PI using the following simple algorithm:

procedure index $- P$ is input PI is output

for each pair v_{xm}, v_{xn} in SP_x **do**

    if $v_{xm}(i) = v_{xn}(i)$ and $v_{xm}(j) = v_{xn}(j)$ **then**

        $\text{rel}_i := \text{rel}_1$;

    elsif $v_{xm}(i) < v_{xn}(i)$ and $v_{xm}(j) = v_{xn}(j)$ **then**

        $\text{rel}_i := \text{rel}_2$;

    elsif $v_{xm}(i) = v_{xn}(i)$ and $v_{xm}(j) < v_{xn}(j)$ **then**

        $\text{rel}_i := \text{rel}_3$;

    elsif $v_{xm}(i) < v_{xn}(i)$ and $v_{xm}(j) > v_{xn}(j)$ **then**

        $\text{rel}_i := \text{rel}_4$;

    elsif $v_{xm}(i) < v_{xn}(i)$ and $v_{xm}(j) < v_{xn}(j)$ **then**

        $\text{rel}_i := \text{rel}_5$;

    elsif $v_{xm}(j) = v_{xn}(i)$ **then**

        $\text{rel}_i := \text{rel}_6$;

    elsif $v_{xm}(j) < v_{xn}(i)$ **then**

        $\text{rel}_i := \text{rel}_7$;

    end if;

    Add $(v_{xm}, v_{xn}, \text{rel}_i)$ to first set of PI;

end for;

for each pair v_{ym}, v_{yn} in SP_y **do**

    if $v_{ym}(i) = v_{yn}(i)$ and $v_{ym}(j) = v_{yn}(j)$ **then**

        $\text{rel}_i := \text{rel}_1$;

    elsif $v_{ym}(i) < v_{yn}(i)$ and $v_{ym}(j) = v_{yn}(j)$ **then**

        $\text{rel}_i := \text{rel}_2$;

    elsif $v_{ym}(i) = v_{yn}(i)$ and $v_{ym}(j) < v_{yn}(j)$ **then**

        $\text{rel}_i := \text{rel}_3$;

    elsif $v_{ym}(i) < v_{yn}(i)$ and $v_{ym}(j) > v_{yn}(j)$ **then**

        $\text{rel}_i := \text{rel}_4$;

    elsif $v_{ym}(i) < v_{yn}(i)$ and $v_{ym}(j) < v_{yn}(j)$ **then**

        $\text{rel}_i := \text{rel}_5$;

    elsif $v_{ym}(j) = v_{yn}(i)$ **then**

        $\text{rel}_i := \text{rel}_6$;

    elsif $v_{ym}(j) < v_{yn}(i)$ **then**

        $\text{rel}_i := \text{rel}_7$;

    end if;

    Add $(v_{ym}, v_{yn}, \text{rel}_i)$ to second set of PI;

end for;

end procedure;

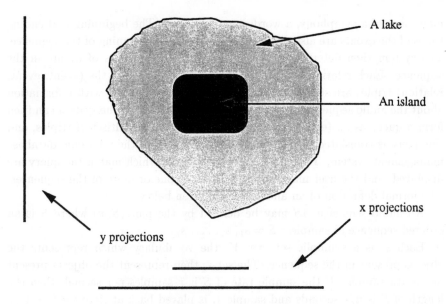

Fig. 6. Pictorial query formation.

A query may be formed either by supplying a pictorial index directly or by giving a query-by-example. In the second case, the query is transformed to a pictorial index using the procedure index given above. In either case, the query is then performed by searching for each of the elements in the two sets of the pictorial index of the query in the corresponding set of each of the indexes of each of the pictures in the database. If a match is found for each element, the picture matches the query and the name of the picture is reported to the user who can choose which picture(s) to retrieve. As an example, the query to find an island in a lake is translated into a search for the triples ($lake$, rel_4, $island$), ($lake$, rel_4, $island$) in the sets representing the x- and y-projections respectively, of the pictures in the database. This translation is illustrated in Fig. 6. The horizontal and vertical lines represent the x- and y-projections of the objects in the picture, respectively.

5.2. *Audio indexing*

The simplest data type to index is audio due to its one-dimensional nature. The user of the system describes each audio sequence in terms of the events (or objects) that occur within that sequence (an event may be a gunshot, first movement of a symphony, a word, a speech, etc.). The beginning and ending times of the events are also given as offsets from the beginning of the sequence. The system then determines the relation between all pairs of events in the sequence. Each relation is represented by the symbol, and the (event, event, relation) triples are stored in the relational database, along with information about the audio sequence in which they occur. The user of the system can then form a query as an (event, event, relation) triple or a multiset of triples, and the query is translated into a query in the language of the relational database management system. The names of the sequences which match the query are displayed, and the user may choose to listen to one or more of the sequences. The formal definition of an audio index is given below.

An audio sequence AS may be defined by the pair (S, r) where S is an ordered sequence of samples: $S = s_1, s_2, \ldots, s_n$.

Each s_i is a symbolic set over V, the vocabulary which represents the objects present in the sequence. The set s_i then represent the objects present in the ith sample. If the sample rate of S is r samples per second, then the length of S is n/r seconds and sample s_i is played back at time $t + (i-1)/r$ seconds where t is the starting time for the playback. The symbolic projection of AS is defined as follows:

$$P_t(i) = s_i, 1 \le i \le n.$$

The t (for time) projection of an object $v \in V$ may be defined as follows:

$$v_t = (i, j) \text{ if and only if } v \in P_t(i) \wedge v \in P_t(i+1)$$
$$\wedge \cdots \wedge v \in P_t(j) \wedge v \notin P_t(k), i \le k, k \ge j.$$

In order to form the index of the audio sequence, sort the t projections of all of the objects on (i, j). The result is an ordered multiset:

$$P_t^* = \{v_{t1}, v_{t2}, \ldots, v_{tm}\},$$

where m is the number of objects in the audio sequence.

Note that an object may occur more than once. From the ordered multiset, form the following multiset of pairs of projections:

$$SP_t = \{(v_{t1}, v_{t2}), (v_{t1}, v_{t3}), \ldots, (v_{t2}, v_{t3}), \ldots, (v_{t(m-1)}, v_{tm})\}.$$

Let R be the set of relations as defined above for pictorial indexes. Then an audio index AI of an audio sequence AS is a set of triples:

$$AI = \{(v_{t1}, v_{t2}, \text{rel}_{i1}), (v_{t1}, v_{t3}, \text{rel}_{i2}), \ldots, (v_{t(m-1)}, v_{tm}, \text{rel}_{i[m(m-1)/2]})\}.$$

The construction process of an audio index, given an audio sequence, is analogous to the procedure given above for the construction of a pictorial index. The processing of a query is analogous as well. For audio data, the query may either be given as a multiset of triples, or as a structured English sentence which is translated into the appropriate triples. For example, the query "Find all audio sequences having a gunshot during a symphonic concert" is translated into the triple ($symphonic\_concert$, rel_4, $gunshot$). The database is then searched for audio sequences having this triple in their indexes. Multiple conditions can be expressed by combining conditions in the sentence using the keyword "and".

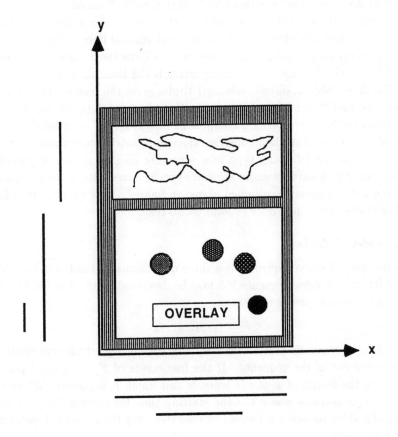

Fig. 7. Projections in x- and y-directions of a multimedia document.

5.3. *Document indexing*

Documents are defined in the prototype as some spatio-temporal arrangement of images, video, or audio created by users of the system [3]. The index for a document is formed by taking the projections of the windows containing the images or video in the x- and y-directions (see Fig. 7) and then taking the projections of all objects (including audio) in the time dimension. The relation between audio events and other objects is a distinguished relation since the audio event has no extent in the x- or y-direction.

Figure 7 shows the x- and y-projections of a document containing three component objects (two images, one of hand drawing and the other of the text "OVERLAY", and a video image of a bouncing ball). Each object is contained in a window whose borders are visible in the figure. The projections of each of these windows are shown as horizontal and vertical lines. The positions of these projections are determined, pairwise, to form the x- and y-portions of the index of the document (the final portion is the time portion).

The three (object, object, relation) triples gives the relation for each pair of objects, and that relation is stored in the relational database for each pair of objects (object here being a component image, audio, or video clip). The user of the system can then construct queries to retrieve documents meeting constraints of the following type in a structure English sentence: "Find all documents which have an audio sequence synchronized with a video sequence, and the video sequence positioned above an image". This query is translated by the system into the triples ($audio$, $video$, rel_1).

5.4. *Video indexing*

The indexing of video sequences is a three-dimensional extension of the indexing of images. A video sequence VS may be described by the pair (F, r) where F is an ordered sequence of frames:

$$F = f_1, f_2, \ldots, f_n.$$

Each f_i is a symbolic picture over V, the vocabulary which represents the objects present in the sequence. If the frame rate of F is r frames per second, then the length of F is n/r seconds and frame f_i is played back at time $t + (i - 1)/r$ seconds where t is the starting time for the playback. A video index of a video sequence is formed by concatenating the indexes of each frame in the sequence:

$$PI_F = PI_{f_1} PI_{f_2} \cdots PI_{f_n}.$$

Since many of the adjacent frames give rise to equivalent indexes, we can form a reduced video index by deleting a pictorial index PI_{f_i} if it is equivalent to $PI_{f_{i-1}}$. It is now necessary, however, to prefix each index with its frame number so that we can reconstruct the original index if necessary:

$$RPI_F = i1PI_{f_{i1}} i2PI_{f_{i2}} \cdots ikPI_{f_{i_k}} .$$

A query can be formed by giving a sequence of pictorial queries-by-example or by giving a sequence of indexes. The query is processed by checking that the individual pictorial queries match in the order that they are given.

6. Discussion and Future Research

We have described the architecture of a multimedia database system which supports content-based retrieval of multimedia objects through media specific indexing. The formalism used to represent video and audio sequences includes the frame or sample rate as well. This information can be used to support time-based queries, though this is not yet incorporated in the prototype system. Another area which needs to be addressed is complex queries involving more than one data type. It should be possible to form indexes of complex objects (e.g. synchronized audio and video tracks) and to form queries based on the properties displayed by this complex object.

References

1. J. F. Allen, "Maintaining knowledge about temporal intervals", *Comm. ACM* **26** (Nov. 1983) 832–843.
2. T. Arndt and S. K. Chang, "Image sequence compression by iconic indexing", *Proc. '89 IEEE Workshop on Visual Languages*, Rome, Italy (October 4–6, 1989) pp. 177–182.
3. T. Arndt, "Iconic indexing of multimedia documents", *Proc. ETCE Symp. on Comput. in Eng.*, New Orleans (January 1994) pp. 339–346.
4. P. J. Asente and R. R. Swick, *X Window System Toolkit*, Maynard (Digital Press, MA, 1990).
5. E. Bertino, F. Rabitti, and S. Gibbs, "Query processing in a multimedia document system", *ACM Trans. on Office Information Sys.* **6**, 1 (1988) 1–41.
6. N. S. Chang and K. S. Fu, "Picture query languages for pictorial database systems", *Computer* **14**, (1981), 23–33.
7. S. K. Chang and T. L. Kunii, "Pictorial Database Systems", *Computer* **14**, (1981), 13–21.
8. S. K. Chang, Q. Y. Shi, and C. W. Yan, "Iconic indexing by 2D strings", *IEEE Trans. on Pattern Anal. Machine Intell.* **9**, 3 (1987) 413–428.

9. S. K. Chang, C.W. Yan, D.C. Dimitroff, and T. Arndt, "An intelligent image database system", *IEEE Trans, on Softw. Eng.* **14**, 5 (1988) 681–688.

10. S. K. Chang, *Principles of Pictorial Information Systems Design* (Prentice-Hall, 1989).

11. G. Costagliola, G. Tortora, and T. Arndt "A unifying approach to iconic indexing for 2D and scenes", *IEEE Trans. on Knowledge and Data Eng.* **4**, 3 (June 1992) 205–222.

12. D. Davcev, D. Cakmakov, and V. Arnautovski, "A query based mechanism for multimedia information retrieval", *Proc. of Workshop on Multimedia Information Sys.* (Tempe, 1992), pp. 21–38.

13. N. Dimitrova and F. Golshani, REVA: A query language for multimedia information systems", *Proc. Workshop on Multimedia Information Sys.* (Tempe, 1992), pp. 1–20.

14. S. Y. Lee, M. C. Yang, and J. W. Chen, "Signature file as a spatial filter for iconic image database", *J. Visual Languages and Computing* **3** (1992), 373–397.

15. D. J. LeGall, "RMPEG: A video compression standard for multimedia applications", *Comm. ACM,* **34**, 4 (April, 1991) 93–106.

16. T. D. C. Little and A. Ghafoor, "Conceptual models for time-dependent multimedia data", *Proc. Workshop on Multimedia Information Sys.,* (Tempe, 1992) pp. 86–110.

17. C. Meghini, F. Rabitti, and C. Thanos, "Conceptual modeling of multimedia documents", *Computer* **24**, 6 (1991) 23–32.

18. G.P. Michalski, "The world of documents", *Byte* (April 1991), pp. 159–170.

19. A. Nagasaka and Y. Tanaka, "Automatic video indexing and full-video search for object appearances", *Visual Database Sys. II*, Eds. E. Knuth and L.M. Wegner (Elsevier Science Publishers B. V., Amsterdam, 1992), pp. 113–128.

20. A. Nye and T. O'Reilly, *X Toolkit Intrinsics Programming Manual,* OSF/Motif Edition (O'Reilly and Associates Sebastapol, CA, 1992).

21. M. H. O'Docherty and C. N. Daskalis, "Multimedia information systems — the management and semantic retrieval of all electronic data types", *The Comput. J.* **24**, 3 (1991), 223–238.

22. P. V. Rangan, T. Kaeppner, and H. M. Vin, "Techniques for efficient storage of digital video and audio", *Proc. Workshop on Multimedia Information Sys.* (Tempe, 1992), pp. 68–87.

23. J. Riedl and V. Mashayekhi, "Continuous media in discrete objects : Support for collaborative multimedia", *Proc. Workshop on Multimedia Information Sys.* (Tempe, 1992) pp. 111–135.

24. D. Swanberg, T. Weymouth, and R. Jain, "Domain information model: An extended data model for insertion and query", *Proc. Workshop on Multimedia Information Sys.* (Tempe, 1992), pp. 39–51.

25. H. Tamura and N. Yokoya, "Image database systems: A survey", *Pattern Recognition* **17**, 1 (1984), 29–43.

26. M. Tang and S. D. Ma, "A new method for spatial reasoning in image database", *Visual Database Sys. II*, Eds. E. Knuth and L. M. Wegner, (Elsevier Science Publishers B.V., Amsterdam, 1992.) pp. 37–48.

27. G. K. Wallace, "The JPEG still picture compression standard", *Comm. ACM* **34**, 4 (1991), 30–44.

28. K. M. Wegener, Electronic Mail Distributed to IEEE Task Force on Multimedia Computing (1993).

29. K. Wolfgang, Electronic Mail distributed to IEEE Task Force on Multimedia Computing (1993).

30. M. M. Zloof, "RQBE/OBE: A language for office and business automation", *Computer* **14** (1981) 13–22.

A TWO AND THREE DIMENSIONAL
SHIP DATABASE APPLICATION

JOHN HILDEBRANDT and KIM TANG

Information Technology Division,
PO Box 783, Jamison, ACT 2614, Australia

This chapter describes a prototype system for querying ship data through a graphical user interface. The queries use symbolic descriptions of component objects of the ships and the objects' relative locations. The basic approach is to encode 3D structure via pairwise spatial relations in a standard relational database. This allows one to take advantage of efficient searches based on standard SQL queries.

1. Introduction

This chapter describes a fast query mechanism for a database containing collections of imagery and CAD data, as part of a knowledge base or as a component of an image understanding system. In a practical system with large numbers of images, a retrieval method is not enough: it must be capable of being efficiently applied to a collection of data. Pairwise spatial relationships have been suggested [4, 9] to allow spatial queries similar to the 2D string queries in [2] but with faster query implementation. This chapter applies this method to symbolic queries on ship class data using multiple 2D levels to encode and query 3D objects. An implementation using a relational database is described and illustrated with the ship database application. To enable effective queries using spatial relationships, a suitable user interface must be provided. A user interface for the prototype ship database application which combines textual data, imagery and spatial data is illustrated. The limitations caused by repeated elements are outlined and solutions proposed. The representation of extended objects is then examined and a method of using pairwise relationships to represent extended features is proposed. A summary and future directions are outlined in the final section.

2. Ship Database Description

The application of interest in this chapter is the management of a data set consisting of a large number of ship images and, in the future, CAD models of ships. The aim of the system is to allow an operator to quickly locate information on a ship for preparation of briefing materials or to compare with incoming data on another vessel. This includes textual information on objects, which may be visible in an image of the ship (e.g. the pennant number, the ships flag and name), and which could be used to retrieve an image. More technical data on the ships such as speed, range, engine capacity and number of propellers may also be stored.

Ideally an operator would be able to query the database based on the content of the image as well as associated textual information. That is, given a new ship image, retrieve all ships that look similar to it. Doing this directly on the image data is not practical at present due to the amount of information in each image and the large number of images in the database. For example, each image may contain more than 9 million pixels and the database will contain thousands of images. So instead of searching directly on the image data one can search on descriptions of the images or properties derived from them. The following content-based image queries can be identified:

1. Retrieval based on textual description of images.
2. Retrieval based on shape and size of objects in images.
3. Retrieval based on position of objects in images.
4. Retrieval based on spatial relationships of objects in images.
5. Retrieval based on statistical information of the images, such as median, mean, and contrast ratios.

Textual and numeric field data associated with each image is stored in existing relational database systems. The image data can be accessed via a file pointer in the database system or by the use of Binary Large Objects (BLOB's), which are supported in some database systems.

A method for recognizing ships, which is used by many navies, is to identify linear features on the profile view of the ship and report these as a code. These features include funnels, masts, cranes, kingposts and gantries and the code is the sequence of features from bow to stern. This simple form of spatial reasoning can be expanded through the use of 2D and 3D strings. For example, information on the spatial relationships of objects on a ship may be stored, in string form, in the database. Then if an unknown ship is observed the operator could enter any objects seen on it and their positions relative to each other. This description could then become part of the query seeking to locate this ship in the database.

3. Extension to Three or More Dimensions

The symbolic pictures and match types defined in [2] and [12] for spatial indexing of 2D data can be extended to 3D data, with CAD collections in mind. In fact one may generalise to an arbitrary number of dimensions to allow for colour, texture, temporal change and other properties. The idea of a symbolic picture and the matching types can be extended to multiple dimensions as follows. A symbolic volume, which can be thought of as a multidimensional array of voxels, is a map $S_1 \times S_2 \times \cdots \times S_j \to W$ where $S_i = \{1, 2, \ldots, p_i\}$. The types 0,1 and 2 matches [2] for such multidimensional volumes can be defined as for the 2D case, allowing queries involving multidimensional spatial relationships. An approach similar to [12] is adopted in that matches are computed from symbolic arrays and not 2D strings. If required the 2D string could be extended to multidimensional strings and used for matching. The algorithms for the 3D case are now described.

The **type-0** match procedure is dimension independent and is applied as described in [12]. If the number of symbols of each type in the picture are stored in the database then the search can be replaced by table lookup.

The **type-1** match in 3D has been implemented with a 1D regular expression string matching routine. The procedure used can be described in three steps.

1. For a pattern $P(i, j, k)$ of dimensions $m' \times n' \times p'$ and picture $F(i, j, k)$ of dimensions $m \times n \times p$ one forms 2D arrays of sets of rows and columns in the picture which have a 1D type-1 match with pattern row and column vectors found using the string matching procedure.
2. In the second step many of the 1D matches can be eliminated if other required 1D matches needed for full match are not present. So from each match in the picture one can check for required matches in directions orthogonal to the 1D string. If the required matches are not present then the match is deleted. This procedure is repeatedly applied to all matches until no deletions are made.
3. Finally, trial solutions for the three-dimensional match can be recursively formed from the sets of pattern row column matches. This effectively gives

the ascending sequences of positive integers $(x_1, x_2, \ldots, x_{m'-1})$, $(y_1, y_2, \ldots, y_{n'-1})$, $(z_1, z_2, \ldots, z_{n'-1})$ used in the definition of a type-1 match. The values in the picture defined from this set can then be matched against the pattern. If all match, the trial solution is added to the solution set otherwise it is discarded.

This algorithm is inefficient at present due to steps 2 and 3. A more efficient method could be developed using 2D string matchers which allow wild cards or by extending the type-1 method in [12] to two dimensions. Optimization of this method has not been pursued at this stage since the use of pairwise relationships, discussed latter, has been found to allow an implementation that fits in well with the application using an existing relational database system.

To describe the **type-2** match, a numbering scheme for the pattern voxels is used. The voxels are numbered from 1 to $m'n'p'$ such that numerically adjacent voxels are always adjacent in one of 3 dimensions. This is illustrated in the following figure for a 3×3×3 pattern.

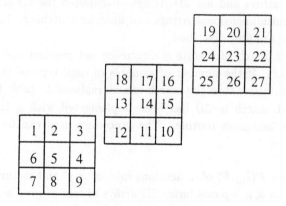

Fig. 1. Pattern voxel numbering.

To perform the match, a 3D array A of the same dimensions as the picture is set up with all voxel values set to one. Then each element of the pattern at position k is considered in reverse order, as per the numbering in the last figure. At each step the following steps are performed.

1. Retrieve the pattern voxel value v at position k and direction D defined as the direction to move to get to the next pixel to be considered. When $k=1$ the direction is defined as halt as the search is now complete.

2. Now check through each element in the picture 3D array, and for each voxel in the picture which does not match the current pattern value v, set the corresponding element in A to zero.
3. Then if direction D is not 'halt', the 3D array A is shifted in the direction D.

At the end of this, all type-2 matches in the picture will be indicated by a one in A, located at the front top left corner of the match.

4. CAD-like Application

An example of the application of these matching methods used a $20 \times 20 \times 20$ voxel model, illustrated in Fig. 2. Such models could be used to index a collection of CAD models and would allow 3D spatial queries. A slice through this model is shown in Fig. 3. A $3 \times 4 \times 2$ pattern used in a type-1 query is shown in Fig. 4. A single type-1 match returned is indicated by the arrows in Fig. 5. This search pattern would be used with the query "Find a ship with 2 kingposts with the superstructure in between them and a mast followed by a funnel above the superstructure".

Fig. 2. Voxel ship model.

```
Level : 10
b b b b b b b b b b b b b b b b b b b b b
b b b b b b b b b b b b b b b b b b b b b
b b b b b b b b b b b b b b b b b b b b b
b b b b b b b b b b b b b b b b b b b b b
b b b b b b b m b b b b b b b b b b b b b
b b b b b b b m b b b b b b b b b b b b b
b b b k b b b m b b b b b b b k b b b b b
b b b k b b b m b b b b b b b k b b b b b
b b b k b b b m b b f f b b b k b b b b b
b b b k b b b m b b f f b b b k b b b b b
b b b k b b s s s s s s s s b k b b b b b
b b b k b b s s s s s s s s b k b b b b b
b h h h h h h h h h h h h h h h b b b b b
b h h h h h h h h h h h h h h h b b b b b
b h h h h h h h h h h h h h h h b b b b b
b h h h h h h h h h h h h h h h b b b b b
b b b b b b b b b b b b b b b b b b b b b
b b b b b b b b b b b b b b b b b b b b b
b b b b b b b b b b b b b b b b b b b b b
b b b b b b b b b b b b b b b b b b b b b
```

Fig. 3. Slice of voxel model: h=Hull, s=Superstructure, k=Kingpost, m=Mast, f=Funnel.

pattern:
Level : 0   Level : 1
k m f k   k m f k
k s s k   k s s k
h h h h   h h h h

Fig. 4. A query pattern.

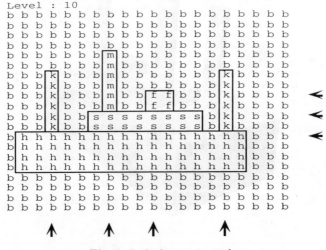

Fig. 5. A single type-1 match.

CAD data is usually stored in one of two forms: the boundary representation or the constructive solid geometry form [7]. In the boundary representation an object is segmented into non-overlapping faces. Each face is modeled by bounding edges and the edges by end vertices. Thus the object is modeled by a tree of depth three. In constructive solid geometry one has a number of primitives such as cylinders, boxes and cones combined and modified by operations such as union, intersection, difference, rotate and scale. Even though CAD data will be stored in one or both of these forms, we envisage that the database catalogue would, in addition, contain a simple voxel model generated from the CAD data for queries.

5. Collections of Images and Pairwise Spatial Relationships

While 2D string based matching methods described in previous sections allow flexible matchings based on spatial relationships, they suffer from the following problem: type-1 match is the most likely to be used as it allows inexact queries which encode spatial relations; however type-1 match is computationally expensive, so performing this on a large collection of symbolic images for database retrieval may be too slow. To overcome this, another matching technique, referred to as matching on pairwise spatial relationships, is introduced [4, 9]. The derivation of local or binary relationships from 2D strings, for spatial reasoning purposes, was discussed in [6].

A pairwise spatial relationship is a triple (O_i, O_j, r_{ij}) where O_i and O_j are two objects and r_{ij} is the 2D spatial relationship between objects. For directions, an integer in the range 1 to 8 was used, where 1 represented "North of", 2 "NW of" and so on. In the applications discussed here single characters are used to label objects and ordered triples used with $O_i < O_j$ in ASCII ordering. Given a symbolic image one can extract pairwise spatial relationships between distinct symbols yielding a set of triples. For the case $O_i = O_j$, two triples are stored (O_i, O_j, r_{ij}) and (O_j, O_i, r_{ji}), to ensure a match on a query with repeated elements. Now if each image has its pairwise spatial relationships associated with it, a query reduces to locating the image with the required pairwise spatial relationships.

To implement an efficient query system we associate a set of image identifiers with each pairwise spatial relation. This set indicates which images contain this pairwise relationship. A database of pairwise relationships is generated from the collection of symbolic images and each triple has a set of identifiers indicating the images containing this relationship. A query will consist of a set of pairwise spatial relationships required in the symbolic image. To execute this query one retrieves each of the triples in the query set from the database of pairwise spatial relationships (if present). The intersection of all associated image identifier sets is formed to give the result.

The pairwise relationships can be generated via a number of methods. First of all, the user can enter the relationships manually after observing an image of the ship. A suitable user interface will simplify this task, particularly if it is to be expanded to the full three-dimensional case. Secondly, textual information in the database may indicate relative locations of objects, which could then be translated into pairwise spatial relationships. If CAD models of ships are available in which components are identified, the pairwise relationships could be extracted automatically from the CAD data. Finally the development of object recognition systems, in the future, may allow the automatic or partially automatic extraction of objects and their relative locations from imagery of the ships.

6. Three-Dimensional Extension and Ship Class Query Application

The pairwise spatial relationship method for retrieving 3D objects was applied to the task of retrieving a ship class using a symbolic description of each class.

Ship Class	DDG	FFG	RIVER	FREMANTLE	LSH
Superstructure level	M F X X F G	R R M G F G	M F R	M R	M F
Hull level	G S X H	X S H	G S X	G S	C C H D S

Fig. 6. Two level symbolic images used (C=crane, D=derrick, F=funnel, G=gun, H=helipad, M=mast, R=radar, S=superstructure, X=missile).

Superstructure Level	Hull Level
(G,M,1)(FFG,DDG)	(H,S,1)(FFG,DDG)
(F,G,5)(FFG,DDG)	(S,X,1)(FFG)
(F,M,1)(RIVER,FFG,DDG,LSH)	(S,X,5)(RIVER,DDG)
(M,R,1)(FFG)	(G,S,5)(RIVER,DDG,FREMANTLE)
(M,R,5)(RIVER,FREMANTLE)	(H,X,1)(FFG,DDG)

Fig. 7. Extract from database of pairwise spatial relationships with the associated image id's.

Superstructure level Query Image	Hull level Query Image
MF (F,M,1)(QUERY)	GS (G,S,5)(QUERY)

Fig. 8. Symbolic query images and extracted pairwise relations.

Result superstructure level	Result Hull level	Overall result
(RIVER,FFG,DDG,LSH)	(RIVER,DDG,FREMANTLE)	(RIVER,DDG)

Fig. 9. Query results.

For this it was noted that most distinguishing features of a class are on two levels: those attached to the hull, and those to the superstructure. So instead of a full 3D description, some of the 3D nature of objects were encoded in two 2D symbolic images, one for objects on the hull and one for objects on the superstructure. The symbolic query then consisted of two images, one for each level, and the queries for each were processed separately. The results were combined by intersection to return structures containing the required pairwise spatial relations on each level. The symbolic images for each level and ship class are shown in Fig. 6. The database of pairwise spatial relationships and associated class identifier sets are given in Fig. 7. In Fig. 8 an example of a query consisting of two symbolic images is given with the pairwise relationships extracted from each. Finally the results of this query for each level and overall is given in Fig. 9.

7. Relational Implementation

To perform queries using pairwise spatial relations, the triples plus object identifier (Ship class in this case) for all objects are stored in a relational table, termed the pair table (pairdb). Then a query is performed by placing all required pairwise relation triples into a query table. The matching using pairwise relationships can then be performed by a standard SQL statement, as illustrated in Fig. 10. Standard relational technology allows this symbolic query method to be quickly added to a textual image database system and exploits the power of relational database optimization technology.

Table pairdb			
Ship Class (class_id)	**Symbol (sym1)**	**Symbol (sym2)**	**Direction (dir)**
DDG	g	m	1
FFG	g	m	1
DDG	f	x	8
...	...	...	...

Table querydb		
Symbol (sym1)	**Symbol (sym2)**	**Direction (dir)**
g	m	1
f	x	8
...	...	...

SELECT class_id from pairdb , querydb **WHERE**

pairdb.sym1 = querydb.sym1 and pairdb.sym2 = querydb.sym2 and pairdb.dir = querydb.dir

GROUP BY class_id

HAVING count = (**SELECT** count from querydb) ;

Fig. 10. Relation tables for pairwise matching and SQL statement used.

As the size of the database grows, the pair table (pairdb) will become large, and so for efficient retrieval special indexing specific to the application may have to be employed such as in [10]. To implement this, an extended relational system which allows the incorporation of user-defined indexing schemes could be used. Keeping the data in a database system allows integration with other data that may be associated with the imagery, and gives a standard framework in which to develop a system.

8. Graphical Interface Implementation

In order for a user to have simple access to spatial queries a suitable interface is required. In our application a graphical user interface was constructed for a prototype ship database application. For textual information associated with a ship, typical database forms were employed. To enter and display the spatial relationships of an object in the database, a graphical interface is

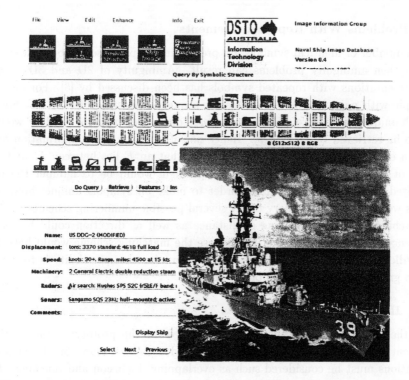

Fig. 11. Graphical interface combining textual and symbolic query with image retrieval.

Query By Symbolic Structure

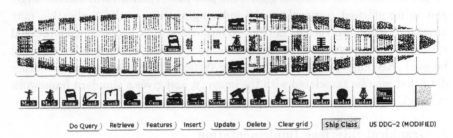

Do Query) Retrieve) Features) Insert) Update) Delete) Clear grid) | Ship Class | US DDG-2 (MODIFIED)

Fig. 12. Query by symbolic structure form.

employed where icons representing objects are placed on the grided outline of a hull, viewed from above. From this input the required spatial relations are determined and placed in a relational table to perform the database query. The interface developed is shown in Figs. 11 and 12.

9. Problems With Repeated Elements

If a number of identical symbols are present in the pairwise symbolic description then ambiguity problems can result. Ambiguity of 2D and 3D string representations with repeated symbols has been discussed by [5]. For an example with pairwise relations, consider a query consisting of FMFKF. Since each unique pairwise relation is only stored once, the structure FFMKF would also be retrieved by this query. Hence not all the structural information has been encoded: for instance the knowledge that an F lies between M and K is not encoded. One solution to this problem would be to number the repeated symbols in some defined order to make all symbols unique; however this would require the query to try several possible numbering schemes in the matching process. Encoding of distance as well as direction could be used to encode more information, in this case the matching scheme would have to handle uncertainty over distance information. Another possibility is to move to a graph-based description of the object.

10. Handling Extended Objects

In the symbolic descriptions used up to now in the prototype, the spatial extent of objects is not considered. For extended objects, more complex spatial relations must be considered such as overlapping, inclusion and touching. To handle extended objects, [3] introduced a cutting mechanism at the extreme points of objects and the generalized 2D string. An efficient variant of this was proposed by [8], referred to as the 2D C-string. The 2D C-string representation also allows hierarchical descriptions to be built up.

At present we have been using pairwise spatial relations to allow direct implementation in a relational database system. In our case the relations between the pairs were the eight compass directions. However the relation set can be expanded to include more complex relations such as those used in the 2D C-string case while still allowing relational database implementation.

For each object, its minimum bounding rectangle (MBR) is considered. If horizontal and vertical projections are used for all objects then two sets of extended pairwise relationships can be generated for each dimension. We refer to these as u pairs for vertical projections and v pairs for horizontal projections, analogously to the u and v components of 2D strings. The cutting mechanism described in [8] can be used to ensure that none of the sub-objects partially overlap and the relationships between any two sub-objects can be described by the symbols $<$, $=$, $|$, %, $[$, and $]$ whose meanings are described in the table in Fig. 13.

With these extended pairwise relations and the cutting mechanism, a symbolic description of extended objects can be stored in a relational database. Further, with the cutting mechanism it is sufficient to store only the pairwise relations within each cut region and between adjacent cut regions (this means the vertical cut regions for u pairs and horizontal cut regions for v pairs). This will reduce the number of pairwise relations that need to be stored in the database

Extended pairwise relation	Conditions	Spatial meaning
(A, B, <)	end(A) < begin(B)	A disjoint to B
(A, B, =)	begin(A) = begin(B)	A has same extent as B
	end(A) = end(B)	
(A, B, I)	end(A) = begin(B)	A touches B
(A, B, %)	begin(A) < begin(B)	A contains B and their ends
	end(A) > end(B)	don't touch.
(A, B, [ )	begin(A) = begin(B)	A contains B and they have the
	end(A) > end(B)	same beginning
(A, B,])	begin(A) < begin(B)	A contains B and they have the
	end(A) = end(B)	same ending

Fig. 13. Relation symbols and their meanings.

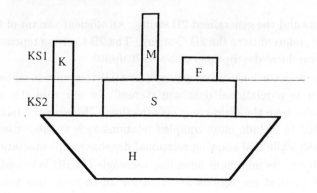

u pairs: (H, K, %) (H, S, %) (H, M, %) (H, F, %) (K, S, <) (K, M, <) (K, F, <)

(S, M, %) (S, F, %) (M, F, <)

v pairs: (H, S, I) (H, KS2, I) (H, KS1, <) (H, M, <) (H, F, <) (KS2, KS1, I)

(KS2, S, =) (KS2, M, I) (KS2, F, I) (S, KS1, I) (S, M, I) (S, F, I)

(KS1, F, [) (M, KS1, [) (M, F, [)

Fig. 14. Example of extended pairwise relationships.

and so improve its efficiency. Relations between sub-objects further away can
be inferred using heuristics on the reduced number of stored relationships. In
fact if the two objects are in adjacent cut regions the only possible relations
are < and |. For sub-objects further away (i.e. not in the same or adjacent cut
region) the only possible relation is <.

An example of the extended pairwise relationships for a simple symbolic
picture is shown in Fig. 14.

In the general case the following procedure will be followed to create pairwise relationships:

1. For each component object its minimum bounding rectangle is created.
2. For each projection a check is made for objects which partially overlap. If
   partial overlapping occurs a cut will have to be made, splitting one of the
   objects into two parts. The choice of which object to cut will be on the
   basis of some policy, such as the use of the right end of the leftmost object,
   for example. The cut line will traverse the image and so may divide other

partially overlapping objects. As each cut is made the need for further cuts can be made on the basis of the divided objects rather than the full objects. This will reduce the total number of cuts required. For example, in the following figure cut, A removes all overlapping objects whereas cut B would leave 2 objects partially overlapping. So performing cut A first would remove the need for cut B but the converse is not true.

3. The divided sections of the cut objects are given separate labels to distinguish parts of the objects.
4. Pairwise relationships between each pair of objects or object parts are then computed for storage. To reduce the storage burden only pairwise relations within an uncut region or a single cut boundary can be stored as other pairs relationships can be inferred.

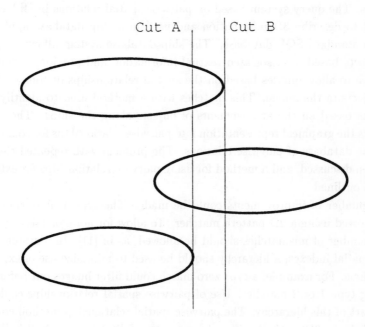

Fig. 15. Alternative cuttings.

Within a single cut region, ambiguity with repeated elements can still result, which could be alleviated by numbering repeated elements within a cut region. The extended pairwise relations will generalize to 3 dimensions by including a third projection.

To allow the user to enter the required spatial relations, a graphical user interface which allows the user to draw objects and label them could be used. This interface would need to allow the user to create extended objects and place objects in the required relative relationships. Such an interface may be similar to a graphics drawing program with some predetermined objects defined to speed data entry. The system would then extract the pairwise relations from the sketch for searching the database.

11. Summary and Further Work

Image retrieval using 2D string matching and pairwise spatial relations has been reviewed. It has been illustrated that 2D string matching techniques can be extended to 3 or more dimensions to form the basis of CAD query systems. The query system based on pairwise spatial relations in [4] has been applied to describe 3D information and used in a ship database application using a standard SQL database. The ship database system allows searching for objects based on associated textual information and provides a graphical interface to allow queries based on the spatial relationships of components of the objects in the image. This matches with a method used to identify ships which is based on the arrangements of objects along the ships. The system converts the graphical representation into pairwise relationships for comparison with the database of pairwise relations. The problem with repeated elements has been discussed, and a method for using pairwise relationships for extended objects outlined.

A number of improvements could be made. The type 1 algorithm could be improved using a 2D pattern matcher. To allow for noise or missing items, some number of mismatches should be allowed, as in [11]. In a system using these spatial indexes, a hierarchy should be used to minimize use of expensive algorithms. For example, a type zero match could filter images out before performing type 1 or 2 matches. Use of pairwise spatial relationships could also form part of this hierarchy. The pairwise spatial relationship method could be expanded to a 3D method using a larger range of direction numbers indicating directions in 3D instead of 2D, but further investigations of problems with repeated elements are needed. Implementation of extended pairwise relationships will require a new user interface which allows input of feature extents. The use of hierarchical descriptions of complex objects may assist in reducing the search complexity as the number of relationships increase.

A number of extensions to the ship database system are envisaged. The use of extended pairwise relationships will allow the storage of a richer set of spatial relationships while the cutting process will reduce the need to store all relationships. A new user interface which allows the user to define extended regions and, there relative relationships will be required in this case. Such an interface will allow a more flexible entry of trial objects to search on. Accessing data sources which can provide information on the relative relationships between objects is an important problem which must be addressed. Sources of such information may include CAD databases and positional information in the textual/numeric components of descriptive databases.

While storage and retrieval of images in imagery management systems has had some study, very little attention has been given to the problem of maintaining the integrity of an image database system. The database may contain information on an object which can also be deduced from a stored image of the object, for example the number of funnels, and the number and types of antennas and weapon systems. Maintaining the integrity of the database will require that any difference between information stored in the database and those visible in an image be resolved. This will require the knowledge of what information may be visible in an image of an object, that is to be stored in the database. Integrity checking of these items could then be performed manually by the user checking the image and the relevant database entries. More details on integrity checking in image databases may be found in [1]. Inconsistencies between images and information in the database and between multiple images will need to be resolved. The inconsistencies may be due to data entry errors or to changes in the configuration of the object.

References

1. J. Aisbett, "Integrity of image database management systems", *Private Comm.* (June 1994).
2. S. K. Chang, Q. Y. Shi, and C. W. Yan, "Iconic indexing by 2D strings", *IEEE Trans. Pattern Recognition and Machine Intelligence* **9**, 3 (1987) 413–428.
3. S. K. Chang, E. Jungert, and Y. Li, "Representation and retrieval of symbolic pictures using generalized 2D strings", *SPIE Proc. Visual Comm. Image Processing* (Philadelphia, 5–10 November, 1989) 1360–1372.
4. C. C. Chang and S. Y. Lee, "Retrieval of similar pictures on pictorial databases", *Pattern Recognition* **24**, 7 (1991) 675–680.
5. G. Costagliola and G. Tortora, "A unifying approach to iconic indexing for 2D and 3D scenes", *IEEE Trans. Knowl and Data Eng.* **4**, 3 (June 1992) 205–222.

6. E. Jungert, "Extended symbolic projections as a knowledge structure for spatial reasoning", *Pattern Recognition* (Springer Verlag, 1988) 343–351.

7. A. Kemper and M. Wallrath, "An analysis of geometric modelling in database systems", *ACM Comput. Sur.* **19**, 1 (March 1987) 45–91.

8. S.-Y. Lee and F.-J. Hsu, "Spatial reasoning and similarity retrieval of images using 2D C-string knowledge representation", *Pattern Recognition* **25**, 3 (1992) 305–318.

9. S.-Y. Lee and M.-K. Shan, "Access methods of image database", *Int. J. Pattern Recognition and Artificial Intelligence* **4**, 1 (1990) 27–44.

10. E. G. M. Petrakis and S. C. Orphanoudakis, "A generalized approach for image indexing and retrieval based on 2D strings", presented at the Pre-conference workshop on Spatial Reasoning, Bergen, Norway (August 1993).

11. S. Ranka and T. Heywood, "Two-dimensional pattern matching with k mismatches", *Pattern Recognition* **24**, 1 (1991) 31–40.

12. G. Tortora, G. Costagliola, T. Arndt, and S. K. Chang, "Pyramidal algorithms for iconic indexing", *CVGIP* **52** (1990) 26–56.